T0084705

Not Yet the Twilight

Books by Josef Pieper from St. Augustine's Press

Christian Idea of Man
Concept of Sin
Death and Immortality
Don't Worry about Socrates
Enthusiasm and Divine Madness
Exercises in the Elements
Happiness and Contemplation
In Tune with the World
Platonic Myths
Rules of the Game in Social Relationships
Scholasticism
The Silence of Goethe
The Silence of St. Thomas
Tradition
Tradition as Challenge
What Catholics Believe
What Does "Academic" Mean?

Not Yet the Twilight
An Autobiography 1945–1964

Josef Pieper

Translated by Dan and Una Farrelly

ST. AUGUSTINE'S PRESS
South Bend, Indiana

Copyright @ 2017 by St. Augustine's Press
Originately published as *Noch nicht aller Tage Abend*
from Kösel Verlag, Munich

All rights reserved. No part of this book may be reproduced, stored in
a retrieval system, or transmitted, in any form or by any means, electronic, mechanical, photocopying, recording,
or otherwise, without the prior permission of
St. Augustine's Press.

Manufactured in the United States of America.

1 2 3 4 5 6   23 23 22 21 20 19 18 17

Library of Congress Cataloging in Publication Data
Pieper, Josef, 1904-1997.
[Noch nicht aller Tage Abend. English]
Not yet the twilight: an autobiography 1945-1964 /
Josef Pieper; translated by Dan Farrelly;
translated by Una Farrelly.
pages cm
Includes index.
ISBN 978-1-58731-575-6 (hardback) –
ISBN 978-1-58731-576-3 (paperbound)
1. Pieper, Josef, 1904-1997. 2. Philosophers – Germany –
Biography. I. Title.
B3323.P434A3 2015
193 – dc23 [B]   2015032126

∞ The paper used in this publication meets the minimum requirements
of the American National Standard for Information Sciences - Perma-
nence of Paper for Printed Materials, ANSI Z39.48-1984.

ST. AUGUSTINE'S PRESS
www.staugustine.net

CONTENTS

I
Starting work in the Zero hour — Habilitation, an undertaking with many obstacles — "Poetry evenings" in Essen — Students' passionate willingness to learn — Drudgery of survival

The military truck which brought me from my strange captivity as a prisoner of war to Münster stopped in front of a military barracks in the outskirts of the city and set me down. The walk home wasn't far from there, but the heavy suitcase with my manuscripts forced me to take my time, and so I really got to see the devastated city. As I later found out, eight out of ten houses were completely destroyed, and not one of the old churches was undamaged. There were almost 1600 dead, not to speak of the injured and maimed.

Our house was completely undamaged, which was hard to believe after my walk through the rubble. At the garden gate beside the hanging larch I was surprised by the message "Property of a British subject" written clearly in ink and covered with cellophane. My wife had thought up this defense mechanism, but unfortunately it would turn out to be ineffective. Our youngest boy, now three and three-quarter years old, was playing outside in the sandpit and was the first to see me. His face became bright red, and at first he didn t say a word. But then he loudly announced all the stored-up news. The most important first: he peed now just like Thomas.

The house was already beginning to be habitable again; there was already glass in some windows. And it happened that right now there was a man with a horse and cart who was willing to transport from their storage place in the countryside some pieces of furniture and, in particular, the books which had been shifted away — of course, in exchange for suitable amounts of cigarettes and a few bottles of schnapps.

At the local administration building I met the senior official in the old office; he would soon be promoted to Minister of State. Almost like at the beginning, two and a half years previously, he allotted me two empty rooms as offices: this time, however, the windows were also missing, even the wooden frames had become detached with the force of air pressure from the explosions. On the floor there were small puddles of water and piles of debris, which at least had been swept into one place. My secretary, now widowed, also arrived. We chose what we needed from amongst halfway usable chairs and tables piled in the cellar and, crucially, we were given a typewriter. And so we set about organizing the first postwar aptitude tests. In cool weather I wore my overcoat under the inevitable white coat.

In my plywood suitcase a manuscript copy of *Wahrheit der Dinge* had made its way home. A few days after my arrival I took it out and brought it to the philosopher Gerhard Krüger in order to set my habilitation in motion. Even he had been summoned to the army as an interpreter, and similarly he had only just returned, from France. Although he had known for years about my ambition to complete my doctorate, he reacted in a friendly but somewhat "official" way. I was surprised and also somewhat disappointed. Probably Krüger thought I was taking it all too much for granted, as if it were only a formality which could be dealt with quickly. In any case I was informed that to start with he, presumably as supervisor, would read the doctoral thesis and then present it, with his report, to the faculty which was just now being re-formed. And if I had expected, as to some extent I had, that it would be made easier for me to skip a few hurdles because some of my *opuscula* had in the meantime been published, the situation in this regard was made clear without anything being expressly said. For better or for worse I prepared myself for a fairly long procedure. However, then it went, at least at the start, with unexpected speed.

Even Bishop von Galen, as my wife had heard, wanted me for the University. But in what manner was this to happen? I was very skeptical, but I went with a certain amount of curiosity to the theology seminary — with which I was familiar and which had suffered hardly any damage — at the Cathedral Square, where the bishop had taken up his temporary quarters. And, of course, nothing at all was then said about the University. Instead of that, to my surprise the conversation began fairly suddenly with a reminder of a socio-political discussion about *Quadragesimo anno* which we had once had with one another. That had been about twelve years previously, and during all that time the Bishop had never mentioned this point again. But now it had suddenly become very important to him; he produced a text of a few pages for me to take with me for critical examination; it was a type of "social manifesto." In our conversation, of course, there was also talk about the times in general. The Bishop was extremely unhappy with the occupation regime; he spoke about it like someone who felt he had been deceived. If the Anglo-Saxon press had believed that they could take him over as an ally because he was a prominent opponent of the National Socialists, that soon proved to be a blatant error. At the beginning of April he had already officially declared, in correcting a Reuters announcement, that he was sympathizing and suffering with the German people, and that he refused to express himself before the end of the war on political questions in public and that he wished his name not to be mentioned in England or America either in the press or on the radio. The ban on "fraternizing," and the dismantling plans in the Ruhr area, which in part belonged to his diocese, exercised him a great deal. "I said to Montgomery's representative straight to his face when he visited me: 'If you continue as you are doing, then the Germans will choose a new Hitler and they will do it in the most democratic way in the world'." The Bishop was now making things as uncomfortable for the new rulers as he had for the National Socialist Regime. And it would probably have come to a public scandal had not the sudden death of the valiant man put an end to it all. I saw Bishop von Galen on 16 March 1946, on his return from Rome, wearing the robes of a cardinal. It was moving to see him celebrated by the people. I stood shivering among the thousands in the cathedral square. For the first time there had been a great drive to move debris to make it possible to move through the city; in front of the west side of the cathedral under the big cross which had been made from half-charred vault beams, a bulldozer had pushed the rubble to form a type of podium on which the heads of the military government sat — likewise freezing and clearly not very enthusiastic — waiting for cardinal, who was very much delayed. With a distressed booming voice the terminally ill man offered his appreciation for the wonderful reception. A little more than a week after that, about a hundred paces from the place of this reception, he would be carried to his grave in his cathedral church — but nonetheless in the open air.

Only a few days passed before Gerhard Krüger wrote that he would recommend me to the faculty for habilitation. And even before the lectures of the winter semester 1945/46 began, this being the first still somewhat irregular semester after the war, the demand came from the Dean to submit three suggested topics for the colloquium. Exactly three months had passed since my release from hospital. With an uncomfortable feeling, I resolved, on the express advice of the Dean, to visit the Rector of the university, since I was after all the first candidate for habilitation in the new era. The prelate Georg

Schreiber, a former influential politician of the Central Party, had been voted into this office. Already at the time of my first doctorate I had persistently rejected his attempts to sponsor me; and so I was not expecting a particularly friendly reception. However, the prelate seemed to be taking a lively interest, seeing my "habilitation" as a "tactical exercise" as he said, and he even spoke of a "plan of action" needing to be drawn up. I replied that at the moment I was not aware of any opponent and that there was hardly reason for any strategic approach. He replied with some anecdotes about the vain attempts of those in power to get him: "but the chaplain was quicker." After a good quarter of an hour I was dismissed with somewhat distant civility.

During these months, of course, I had duties throughout the whole working day; sometimes I was out and about for a whole week carrying out aptitude tests, incidentally also in Bigge. And looking back, I ask myself what time could have been left for me to prepare for the quite daunting undertaking of the "habilitation." Besides, there were in late 1945 some other unforeseen decisions to be made which still affect my life right up to the present.

In November came the direct inquiry from Düsseldorf, from the office of the president of the North Rhine Province, about whether I would take up the position of lecturer of Philosophy at the Essen Pedagogical Academy which was about to be founded. Despite its reference number and official letterhead, it was less an official letter than a very personal, almost canvassing invitation. It was signed by Professor Joseph Antz, an old acquaintance from the job in the Dortmund "Institute"; we called him "Father Antz." Having been involved with adult and teacher training for many years, he now had the remit of rebuilding the pedagogical academies for the provisionally redrawn administrative region called North Rhine Province. But I had very little desire to give up the house and garden which we had only just reclaimed and to move into the place of devastation that was Essen. Still, the offer in itself was attractive, and without giving a final acceptance I sent to Düsseldorf a *curriculum vitae*, a list of my writings and, of course, the ominous political questionnaire of the occupying forces. At the same time, however, I inquired, with the letter from Düsseldorf still in my pocket, about the prospects of a pedagogical academy in Münster. The schools inspector Johannes Brockmann resided in the presidium at the Palace Square. He had now been named "general consultant for culture" by the military regime. He had been a Center politician until 1933, had been recalled from his enforced retirement, and was now to be the hapless re-founder of this same party. He seemed immediately pleased to see me and even offered me the direction of the Academy which was in fact being planned for Münster. It was awkward that the regional occupation officer, clearly out of fear of the infamous German "centralism," had divided the formal responsibility for teacher training among the three Westphalian regional districts. I therefore had to turn to the governing president of Münster, whose provisional seat of office was situated not in Münster but was still in Warendorf. Brockmann's strongly expressed assurance that there would not be the slightest difficulty soon proved to be false. Not alone was there not a trace of special interest in me, but I actually appeared to be totally unwelcome. The offer of a post in Essen clearly hadn't made the slightest impression. The General Consultant, very annoyed, became involved, but this seemed to make things worse. As at this stage it was Christmas and nothing would be happening in Münster, for better or for worse I had to seize the Essen offer. So I resigned my Local Administration contract on 31 January, 1946. Immediately after that, on 1 February, the lectures in Essen were to begin. In 1946, on the day before the Feast of the Epiphany, I traveled to Düsseldorf to sort everything out definitively.

Chapter I

Professor Antz was delighted and proved to be very generous. But on my return home that same evening there was a letter from Brockmann waiting for me: he had now taken on the responsibility for teacher training in Westphalia, and so the way was now clear. But it was too late — thankfully, as will become clear later on.

A fortnight later, the habilitation colloquium took place. However, just about a week before the appointment there was another incident, which almost threw me again. Gerhard Krüger wrote me an eight-page letter, which was very personal and perfectly friendly, in which he expressed his misgivings about me entering on a career at university at all. The bad thing was that the letter confirmed certain self-doubts I already had and also awakened others. Luckily, I say today, I did not worry about it at the time. Something which immediately struck me as suspicious was that Krüger's letter started off by extolling the virtues of my writings, my ability to bring to mind forgotten thoughts, and my "philosophical disposition." But then came talk about the demands of the "academic trade" and "scholarly research"; both seemed to be much less my leaning. So why would I direct my "academic ambitions" in that direction? He then mentioned significant philosophical outsiders like Theodor Haecker and Romano Guardini, and whether he meant them as role models or as warning examples I was not sure. I felt myself totally misunderstood; I did not really have the least amount of the usual academic ambition. At that time it was not completely clear whether it was a question of my personal problems or, in addition, the position of philosophy within the remit of the university as such. "Research" seemed, in the area of philosophy amounts to the history of ideas — basically history — and added to that the effort "to find out what others have thought," of which Thomas says it has nothing to do with the true meaning of philosophizing. In 1940 I had already used this sentence — its appeal lies in the fact that it is used precisely in a commentary on Aristotle — as a preface to my essay "On Thomas Aquinas."

I have always had deep and grateful respect for the individual knowledge and learning which was always at the fingertips of the specialist, who along with a thorough knowledge of his area keeps up with all the latest publications; but philosophy has always been somewhat different for me. And to be able to have my say as a teacher of philosophy in the university context — this was what I wanted now. That I might not fully — if at all — fit the image of the "scholar" and also of the "university professor" was completely clear to me; but I accepted that, even if always with a somewhat disturbed conscience. In reality, this constantly remained my "problem" during the first decade after the habilitation: how can I legitimately be a university teacher without becoming a "professor"? And also later as "Ordinarius," for example, I did not once undertake to supervise a doctorate, just as I was never the "director" of a seminar, not to speak of an institute.

But at that very critical time, when as I was burdened with the many demands made of me and read Gerhard Krüger's letter, such developments and particularly some unexpected helpful strokes of fortune were all still in the future. For the moment I was deeply affected and even somewhat distraught; as I said, I would almost have resigned. The theologian Joseph Pascher, with whom, in my helplessness, I spoke of my worries, recommended me dispassionately to examine myself and then to do exactly what I saw was right. A long conversation with Krüger — in which both of us were resolute and matter of fact — clarified everything. He immediately admitted to me that it was impossible for him to voice his worries at this stage, as the procedure had already been started; and now the affair could only take its course.

Chapter I

"Colloquium" was of course only a discreet name for a type of examination; and it was said that some of the professors were actually feared as "examiners." In fact, Heinrich Scholz the logician did not refrain from asking me the examination question which had become a classic: when is the statement "There are people on Mars" true?

Heinrich Scholz was one of the most remarkable figures I met at the university. At the time of my habilitation he was a very determined advocate of separating the natural sciences from what was at that time the unified Philosophy and Science Faculty. Above all, he himself wanted, as happened a short time later, to move with his "mathematical research of fundamentals" across to the "exact" sciences. He maintained that he was ashamed to be called a "professor of philosophy." Originally an Evangelist theologian who did his habilitation with Adolf von Harnack, he was always inspired with the ideal of exact ways of stating things and went over to the philosophy faculty, only to leave it again later for the very same reason — in other words through the door directly opposite the one through which he had entered. But the more consistently formalized his statements were, the less content they had. And since Heinrich Scholz had a personality which, besides its religiosity, was strongly influenced by art, he managed all of this only at the price of seeming bizarre and tensed up — which was manifested even in his words and gestures. The image he often invoked of the "philosopher in the white coat" was basically a romantic idea; and his consciously banned feelings repeatedly slipped in through the back door of his numerous "aphorisms," which often enough degenerated into sentimentality. Besides, Scholz understood his hunt for complete precision, which really in every conceivable world should have a claim to validity, always as a thoroughly theological matter, as he himself formulated it in an essay for Guardini's fiftieth birthday. And the puzzling observation, which he made at his first wife's grave to his friend Eduard Spranger, always seemed to me worthy of deep consideration; Spranger used it in a letter, which was read at a memorial function for Heinrich Scholz in the Aula of the university: "You understand, I cannot deal with the content of things anymore." His almost neuralgic sensitivity against people for whom the "content" was important could lead to unusually sharp outbursts. In this way he had made the particularly sensitive Peter Wust's life very difficult — and yet Heinrich Scholz could write him a very noble obituary on the occasion of his death in 1940.

For my colloquium lecture the faculty had chosen the topic "Heidegger's concept of truth." I had, of course, suggested it myself; but from the start it did not sit well with me, and I never thought of publishing this text. Not only was I not sure that I really understood what Heidegger meant ('The being of truth is freedom": what kind of "definition" is that, in which the definition is less known and clear than what should be defined?); in truth at that time my initial fascination gave way to a deep distrust. I simply could not trust the language of this author, and as a result I could not trust the author himself. "I just don't trust him" was later on the answer I sometimes gave to American friends when they absolutely insisted on hearing my opinion about Heidegger.

Although I completed my "colloquium" successfully in January 1946, it still did not bring me authority to teach; this came only after a public first lecture. In those days permission for this had to be granted by the English. They took their time, however. Way into the summer — almost another six months.

Despite all of my angry impatience, this time of waiting was to my advantage; it was precisely what I needed. It was not possible in those days simply to sit down at the desk and work. For example, I made my desk from fragments of our "reaction time testing device" which in October 1944 I had picked out of the rubble; and it was put into our kitchen for the winter of 1945/46, as this was the only room which could be heated — there were seven of us there. The cooker swallowed endless amounts of wood which had to be collected every couple of days from the rubbish heap of some destroyed house, a resource for which one began to develop an eye. As our children's handcart was limping along on one wheel, we had to push it and drag it instead of it rolling along; and even today it is easy for me to recall the miserable drudgery of this transporting, during which, despite the coldness of the winter, the sweat ran down the backs of my knees. Luckily we had a saw for cutting the beams to the right size for the stove. My wife traveled for whole afternoons throughout the countryside with sewing thread and cigarettes, with my officer boots, with a wristwatch and other valuables, in order to bargain for some bacon from the farmers, a pound of butter, eggs and milk. A good deal of our waking day was used up in managing mere survival.

At the same time I had to prepare my lectures and seminars for which I had been travelling to Essen for two days each week since 1 February 1946. At the beginning, just getting there was an adventure in itself; as I had books, manuscripts and whatever else I needed packed in my Air Force rucksack, at least on the open platform of the train carriages, which were constantly overfilled, I had both hands free to hold on. I quickly found a night lodging; from a tiny ice-cold garret I went down two floors each morning to wash in the bathroom of a lower middle class family. The Pedagogical Academy had been housed in a fairly desolate and much too small school building of the workers' suburb of Kupferdreh. There was only one auditorium, with the result that some of the lectures had to take place in a cinema which was rented for the afternoons. The air-raid shelter deep under the school yard was our "mensa"; in the afternoons there was a long queue of students and lecturers passing the huge tub out of which one's plate was filled. A paltry stock of books was called the "library." None of the lecturers had his own office. And the students did not really know where to go when they had breaks or lecture-free periods; in the summer they just sat outside on the wall in the schoolyard.

It was therefore clearly not external comfort which made the first post-war years into an incomparably happy time of intense learning and teaching. I never again experienced such an industrious intellectual curiosity as was shown by this generation of students who crowded into the lectures and seminars in their unsightly military uniforms, which the occupation force required to be re-dyed.

Clearly our start in Essen took place under a particularly lucky star. Firstly, we could pick the best three out of every ten students who applied; there was simply no room for more. The atmosphere of the house from the start was helped by the fact that the teachers unexpectedly got on really well, both personally and in their ethos. It was clearly to the credit of Helene Helming that this came about. She had been involved in the management from the first day, and that remained the case for more than a decade. She had been involved with the Catholic youth movement early on and had published the magazine *Die Schildgenossen* with Romano Guardini; although she had been forced out of work for a long time, she was internationally known in the field, particularly through her studies on Maria Montessori. And if the style of personal interaction became a little like that "cheerful respectfulness" which Goethe had extolled, this was doubtless thanks to this woman's personal caliber and ability to balance things.

In my lectures and seminars I at first lived from hand to mouth. But then, when you have reached a certain stage in life, such elemental new beginnings have their good points. For the seminar about Plato's *Symposium*, for example, I got the simple idea of establishing, with the help of Otto Apelt's

Plato-Index, in which dialogues the various people keep on appearing and what they say there — so that individual figures, like that of Criton, came to life in an unexpectedly concrete way. When I happened to tell Guardini later about this "method" he slapped himself on the forehead saying: "I should have thought of that." By far the nicest and most fruitful of my undertakings was an evening colloquium whose theme, ambitiously called "philosophical poetics," could have been changed: the students simply called it "Writers' evening." It began completely unintentionally because the landlord of one of the students gave her the use of a heated living room once a week to be used for a social meeting of five or six friends. Soon I was also invited; on this occasion they put together a real party meal from the items which everyone brought; there was even a bottle of wine. I had a few magazines and poetry books with me in which, for the first time, names like T. S. Eliot, Thornton Wilder, and J. P. Sartre occurred. We began to read aloud and interpret; and suddenly, following on from the poetry, there would be talk about anything and everything. After three or four weeks this colloquium had already become an institution. And, of course, what we were doing could not be kept secret; so it was asked, with a friendly tone of criticism, if the conversation evening could not be moved to an establishment which was accessible to everyone. For me, this interest in philosophizing was something very welcome; on the other hand, the more personal style could not possibly be maintained — that was my fear anyway. And when I suddenly stepped into a circle of more than a hundred participants I was gripped by fear. But after a moment, in fact surprisingly quickly, the unforced ease of the conversational exchange re-established itself. And with the interpretative and evaluating discussion of individual poems the more fundamental questions were again sparked off about the place of poetry and the arts in general in the totality of existence. My request not, for the sake of what is currently in fashion, simply to give up things which one spontaneously liked and found "beautiful," but, on the contrary, occasionally to have the courage to entertain kitsch, resulted in my regularly finding a piece of paper with a love poem on the desk, sometimes an original one; I would read it out and in no time the most lively discussion was in progress. Whole evenings were filled up with the reading of a single work: Eliot's *Murder in the Cathedral*, Sartre's *Flies*, Wilder's *Small City*, single chapters from Thomas Mann's *Dr. Faustus* novel. But again and again we ended up actually philosophizing; and far from engaging with technical terminology, all were confronted with the impenetrability of the world. Often enough on summer evenings when we had the discussions along the paths at the Baldency Lake, called "Lake Genesareth" by the students, we went on so long that when the sirens announced the midnight curfew, we had to run home at the double. I am fairly convinced that during these "Writers' evenings," which went on for many years, more philosophical awareness was awakened than in the actual lectures and seminars which were designated as being "philosophical."

In Münster the British University Officer had meantime granted me clearance for my public inaugural lecture, which finally took place on 5 July 1946 in the auditorium of the medical clinic — the only large lecture hall which had not been destroyed. I would be giving my lectures there in the years that followed. The topic which the faculty had chosen was called: "Philosophical training and intellectual work." With this formulation I wanted expressly to establish a contrast between both of these ideas which were understood to be almost synonymous and certainly mutually compatible. It was my wish to highlight the contemplative element of philosophizing and to restore the old concept of leisure (*scholé*) with new arguments — *in opposition to* the over-evaluation of both rational discursive activity and the function of thought understood as purely social. And I found it totally acceptable that Heinrich Scholz, as I later heard from Krüger, reacted to the strong applause of the audience with a perplexed shaking of his head. Incidentally, it was only through my stubborn resistance that the Dean agreed that I should not appear at this first inaugural lecture of the post-war period in tails; he had even been willing to lend me his, since I had never owned any. Anyway, it was all to be as formal and celebratory as possible; so I was told several times that when greeting him I was to call him "Spectability," a title which, in dealing with Dean of the Faculty, was hardly ever used any more even at the time of my first doctorate. However, this was not about personal vanity but about the view — understandable and shared by a considerable number at the time — that one must, after these twelve years of barbaric formlessness, restore to the traditional academic ritual its due importance. All of this did not make sense to me; and later on I seldom could decide to take part in academic ceremonies at which the teaching body appeared wearing robes. Nowadays nobody doubts that it would have been better, immediately after the war, to have found more modern forms of academic life than, a good twenty years later (or — too late), to have to let the newly retrieved old props soundlessly disappear under the pressure of rough student protests. At that time, however, before the beginning of my first semester as a university teacher, I had worries of a completely different sort. I was in the meantime forty-two years old, and I had the feeling that I had reached a certain age limit in my life; even a year later I don't think I would have taken on the stress of the habilitation.

But now that I possessed the *venia legendi*, what was I to say to the auditorium from the podium? I had vaguely imagined, in accordance with my studies to date, to espouse the cause of some kind of neo-Scholastic philosophy modified by phenomenology and existentialism. But then that was exactly what I had never done. Because of the student body which was mainly composed of people who had just returned from war and captivity, as I knew from my experience in Essen, I could not imagine offering an abstract systematic lecture, for instance about epistemology. In the midst of this devastation was it not obligatory, firstly, even for myself, to clear up again what this whole business of philosophy meant and what philosophy was in fact for? "What does it mean to philosophize?" This was the title I wanted to use for my first university lecture. Gerhard Krüger, however, felt that this, as he put it, too "unusual" formulation lacked due academic discretion; and so I made do, although not particularly enthusiastically, with the title: "Introduction to Philosophy." The students admittedly were clearly not frightened away by this traditional formulation. Furthermore, although, as the youngest private lecturer, I was given the least popular time, namely late on Saturday morning, they came in such crowds that, despite using a large lecture theatre which had about 400 seats, from the beginning of the year 1947 in the middle of the first semester I had to halve the audience and hold each lecture twice: from ten until eleven and then the same again from eleven until twelve. The same was repeated then in the following years. Besides, the Saturday morning proved not to be as unsuitable as might have been expected; the science students, for example, and the medical students could not come any other day; and so I kept this slot later, long after the five-day week was being introduced — for more than twenty-five years, in fact.

In yet another point I met with Krüger's complete disapproval; however, happily this time it came too late. Since my habilitation he had moved to the university of Tübingen. Immediately after my inaugural lecture I was offered an appointment to the "Research Examination Office" by means of an official communication. I replied in all innocence by post that

Chapter I

I was very tied up in Essen with my official occupation and that I hoped I could be relieved of the work envisaged for me. This invitation, according to Krüger, had been meant as an honor, and I was guilty of gross impoliteness. Perhaps he was right. In any case, no such invitation was ever repeated. But how much this *faux pas,* if it was one, saved me futile work in the following period with its huge amounts of compulsory examinations in the subject of philosophy, and how many genuinely interested students it sent me, nobody could know in that summer of 1946.

One evening when I came home exhausted from Essen, the news awaited me that a commissioner of the British Military had been looking at the house; the well-preserved sign which was still beside the garden gate had not put them off. At least from now on I had access to the Officer for the University who resided in the former building of the General Command; so one day I was wandering unexpectedly through the familiar corridors which still smelled the same as ever. I tried to make it clear to the young intellectual in uniform that a library with an inaccessible set of books packed in boxes was as good as no library at all. But clearly he held my mention of three to four thousand volumes as considerably exaggerated; and with a surprising willingness, I thought, he jumped up to look at what to him seemed a "very interesting" private library. Visibly surprised, he found my statements confirmed, perhaps even understated. First and foremost, he realized that an evacuation would mean the loss of the job offer which I had only just received. As he left, he promised that he would do his best. As a matter of fact from that point on we remained undisturbed.

II

New colleagues and the return of old friends —
Ecumenical workgroup — An odd private lec-
turer — Contact with the occupying forces and
English friendships — *Leisure and Ritual*

During the second winter after the war we wanted, at all costs,
to avoid the misery of everyone having to be in the narrow
kitchen, huddled together around the stove. I just needed quiet
for writing down my lectures, for which I was of course completely drawing on my own ideas. You could not force the children to be silent; they were by now four, eight and ten years
old; Thomas was already attending secondary school at my
old Schola Paulina. So we had the truly utopian idea of building a tiled stove in the doorway between my room full of
books and the living room, so that it would heat both rooms.
The stove builder, a small man who made a shy impression ,
listened to our plan with an indulgent astonishment; nevertheless he found the position of the fireplace quite reasonable.
"But do you have a stove? And the tiles?" And then he wished
us good luck and went; it was not profitable for him to speak
further with such hopelessly unworldly people; for him it was
over. However, we were not ready to give up. In the early summer mornings, on the lame hand-cart we carried tiles gathered
from the piles of rubble in the city; they were scraped clean to
some extent and piled up in the garden; actually the traces of
grout proved later to be particularly ornamental. Unbelievably, we acquired the stove in a similar fashion. In Wetzlar the
former librarian of the Plenge Institute was working as a

bookseller. She had converted to Catholicism years ago, partly with my help, and we had remained in informal but constant correspondence. With an unusual instinct for everything which could be of any interest to me, for a couple of decades she would note down for me, on calendar pages, unusual journal articles and forgotten books. Among her current customers there was one of the directors of the Wetzlarer Eisenwerke Buderus (Wetzlar Buderus Ironworks), for whom she must have done the same thing. And since books were almost as difficult to get as Iron Industry products, a most unlikely thing happened through negotiations on the part of the unknown book lover: in exchange for a parcel of Guardini and Pieper books taken from my bookseller and my own stock, with, of course, the normal payment, one day the stove arrived into the house packed in a crate! Our master craftsman heard it in disbelief. And once the stove pipe was procured — an issue which could have caused the whole project to founder again — he actually enjoyed making a work of art out of the unusual tiles.

In the middle of this undertaking — the hall and rooms were packed full of sacks of cement, piles of bricks, tubs of grout, and furniture which had been pushed aside — Joachim Ritter, the successor to Gerhard Krüger who had just been appointed to Münster, arrived out of the blue. He dismissed my apology about the discomfort of the reception with the words of Heraclitus: "Here too are Gods." I was happy with that. And when I visited him on that same evening — we were almost neighbours — a spontaneous friendly bond developed which was fruitful for both of us. After more than a decade, however, it dissolved because of a specific academic conflict.

In the first semesters working together, after my Saturday morning lectures I used to call in to my colleague who was only a year older than me. And at one time, during the holidays we met day after day in my office for a shared reading of

Aristotle's metaphysics. I had hesitantly suggested including Thomas Aquinas as well as other commentaries. Of course, this late work of my revered master was not unknown to me; but I had never read it in terms of whether and how far his interpretation, which was based on a fairly flawed Latin translation, really reflected the meaning of the ancient text. So I was delighted and also a little surprised when Ritter said one morning that we should put away all except the Thomas commentary which had been unknown to him until then: only this commentary made Aristotle's opinion more deeply accessible. — This is when I heard the name C. S. Lewis for the first time and the title of his wonderful book *The Problem of Pain*. Ritter had come across it during his time as a prisoner of war in England. Some years later I translated it, in collaboration with my wife, for the newly founded Jakob Hegner Publishing House.

During the same winter semester of 1946/47 a third person along with Ritter and me took up his teaching post in Münster: the theologian Hermann Volk. And it happened that we three, together with the Latinist Franz Beckmann, soon formed a type of club which met regularly on Saturday afternoons for cycling and walking. — In the first post-war years there was no such thing as "lay theology" — in other words, the later massively practised and by no means unproblematic study of the subject "theology," where one could take a state exam which would qualify one for teaching at second level, as one could in German or history. Actually there was something else happening: there were countless students of all faculties who were completely unconcerned about any eventual grade in an examination and were urgently seeking a higher than empirical justification for their own world view. These students went in droves to the constantly overcrowded dogma lectures of Hermann Volk. There were several things which fascinated his listeners. First and foremost was that in him were to be found together, in an exemplary way, spirituality and speculation. Volk did not teach theology as a type of "information." As a person he stood for what he believed. It was impossible for students not to notice that. Besides, this theologian, with his vehement vitality, took part in the cultural life of the time. He might travel to Frankfurt specifically for a five-hour performance of Eugene O'Neill's *Mourning becomes Electra*. Often enough his own excellent lectures had to be repeated because of overcrowding due to the particular brilliance of his words about the problem dealt with in a film or about Claudel's *The Satin Slipper,* a play which he particularly loved. When someone ironically asked him in Bochum Theatre, at a discussion about the dramas of Jean-Paul Sartre which at that time were now reaching their German audience, why a Catholic theologian was so interested in these atheists, he answered to the applause of the auditorium: "If Sartre is showing what it is like in a world without God, then I don't need to do it." These things were not a hobby on the side for Volk, but as every listener could sense, they were related very directly to his post as a teacher of theology.

At the universities at that time the catchword of the decade, or let's say of that five years, was *General Studies.* The British occupying forces, in the course of the disastrous re-education program, were striving to set up — along with the normal academic subjects — general education courses on philosophy, the history of ideas, and later also sociology. As was to be expected, not much came of it. The universal study which was comprehensive and profound and went beyond individual subjects and which focused on whole world issues was done in a much more undeclared and completely different way. An attendance count, for example, showed that for the two three-hour lectures of Ritter and Volk — which took place simultaneously — for a whole semester there was more than a quarter of the complete Münster student body in attendance, over a thousand. In today's figures, given the overcrowding of the university, that would amount to much more than 5000 students, a fantastic and unbelievable figure.

Hermann Volk, who was at that time over forty the same as Ritter and myself, unfortunately did not work at the university very long; in 1962 he returned as Bishop of Mainz to his Rhine-Main homeland. When the appointment was made I was just on the point of setting off for a semester in America as a guest lecturer, from where I sent him a traditional red rug of the Navajo Indians to mark his consecration as bishop. During my quick visit to congratulate him and say goodbye, I could not resist reminding the dignitary, half-jokingly and half-seriously, about the warning which the head of the Dominican Order gave to Albertus Magnus when he was about to exchange his teaching post for the bishopric: "I'd prefer to see my beloved son on the bier than on the bishop's throne in Regensburg." These strong words, quoted on such a festive occasion were understandably not seen in a particularly positive light. The sister of the honored man who ran the household replied spontaneously: "That's not the way we think." None the less, that sentence sometimes came into my head in the meantime when I saw my friend almost break down under the strain firstly of the Council and then of the post-Conciliar confusions. He was always overstressed and exhausted and hardly had time and energy to do any of the theological work which he urgently needed to do. His vitality seems to have come to the fore again and again, particularly in his hard-hitting words born of the moment; it is said that he replied to a young cleric in response to the "progressively" typical question doubting what liturgical dress was good for: "Good for the fact that you disappear under it!" — And with regard to the almost anonymous selfless work of the academically trained theologians within the leadership committees of the church — who will say, even if it is not rewarded with any

public glory (still he was acknowledged by his unusual eleva-
tion to the status of Cardinal), that it was not perhaps more
fruitful and maybe still is than academic lecturing?

These matters, however, were not yet bothering us in the
first happy and successful years of teaching at the university.
No one knew how things would develop.

At that time, friends with whom we had lost contact during the last war years gradually began to get in touch. At the
end of 1945 a soldier coming home from a south German hospital brought us a letter written in pencil by Heinrich Wild.
Wounded in Italy while being captured by the Americans, he,
too, was about to be released. And it was not long until he
wrote from Munich that the Hegner production for which he
had the rights would, in conjunction with Kösel, be taken up
again as soon as possible and continued. It could not have
been better news for me; I was already able to name a few titles of future books.

My wife's brother came unexpectedly from England. He
had meanwhile become a British citizen and had a large legal
practice. He thought that the whole of Germany smelt like a
public convenience. Peter Suhrkamp also got in touch before
the end of 1945. Since our previous meeting in Berlin in the
spring of 1943, dreadful things had befallen him. A few weeks
later his tower apartment had been destroyed and his library
had gone up in flames. He sent a Christmas parcel of books
from the firm, which had remained intact; a page with his own
verse, which had been supposed to arrive with the parcel,
came in the New Year: "We are not the same as before/nothing
stops us from keeping up our friendships/the city has fallen
asunder/we are sending around the year's greetings." We were
much less than halfway through the new year of 1944 when
we received an ominous message that Peter Suhrkamp was ill
in a sanatorium, and for the moment could not be reached by
letter. Then we got the unvarnished truth from his wife: her

husband had been arrested. "None of us knows about the reasons and how long it might last." Strangely enough he was then released before the end of the war and ultimately, in a miraculous way, escaped death by bombing: while he was lying in a Berlin clinic with a serious lung infection which meant that he should not be moved, they had not wanted to bring him to an air-raid shelter which then, having been totally destroyed by a mine, became the grave of everyone who had fled there. A good six months later he sent me his first postwar letter and asked for my collaboration with his "Book for young people," a large number of copies of which were soon to be published and distributed. He did not say a word about any of these dreadful events.

At the same time I was unexpectedly able to see Gerhard Krüger, who at this stage had for a long time been back living in Tübingen. Paul Simon, Robert Grosche and the Archbishop of Paderborn, later Cardinal Lorenz Jaeger, had in conjunction with some Protestant friends — among them Bishop Wilhelm Stählin — put in place the long-cherished plan of establishing a discussion group in which controversial theological questions were to be openly discussed. Meantime, this group continued to exist for a quarter of a century. Cardinal Bea claims that without this groundwork the Second Vatican Council's decree on ecumenism would hardly have come about. Paul Simon encouraged me also at that time to become involved; given my half-hearted commitment at the time I could not yet know what an enrichment these meetings would be for me. Almost the best thing about it was the absolute lack of publicity; the press reported not a word either about the existence or about the subject matter of the discussions. That made it easy for the participants to speak without any concern for confessional prestige; and, in fact, divisions in the debates sometimes ran diagonally across both groups. And, of course, there was often very sharp-edged debate, so much so that we sometimes wondered if another meeting would happen at all. But such crises were sorted out every time — characteristically less through theological farsightedness than humanity and humor: for example, through a lusty interjection from the Rhinelander Robert Grosche or through von Campenhausen's wonderful nonchalance. One evening, when the discussion could not be reconciled, he announced with Baltic directness that, as for him, he was unfortunately unable to think clearly after nine in the evening.

The leading minds of the first sitting apart from those named already were: Gottlieb S hngen, Hermann Volk, the Benedictine Viktor Warnach on the Catholic side; the evangelical theologians Hans Asmussen, Peter Brunner, Heinrich Schlier, Edmund Schlink and the Dane Skydsgaard. Later there were also Joseph Lortz, Karl Rahner, Joseph Ratzinger, Rudolf Schnackenburg, and in the evangelical group the two Lohse brothers and the young Wolfhart Pannenberg. Of course, in the first meeting — as "paragraph one" of our unwritten statutes declared — no side had the intention of proselytizing the other. However, there were some conversions, not of course from Catholicism to Protestantism, but the other way around. The first convert was Heinrich Schlier; soon he was followed by his friend Gerhard Krüger.

I met Krüger again when I was getting out of the train at the small railway station Scherfede at the beginning of September 1946. Carrying my military rucksack just as he was, I was about to set off on the walk to the conference place in the Cistercian Convent of Hardehausen in Warburger B rde. It was a wonderful late summer's day, and we took many hours to get there, as we kept lying down on the side of the road in the grass and, while looking at the wandering clouds, told each other about our experiences during our time in the military. For the first time there were no official matters involved, and our relationship became closer and warmer and involved a lot of laughter. And the controversial theological discussions which had now become the order of the day for us and which had even in earlier days occasionally been sparked off by a statement of mine that Krüger vigorously opposed — that Thomas Aquinas was the last great teacher of the as yet undivided Western Christendom (Augustine — yes; but Thomas? Surely he is overpoweringly Catholic) — even such disputes became relaxed and cheerful conversations between friends. But after only a few years our connection was suddenly interrupted. Krüger, who was just fifty years old, suffered a stroke which luckily left his mental capacity unaffected but which affected him so much otherwise that he was now no longer able to take part in discussions or to teach. The physical paralysis did ease gradually, but a speech disorder made it ultimately impossible for him to form grammatically correct sentences. For him the most painful thing was that, despite his sight remaining fully intact, he could no longer read; he simply could not grasp the sense of what he had read and yet he could understand the most complicated of texts if they were read aloud to him.

Years later, when I made my first visit to Gerhard Krüger in Munich, I was very taken aback when I saw him, but I quickly got used to what was in fact an insignificant impediment of speech. What amazed me was the cheerfulness of a man who normally was rather too serious. Without any reserve he told about his conversion to the Catholic faith. I reminded him of our dispute about Thomas and asked him how he now judged his (Thomas's} previous writings. But he said they had always basically been totally Catholic. More than a decade after this meeting I used as a preface to my short book about *Concept and the Claims of Tradition* his melancholy words: "We live now only from our inconsistency, from the fact that we have not silenced all tradition." He then let me know that he was glad he could be part of present-day debate in this way. In February 1972 Gerhard Krüger died at seventy years of age. The eulogy for him which Edmund Schlink delivered shortly after that to the ecumenical work group spoke again of the *hilaritas mentis* which had radiated from him in the last days of his life. The true root of this was, as I am convinced, what his friend Heinrich Schlier called: an existence which is completely based on the sacramental.

Hence for me, at the beginning of my first university semester, work opportunities and other opportunities of influence opened up on all sides, even in the university itself. But I consistently refused to exchange the position of private lecturer too readily for that of a full professor. Some colleagues openly and emphatically shook their heads about this strange attitude. But I simply had too much to catch up on in my own basic education. Besides, I needed more than a full day to write out a forty-five-minute lecture and often half the night as well. Only seven years after my inaugural lecture did I risk announcing my first seminar at the university; its theme was, by the way, the relationship between active life and contemplation.

But the temptations already began during my first semester in the winter of 1946/47. On one icy morning, announced by telegram and dressed in a fur coat, a representative of the Philosophy Faculty of the University of Göttingen stepped into my office; he had arrived by car, for which, as he told me, the Bishop of Hildesheim had provided the petrol. My guest did not wish to sit down until he had delivered the "message" for the sake of which he had undertaken the journey — which seemed unnecessary, given the fact that the postal system was now working well. So I heard — while of course still standing — the "message" that his Faculty had listed me as the only candidate, *unico loco*, for the newly established "Professorship for Weltanschauung." Before I could say anything, my clearly anticipated objection was answered with: it is, in fact, a chair to be occupied by a Catholic Christian, but formally it would be simply run as a Chair of Philosophy (an all too cleverly calculated regulation which would very soon prove to be absurd). Now I had to declare my intention, for better or for worse, of not taking on a full university professorship Chair for the moment. The old gentleman thought he had not understood me correctly at first, but then he could barely hide his boundless disappointment, indeed his displeasure — which I actually understood very well.

My Münster colleagues also clearly found my attitude difficult to understand; they did not completely accept the seriousness of my justification. And I really had several reasons. For example, I wanted to keep on the work of teacher training. And there was another reason which I could, of course, only confide to some friends but could not divulge in an official interview for the post: that one does not easily leave a garden in which one has personally planted trees.

Then a remarkable thing happened in Münster: the successor to Peter Wust gave up his university professorship in order to teach in a small episcopal academy. And I was encouraged from various quarters to take up his position. Beckmann and Ritter also maintained that the Faculty would be completely in favor of it. When I still refused, this was again followed by surprise and resentment; it was gradually seen as total eccentricity. An Emeritus professor sought to make it clear to me in a long letter that when I completed my habilitation I had taken on the ethical commitment of accepting a Chair when the occasion arose. For me, however, there was still, in this particular case, a quite different important reason. The occupier of the so-called "Concordat Chair" had, by virtue of customary law, the duty of looking after the philosophical instruction of theology students. For that it was not only usual but also necessary to give a course of recurring systematic lectures which I felt absolutely unable to do; besides, the complete philosophy degree lasted only four, formerly only three semesters, and then ended with a final exam called the *Philosophicum*. I knew this setup from the inside and from my own experience, very precisely. At the exact moment when one was at best just beginning to understand philosophical questioning, the students of theology were already "finished with philosophy"; after the exam they would as a rule never touch a philosophy book again; the theology course also left no time for it. The only person who gradually understood my unyielding refusal, and finally also supported it, was the Latinist Franz Beckmann. Almost a decade older than I, he had many times acted as my mentor.

At our Saturday discussions he was the quietest of the four of us; but he listened very critically, which often enough later became apparent from a surprising comment. For myself I called him a "Roman," not only because he was quiet but also because he had this very particular sense for the wordless business of legitimate exercise of power, which he himself understood absolutely. Even had all his own library and also all his notes and lecture notes not been destroyed by an early air strike on the city, he was hardly likely to have published large books; he also had the ability, as the example of a small publication about Virgil proves, to write impeccable German — a rare thing amongst scholars. Beckmann had been involved in both World Wars as an officer — most recently as a regimental commander on the East Front. However, he rarely spoke about his war experiences; the only comment which he let slip to me once implied no more than there was often "death on all sides." For rebuilding in the post-war years he was the ideal Dean of Faculty. Ritter told me once that he had come to Münster principally because of the forceful personality of Beckmann. And when in 1949 it was the turn of the Faculty of Philosophy to supply a Rector of the University, Beckmann was chosen and a year later was voted in again for a further term of office. He was generally baffled by the early, relatively mild lack of discipline of the students; he would have preferred to react as an officer; but of course it was clear to him that this was not possible. In the last years of his teaching career he had withdrawn from academic concerns with a certain kind of stubbornness. Many regretted that, but I could understand it. — When he died not long after becoming an Emeritus professor, it emerged that he had requested that the date of his funeral be not published; that fitted in with his personality. Also the burial service was not carried out in the usual way. I wrote his wife a verse from the *Divina Comedia,* which seemed to me to be the right epitaph for my friend; it is the promise which Beatrice makes to the poet: "You are here for a short time as a guest/and then a citizen beside me/ in that Rome where Christ is a Roman."

Despite his different opinion at the start, Beckmann encouraged me in my concern about taking on the Münster Concordat Professorship. Otto Most, who was appointed shortly afterwards, found my refusal so unbelievable that, in his almost exaggerated decency, he visited me before accepting in order to assure himself that I was really serious. — During the course of the next years a string of similar offers followed; but I refused most of them at the preliminary enquiry stage. Curiously enough that earned me the reputation of being particularly arrogant. In this situation I was leaving myself open to not inconsiderable disadvantages. The "professor" at a Pedagogical Academy was at that time — and not completely unjustly I think — perceptibly worse off than the University professor; he not only received less money, but there was not yet the institution of the emeritus system instead of retirement.

When Michael Schmaus, in Münster again for a lecture, told me — according to his instructions — that I should send on my curriculum vitae and list of publications to the Philosophy Faculty in Munich, I answered him as a good acquaintance, but perhaps a little too bluntly or too casually, that we could save ourselves the trouble of all of that. Shortly afterwards, a mutual friend told me that Schmaus had expressed himself a little indignantly about my answer (What is this private lecturer thinking, to react like this to the greatest German University?).

One day Max Horkheimer, who was then Dean of the Faculty of Philosophy, sent me an invitation to give a "guest lecture" in Frankfurt. Of course, I had half a suspicion about what that meant. But I accepted with thanks and suggested as a title: "About the negative element in the philosophy of Thomas Aquinas." Then it happened that the Hessian University Consultant in Hessen had traveled from Wiesbaden. In any case there was a particularly stimulating night discussion with Horkheimer and his friend Adorno. To the inquiry that followed shortly afterwards by telegram as to whether I would be willing provisionally to accept a Chair of Philosophy I was able to reply with the understandable argument that this was not possible because of my permanent position in Essen.

Dealing with the British Occupying Forces was a particularly delicate matter in those years. They were not only represented at every university by a "control officer," but they had also employed an Educational Advisor responsible for the whole occupation zone and a special representative for church matters. On the one hand it was repugnant to tell those in power what they wanted to hear in order to gain advantages, as some, though very few, colleagues did; but the idea of discussing the absurd idea of the victors undertaking the re-education of the Germans was even worse. On the other hand, it was difficult to ignore the intellectual standing of a humanist like Robert Birley; and the discussion sessions organized by him about general cultural questions were simply unique opportunities to break through the twelve-year block which had been decreed and to speak with people of different nationalities and minds. However, one felt a little like an opportunist and collaborator on climbing into the Mercedes which was in front of the house in order to be driven for a weekend to the Westphalian country residence of the British Educational Advisor. And there were more than a few among my University colleagues who strictly refused to attend such things or would have refused them had they been invited. Even Joachim Ritter, I knew, observed my occasional attendance with silent disapproval. Then, I had contributed, though with a certain feeling of unease at first, to the commemoration book for Robert Birley when he left Germany in 1949 after three years of service in order to become Headmaster of Eton College. Only when I showed him the text did Ritter admit: yes, one could do it that way, that is "different."

I formulated my farewell as follows: "Dear Mr. Birley, I am one of those Germans who are of the opinion that we lost the war for good and right reasons, and that we must therefore accept the consequences of the defeat as a burden which is by no means coincidental; at the same time we cannot see this burden, meaning the occupation of our country by the victors, as something quite pleasing. It seems to me all the more reason gratefully to accept as a gift, in this difficult situation, the encounter with people whose personal culture of mind and heart is able to make us forget all politically rooted problems and embarrassments by unexpectedly shifting the encounter out into the clear sky of great and eternal things.

"I believe, Mr. Birley, that you will feel somewhat uneasy at reading these 'high-sounding words.' But allow me to say to you in this farewell that I am very grateful to have met you. A short relaxed evening conversation in Hilter about Newman and T. S. Eliot, as well as your last lecture in Münster about the education in the arts in which, in such a revolutionary way (as is typical in true tradition), Plato, Dante and Milton were being spoken of, are particularly fond memories for me. —

With best wishes and in the hope of our meeting somewhere again, yours faithfully . . ."

Actually I never met this wonderful man again. I did see him almost twenty years later (1967) in Toronto where I had been invited by the university there as Centennial Professor, on the occasion of the Canadian 100-year celebration of Dominion Status. As I was walking through the foyer of one of the big hotels in search of a hairdresser, I was surprised by a face well known to me and unmistakeable; but I could not remember at all where I knew it from and to whom it belonged. It was only when I was back in my apartment that, while leafing through a calendar of events, I saw the name Robert Birley, and it all became clear. But when I tried to reach him the next day by telephone, I found out that he had indeed been staying in that hotel but had just checked out.

In the spring of 1947 I was introduced by Franz Joseph Schöningh to two English people who were to stay in contact with me for decades. Through the Americans Schöningh had become the licensee of a large Munich newspaper publishing house; the *Hochland* appeared again, edited by him, as a bi-monthly paper; and, as before, our friend drove in his own car throughout the country and told highly dramatic stories, especially about his curious activities during the last years of the war. He had arranged to meet in our house a British friend who also wrote for *Hochland* from time to time. He hid his real name (Count Alexander Dru de Montgelas) and called himself simply "Mr. Alick Dru." He was particularly knowledgeable about French intellectual life and he could laugh in a delightfully boyish and innocent way. Above all, he had the talent of making the other person speak. In any case, I told him in detail about two of my books which were only at the planning stage. This was a little out of character for me. To my surprise he immediately said he was prepared to translate them into English. This did actually come to pass a few years later.

Of the books which, as I said, still had to be written, one of them was under the beneficial pressure of a deadline: for the Bonner Hochschulwochen of the same summer I had to distil four lectures from my first Münster course — an unexpectedly arduous task. Those weeks in Bonn, however, were an also unexpectedly exhilarating experience. We witnessed the combination of more or less successful improvisation, the good-humored manner in which people managed to do without external comfort, the generosity of foreign food donations — with the difficulties of sharing them equally — and, above all, the enthusiasm and stimulating attentiveness of the mostly young listeners who every morning pushed their way, in this sunny summer weather, into the hall of the Pedagogical Academy (later the seat of the German Government). — All of this generated a dense atmosphere of intellectual vitality characteristic the first post-war years which were passing much too quickly. In a circle of old friends whom we had not seen for years, and also new ones, we went with our wives to adventurous banquets at which there was no end to the talking, discussion and laughter. My publisher friend Dr. Wild was also there, and he took the manuscript of the four lectures, just as they were, to Munich and printed them. They appeared in the following spring under the title: *What does philosophizing mean?* which had been planned from the outset.

Directly after these days in Bonn, and almost still fired up by the same impulse, I sat down to the task of dealing with the much more difficult small book which, in various drafts, I had carried around with me for some time: *Muße und Kult* (Leisure and Ritual). The family of a children's doctor, a friend of ours who sometimes kept an eye on our children, had given me a tiny room in her Sauerland holiday home "on the Böhre." Sometimes his own children who were of student age and their friends were there in the overcrowded house, but my retreat was away in the upper floor of a wooden shed. There was a bed, a chair and a table which was pushed in front of the window through which one could look at the hilly landscape without seeing any housing. Now and then there was the screeching of the buzzards circling above the forest whose play could fascinate and distract a person for minutes; otherwise there was absolute silence. Only for meals — that was how it was arranged — did I go over to my friends. And because I began work early in the morning, the evenings were there for sociable conversation and diverse preoccupations with the muse thought up by the young people; I myself contributed to a Konrad Wei evening on one occasion. During those unforgettable three weeks, which benefited from the brightness of the late summer and the fresh cool of the morning hours and were spiced by the ingredients of human closeness and friendship, the manuscript grew rapidly into a complete *opusculum*. And when the prettiest of the four charming daughters, who was a student in Göttingen and recently engaged, readily and undaunted sat at her typewriter in order to convert my handwriting, at my dictation, into a readable form, I was actually able at the beginning of October to send the publishing house a completed manuscript, dedicated to the hospitable family. In the spring of 1948 it was already on the book market. None of my other writings were written under more favorable conditions; maybe it is even noticeable in the text.

The second Briton, with whom I had become acquainted a couple of months earlier, was Hubert Howard, a friend of Alick Dru. He was the Military Government's official representative in charge of church affairs. It never really became clear to me what he actually did and achieved in this position; however, one could well imagine this sincere, aristocratic man as a negotiator and peacemaker. Although at first he seemed to have a fragile sensitivity, he proved in discussion to be unexpectedly firm in matters of principle. He belonged to the

Catholic noble Howard family whose head is the Duke of Norfolk. One day, after a long period of silence, he sent us news of his marriage to a Roman Princess along with an invitation that, whenever we were in Rome, we should visit him without fail in *Palazzo Caetani*. To us that sounded at first like pure fantasy; but at Easter 1953 — the Essen students had organized a trip to Italy — Thomas, Monika and I wandered into the *Via Botteghe Oscure*, past the Communist Party Headquarters, and on to the Palace of the Boniface VIII Dynasty. We were shown some of the hundred sights of the house: famous paintings, golden wallpaper, expensive furniture; we were allowed to see the private studio of the Princess who was absent at that time. An American by birth, she was publishing the extravagant literary and artistic magazine *Botteghe Oscure*. Howard's wife, a not insignificant painter, did not speak German, and so the conversation had to be held in English. Monika, who was so bemused by all the splendor that she had hardly spoken a word, now went completely silent; the white gloves of the servant, who was suddenly placing the soup in front of her, were simply too much. Thomas, on the other hand, almost seventeen years old, chatted on without embarrassment, and every now and then even dropped a newly acquired Italian word into the mix. Howard clearly enjoyed all of this; he particularly liked Thomas, with whom he had a special bond. And as we departed he urgently requested that we get in touch with him on our next visit. — When we did that eight years later, on the occasion of Michael's final school examination, despite the invitation and arrangement we arrived at an inopportune moment: the old Prince had died a few days previously. The name and dynasty of Caetani died with him; the only son had died in the Second World War and the Howards had no children. A gleaming car was sent to the door of our cheap hostel with provisions for the whole day. The discreetly uniformed chauffeur was to bring us to Ninfa, south of Rome. In old travel guides one finds ruins of a city given three stars as a special sight, although the city is overrun with flowers after being abandoned because of malaria; for some time, however, the Caetanis had blocked public access to their property and Howard had ordered hundreds of roses and large-bloom types of clematis from England and turned the whole into an enchanted garden. Monika and Michael were at first not very enthusiastic about having to devote a whole day to a sight which seemed so unattractive, but then, when the pre-arranged sounding of the horn came from the chauffeur, it turned out to be much too soon.

But this is jumping ahead by almost one and a half decades. In the year 1947 it was impossible to contemplate such trips; there were enough problems traveling from the British into the American or even into the French occupation zone, not to speak of the Russian zone. With us the different "victorious powers" had varied and — rightly or wrongly — fairly solidly established reputations. The Americans were considered to be consistently generous but unpredictable; the English bureaucratic but dependable, the French politically and culturally undogmatic, though bloody-minded in small things.

III
The gate to the world opens up: Trip to Switzerland — Richard Seewald and Eckart Peterich — First invitation to the USA: Waldemar Gurian — State of emergency in Germany and currency reform

The first trip abroad after the war arrived as an unexpected bonus for my wife and myself in the spring of 1948, fifteen years after Hitler's Germany had closed the borders behind the people arriving home from the *Primavera Siciliana*. In the Swiss town of Olten, Jakob Hegner had founded the Summa Publishing House together with the Publishing House Otto Walter. A typical Hegner company name, but, as soon became clear, also not a very successful venture. All the same, Dr. Wild conceded to him the rights for Austria and Switzerland — which could not be used in any case — and also the rights to my books which began to appear in wonderfully printed editions. They made me a considerable advance payment on the expected fee, and we used that to travel to Switzerland. There were unending problems with visas, but finally we sat on our suitcases and waited for hours on the windy platforms for an uncertain connection. In the first-class waiting room of Cologne there was at least a warm soup that you could buy on paying a deposit for the plate and spoon; there were signs on the walls forbidding you to sleep on the tables. On the night train to Basel, for which one needed a special certificate as well as the ticket, we were relieved to have finally installed ourselves, when after a few stations the ticket inspector put us out of the compartment; it was apparently reserved for foreigners. Our fellow travellers, shaking their heads in embarrassment, carried the suitcase out for my wife. In the part of the train which was reserved for Germans and which was separated from the other part by a luggage wagon you could not pass through there was neither light nor heat; still, the window panes were intact. Then the next morning we were alone in the compartment and, as we passed the border feeling completely tired out and arrived in the Swiss railway station, after all the hardship we were suddenly taken over by a rush of a newly awoken *joie de vivre*. At a pre-arranged point we collected a letter addressed to me with one hundred Swiss Francs in it and sat down in the morning dining room. The aroma of fresh rolls and coffee (at that time we still said: "real coffee"), the sight of the little plates of butter on the table, just there as a matter of course — all of this was simply overwhelming; it almost took our breath away. My wife was particularly amazed by the immaculate, undarned stockings of the waitresses. And in fact that was the first thing we bought when we timidly walked around the area near the station: a pair of pure silk Italian stockings for Madame. It was completely wrong to do this, as we knew nothing yet about the secret "nylon"; but a symbolic act like this just had to be performed.

Wide awake and refreshed, we then traveled on the left side of the Rhine through this carefully tended Swiss garden; and we could hardly believe that just over on the other bank, and often visible, lay miserable Germany. That the separation was clearly not so neat and that the whole thing was much more complicated became clear to us a short time later. For example, when I turned up in an overcoat I had just bought, the young wife of one of our friends said: "Chic — like an SS man!" I looked at her somewhat taken aback; but it was without doubt quite innocently meant as a compliment. Finally we were even able to understand the art historian of the Münster University: soon after the end of the war, as a native of Basel, and envied by everyone, he went home, but then returned to our ruined city, which in his view was more intellectually alive. But to begin with we found it wonderful to wander through the streets of a city which had not been destroyed, to look at the shop windows and to spread butter thickly on the bread. We were amazed at the carelessness with which bicycles were left unlocked against the house walls while their owners shopped. And that people just got out of an overcrowded carriage and could wait while another carriage was added seemed unbelievable; but even the fact that when you were going into, say the post office, you would hold the door open for the next person, was a custom we had almost forgotten in the rough circumstances of wartime Germany.

The reception by colleagues of the Publishing House, all much younger than ourselves, was immeasurably warm; and then, when Jakob Hegner turned up for a day, it was almost as if we had known one another forever. We were driven all over the place. We visited Peter Schifferli in Zürich and traveled to the theatre in Basel in the evening. Even the misfortune that a performance of *Hamlet* had to be stopped after a few minutes because the main actor had jumped too violently off the stage and sprained his foot — even this mishap gave us the opportunity to spend the evening with the actor Ernst Ginsberg and the director Kurt Horwitz. In Basel there was also a meeting after more than twenty years with an old acquaintance who in the meantime had become famous. He was a few years younger than I and, formerly a student of Germanistics, had become part of the Erich Przywara circle; I had at the time greeted the piano player, at once fascinated and annoyed, who had interrupted me in a highly philosophical discussion by playing a Viennese waltz in a very sensuous and subtle way. He then introduced himself as Hans Urs von Balthasar. As our reunion took place on Josef's name day, I received his wonderful translation of Claudel's *Satin Slipper* as a present. For the Easter weekend they had been able to organize a holiday house at Lago Maggiore to be made available to us by friends. At the bus stop in Ronco, Richard Seewald and Eckart Peterich met us and led us to a completely secluded retreat which had all modern conveniences. Peterich, who lived alone nearby, showed us where to shop and where one could get fresh spring water, which was watched over by a snake that, at the time, appeared very real to us. In the evening we were at Seewalds in the *Casa di Leone* as guests. There were conversations about everything and anything, accompanied by red wine and chestnuts from the trees around. All of this had for us the smell and taste of the unreal, as if it were taking place in a dream world on another planet, *out of this world.* In the middle of the night we got up to look down at the lake onto which the pre-Easter moon was shining. In the morning before Madame got up I lit a crackling fire in the fireplace with wood from a fig tree which had fallen down in the yard.

With Richard Seewald I had a warm if sometimes problematic relationship. Up until then we had never seen one another. But I knew many of his paintings. I particularly loved the earlier ones and, perhaps even more, his drawings; his triptych of the dreaming boy, done on a glaring red plywood, had its place above our Thomas's bed, and I often wondered to myself what kind of dreams he must have had. Seewald, for his part, praised my books to the skies. The tricky part was just that I felt myself to be ever so slightly over-interpreted. Of course, I was delighted a short time later, in the acknowledgements of his Giotto book, to read that I knew how "to lead the waters of wisdom of Saint Thomas to the mills of painters." But Seewald's concept both of the "classical" and the "Catholic," and also some of his later pictures, were too "positive" for me; they lacked the grain of the "negative" philosophy and theology, without which the world seems far too unrealistically harmonious. A few years after this first meeting I tried to explain this in a long letter; but his reaction was, I felt, not without a touch of annoyance; and we then agreed that he should paint and I should philosophize. Eckart Peterich also invited us one evening to an exquisite meal he cooked himself on his balcony, which literally seemed to hover over the lake. His brilliant *Theologie der Hellenen*, which was accepted by Jakob Hegner but only appeared in 1938, was well known to me; I did not believe everything in it, but I had a lot to thank it for. In that spring of 1948 he was working on his dramatic piece *Nausikaa*, the first act of which found in us its earliest and unusually receptive audience. As I never read the book later, I do not know what moved us more at the time: the poetic quality of the piece or the poetry of the evening glow over the lake, which won our approval, without much criticism, of whatever happened.

When I returned to the publisher's office there was an English telegram for me, saying that a representative of the American University of Notre Dame (Indiana) would be passing through Olten on the Rome to Amsterdam express train in the late evening of the following day and that he would come out of his sleeping carriage onto the platform to talk to me. According to the timetable the train only had a two- to three-minute stop; not much could be said in that time. — Waldemar Gurian was behind it. He had taken the notion of inviting me for a semester as guest lecturer at the university. Gurian, who had moved to Germany as a young Russian in the pre-Bolshevik era and had converted from Judaism to Catholicism, had made a name for himself in the twenties as a political publicist, in the first instance, because of his book about Bolshevism, which was the first one to go beyond impressions and reportage. In Paris, Franz Kramer, who later founded the *RheinischerMerkur*, arranged our first meeting.

Chapter III

We met in a fairly noisy café in the Montparnasse Quarter where Gurian liked to work, something which was inconceivable to me; but he actually took up a pile of books and papers from the chair beside him and put them on the table when I took my leave of him around midnight. Shortly after the beginning of the Nazi Regime he had traveled with his wife and daughter, without letting them know his intentions, into Switzerland, not intending to go back to Germany again. More than fifteen years later his wife told me what a shock it was for her never to be able to see her homeland and her house again and to be permanently in a foreign country with only the belongings that had been packed for a supposed two-week holiday. At first Gurian continued to write from Switzerland under a pseudonym for newspapers and magazines. Among other things there was a short essay about my *Basic Forms and Rules of the Social Game (Grundformen sozialer Spielregeln)*, particularly highlighting the latent anti-totalitarian character of this book, which perhaps contributed to the ban on a reprint. After some years of exile in Switzerland the final move to America followed. At the University of Notre Dame he had a teaching post for political science and founded there the *Review of Politics* which was later widely respected. His first letters of encouragement likewise to come to Notre Dame I had answered with thanks but never with a clear "yes." On the one hand, I was attracted by the "New World," but on the other hand, added to the general anxieties of my first university years was the language difficulty; my English was quite bad. I did intend to change this soon; but in the spring of 1948 this was not a priority. And understandably I was told later that the result which the young philosophy professor Fitzgerald brought home from the two-minute conversation in Olten station was: "A nice man, but he doesn't speak English." In fact, my first American semester as a guest lecturer began in Notre Dame less than two years later. It was only when over there that I discovered that it was Gurian who immediately after the end of the war had sent friends a list of German intellectuals and that the first two names on the list were Ida Friederike Görres-Coudenhove and mine. We also had him to thank for the CARE parcels which arrived now and then. They were a life-saver for the children. We were very happy about the present which was announced to us in Olten as we departed: Thomas and Monika were to spend the holidays with the families of two of the publisher's secretaries.

On the evening before the overnight trip home we were in Basel as guests with the publisher of *Christenfibel* and his Spanish/Swiss wife. Then the wonderful time "outside of time" ended quite drastically. Shortly before the train left I had taken two seats in a half-empty compartment and stowed our suitcases, when a youngish man told me that as Germans we could only stay in that compartment for the few minutes to the Baden station; he and his comrades were Allied Officers and on the other side of the border we were to leave the compartment. Our friends on the platform could not believe it. Although we were still in Switzerland, we had already arrived back into the reality of "Germany."

Still, in this emergency setup which we got used to fairly quickly again, it was quite lively. There were more than four hundred people gathered in a medium-sized town for my lecture series on "Plato's Symposium." Or I stood in a half-destroyed city along the Rhine, wrapped up in winter clothes, in the pulpit of an ice-cold church and spoke to a big auditorium — with people who used woollen blankets to keep warm — about the connection between leisure, celebration and ritual. And the speaker traveled home in the unheated train, perhaps with a packet of soap or some treasures from the CARE parcel, but mainly absolutely delighted with the large enthusiastic audience. Even the rare parties had a very special and incomparable magic — a mixture of blatant departure from the everyday, half illegality, unplanned good luck and the relatively inexhaustible store of the newly-won feeling of freedom. An example of just such a mixture was the first German writers' congress in Frankfurt during Pentecost in 1948. Peter Suhrkamp had immediately placed me as his author on the list of invitees. Saint Paul's church, which, for the centenary celebration, had been renovated with assistance from the Americans, was in the middle of a city which still lay in ruins. It was in itself an amazing phenomenon.

I met a dozen friends again; and a trip to Rüdesheim on a steamship with a shared meal and plentiful wine made for a boisterous conclusion. At the same time, during these celebratory roundtable sessions the first conversations about the founding of the Deutsche Akademie für Sprache und Literatur (German Academy for Language and Literature, Darmstadt) were held.

Surprisingly, we had difficulty in getting the money together for the ticket when Thomas and Monika set off towards the end of July 1948 on their Swiss adventure. A good month before that, one Sunday was declared "Day X" and the old currency was invalidated. Suddenly no one had a penny and we were only given twenty Marks to start with. They were clearly now worth something since the black market and the use of cigarettes as currency were suddenly a thing of the past. The suddenness of the change happening like this will not be understood by anyone who has not experienced it. Germany acquired, purely optically, a new face overnight. Suddenly it did not smell like a public lavatory any more. And in the autumn, when I went on a lecturing tour for the second time to Switzerland, the tables in the waiting room in Cologne on which it had been forbidden to sleep only a few months previously were now covered in white and one could order from a menu.

Everyone knows that, with the end of the period of emergency, the "member of the affluent society" and some other unpleasant things made their appearance. A friend who was visiting from the Eastern bloc said, half sceptically and half enviously quoting Tolstoy: "War means rape, peace means adultery." That is all well and good; but nevertheless you cannot wish for the emergency time to return.

IV

"End of time" — Conversation with T. S. Eliot — One allegedly destroyed, and one really destroyed city: London and Berlin — The "Free University" — Reunion with Peter Suhrkamp

It never crossed my mind to think of Adolf Hitler as the Antichrist incarnate; for me he was too small in stature. But it became more and more conceivable to me, from what happened in front of my eyes, that the most recent epoch of human history, instead of being seen as a victory for reason or good, could possibly take the form of a pseudo-order — through the exercise of power, in which everything purely technical would function perfectly and at the same time be the embodiment of injustice.

In 1943, during a night-time air raid alert, I had already written down what Thomas Aquinas has to say about the Antichrist: an eminently political figure of monstrous, not to say miraculous worldly power; the despots and tyrants of history were his precursors; all persecutions were just a premonition of those last ones which were directed against everyone who was good. Solowjew's *Legend of the Antichrist*, which was repeatedly read aloud among students in Siedlinghausen and later in Essen, seemed to me to be more and more a vision of contemporary relevance. And then, when I got the 70-year-old Kant's essay into my hands, which was both intellectually complicated and obscure and had been written thirteen years after the *Critique of Pure Reason*, I announced lectures on the theme "The end of time in the history of Philosophy" for the winter semester of 1948/49. I did not realise what a gruelling effort the writing of this manuscript would be. My colleagues in the field did not exactly conceal their critical astonishment. Heinrich Scholz, whom I met by chance in a bus, happened to ask out of pure politeness about plans for my lectures. He raised his narrow hand in a gesture of extreme dismay: "Oh, for me that is much too up in the air." Even the Berlin historian Friedrich Meinecke, who at 86 years old was chosen as honorary rector of the newly constituted Free University and whom I had to visit on my arrival there when I was guest lecturer in the summer of 1949, was shocked at the announcement of such an unusual topic. And it was not until I cautiously said that Kant himself had spoken not only about the supposed *beginning* of human history but also — something which the educated man clearly did not know — about the *end*, that I succeeded in calming him down somewhat.

Before my term as guest lecturer in Berlin the British Council invited me quite unexpectedly for a three-week trip to England. I was not to be given any duties whatsoever: I just had to indicate what cities and which personalities I wanted to see. After that, the itinerary and accommodation would be planned. Then, in fact, in the hotel foyer, a very correctly dressed young man, with his hat and also the handle of his umbrella in his left hand, was waiting to bring me to the train or to accompany me to the theatre or to the anteroom of the Publishing House Director T. S. Eliot. — Unfortunately, I had not realized quickly enough that the money which had generously been given to me on the journey was "occupying forces currency," which, on the ferry, was not even enough to purchase a breakfast. The result was that I arrived at the London Liverpool Station very hungry. In the middle of the hopeless turmoil on the platform, I had just started to wonder with some amusement how things would work out, when someone rather hesitantly addressed me by name. And fortunately we set off straightaway for the very well-known Café Royal, where at that moment its former famous regulars, Oscar Wilde and Aubrey Beardsley, interested me a lot less than the excellent lunch.

At the Headquarters of the British Council the impoverished German was given a considerable sum of money for possible personal needs. Recklessly I immediately spent it at Blackwell's on Broad Street in Oxford — which was the first stop on my trip — on an edition of Aristotelian metaphysics annotated by W. D. Ross and an antiquarian complete edition of Plato's dialogues. In Oxford I was staying at the Jesuit College Campion Hall, a clubhouse of exceedingly nice individuals. Frederick Copleston, the philosophy historian already known to me through his lectures in Germany, showed me around this remarkable city which was full of grey sandstone buildings and was now a beautiful spring green. In the Bodleian University Library in Oxford, for better or for worse, I had to disgrace my protector. Presumably he had given notice that a specialist in medieval philosophy was arriving; and so one of the librarians was ready to assist this guest of the British Council by bringing out old codices and manuscripts and that type of thing. And, of course, he was then disappointed when I was not looking for anything of the kind. Instead, I just asked if the long-promised Greek-Latin edition of the Thomas commentary to Dionysius the Areopagite's *About the names of God* had appeared at last from the Turin Publishing House Marietti. The librarian referred us to the catalogue and hurriedly took his leave. I was interested above all in any sites which were reminiscent of John Henry Newman; and I was able to see a lot of them, some near Oxford.

On the feast of the Ascension, the Anglican "Thomist" Mascall awaited me at the gate of Christ Church Cathedral wearing the wonderfully colorful vestments of Doctor of

Divinity. Copleston, a Jesuit and therefore a Roman Catholic priest, took his leave of us discreetly, but I was ceremoniously led to my place in the choir seats. It had been said to me many times that the Church of England is nothing but a shiny façade, that only about a dozen people came to church and certainly not the young people. In reality, I saw in this festive Pontifical Mass an amazingly big number of students, many of them sunk deeply in prayer, with perhaps a new Newman among them.

One afternoon, as I had requested, had been set aside for the visit to Christopher Dawson, whose critical and cultural views about "Religion and Progress" had made him well known in Germany before the advent of National Socialism. I had noted a passage from it: "We have entered a new phase of culture, where the most amazing advance in technology serves purely transitory needs. It is clear that, in a civilization of this kind, instead of a nucleus of the future there lives only a nucleus of decline." At the bus-stop in a rural leafy suburb stood a thinly bearded and slender man who seemed unwell and who looked older than his 60 years; even so, a decade later he was invited to Harvard University, where he worked for another four years. In his library there was hardly room to sit down. On the floor beside a low armchair in front of the fireplace were two or three meter-long rows of books all within reach, with their backs turned upwards next to one another. Dawson's first question brought us immediately into a long discussion where he himself spoke somewhat hesitantly with a so-to-speak quiet seriousness. He wanted to know from me whether the Germans had learned anything from their encounter with the Antichrist and the totalitarian regime which would be of benefit in a second encounter. Probably, I said, a concrete attitude could not be anticipated and so a "once and for all" decision would not be helpful; one would have to first know whether the regime really was an antichrist one or not;

and one would have to be prepared to admit it was true. This is the decision that would have to be made. Dawson, pensively agreeing, then spoke of the apocalyptic situation that was becoming ever more apparent — that martyrdom was being rendered unrecognizable because the totalitarian state, as, for example, in the case of Cardinal Mindszenty, had developed a technique of preventing the profession of faith or of making it seem inconsequential. In response perhaps Christianity must try to win back the possibility of public testimony. Perhaps, I answered, it may belong to the current conditions of witness by blood that it must remain "undeclared." — We came to speak of the Anglican Church, of which Dawson, himself a Catholic, very decidedly maintained that it was not a mere façade. With regard to Anglicanism there were two different opinions amongst English Catholics. The first one: if the State Church — for example through a Labor Government — were to be rescinded, the situation would immediately become clear, and for the Catholic Church there would be the opportunity of a new revival; the other: the Church of England was the only power which could protect public life against a complete paganization, if perhaps only because of its institutional nature; the Catholic church was not in a position to do this because it was seen as un-English and foreign — even Irish. I asked why a man like T. S. Eliot, being already a "convert" did not just immediately become a Catholic. Probably, says Dawson, because the barbaric — more exactly, the Irish — element in American Catholicism had frightened him off; still, in the America of the last decades much had changed; between Eliot's early years in New England and, for instance, Thomas Merton's *Seven Storey Mountain* the gap was much more than that of a generation.

I met Alick Dru in the Benedictine Downside Abbey. The Abbey was founded in exile in the French town of Douai hundreds of years ago at the time of the persecution of Catholics.

Many of the monks who went from there to England suffered a fearful martyrdom just because they had secretly celebrated mass. The Church canonized six of them; their names can be read on a stone tablet in the monastery church. I arrived just in time for Vespers on a very special feast day; it was the day on which the Roman Benedictine Missionary Augustine died in 606 as the first Archbishop of Canterbury. The Gregorian choral music sounded wonderful in the unusually high nave of the church; it was sung with a discipline and reserve which allowed the amazing musical impetus to come through clearly. Life in the monastery was shaped by the monastic routine also in other respects — by the silence in the refectory, of course, and the sung prayer at table. As Alick Dru arrived by chance during lunchtime, we could, for the moment, only greet one another silently with our eyes. Otherwise there was a lot of informal human warmth. An old monk who during High Mass had missed an entry during the singing of the Graduale and had caused some confusion, got off the seat smiling and knelt down in the middle of the choir, at which moment the Abbot, also smiling, with his hammer gave him the sign to stand up. And the white-haired organist, who illustrated the workings of the organ which rested on the organ table at ground level, while pulling out all the stops pulled up his soutane to reach the pedals without hindrance and let his hairy bare knees be seen. It was also with a smile that, when I went into my guest room, I saw a huge orange-coloured chamber pot.

I also happened to meet there an acquaintance who was well versed in politics and who was also a man of some influence. After a trip, initiated by the *Foreign Office* itself, through the university cities of the British Zone he had written a clearly critical report mainly about the activities of the supervising officers; because of some remarks in the report attributed to me I was later drawn by the Münster University officer into an embarrassing conversation. It was the same officer who had prevented the confiscation of our house. In the spacious monk's cell I was surprised by the unexpected presence of a huge black dog which the priest then explained was one of the privileges of his office: he was the Cellarius of the monastery, the head of the economic administration. During the daytime with him and Alick Dru I drove around a little in the Somerset countryside. We visited the country house of Lady Catherine Asquith as whose guest Ronald Knox was just finishing his history of Christian "Enthusiasm." An embarrassing moment of silence arose when, on the way, I randomly and quite innocently asked about the meaning of a word which I could not find in any of my English dictionaries, but which I constantly heard being used loudly by the occupying forces. The priest who, at the wheel, had been dominating the conversation, fell silent; Alick Dru explained to me in a low voice that it was a very vulgar expression for copulation. "And you hear our soldiers saying that all the time?" I could only confirm this information, which must have been of interest to an educated Englishman. Twenty years later I saw the same word in the entrance hall of the Münster University on a poster advertising a student party. — On a walk around the monastery buildings, to which a second-level boarding school for about four hundred pupils belonged, I noticed in the changing rooms whole rows of colorful uniforms; I expressed open surprise about it and was told that naturally the school had its Training Corps which provided a pre-military training.

We drove off next morning to Alick Dru's farm in Cornwall; he said that, from the fields, you could already see the sea. His three young daughters, between 2 and 5 years old, were each carrying a cat in their arms when they greeted us. The lifestyle seemed completely foreign to the grandson of Münster farmers. One did live "in the country" and farm and breed cattle; but one lived in the same way as in the cities —

in a mansion with a library, bathroom and hot water. The housewife, who during the Spanish civil war had run a military hospital on Franco's side, clearly felt that she was in a type of guest house; so she found it not very *satisfactory* when one morning there was no hot breakfast; the Polish cook was in charge of that; they spoke French with her. The farm was mainly run by two former German prisoners of war who had no inclination to return home to the Russian occupied zone; their names Siegfried and Fritz presumably came from Alick Dru whom they addressed as "Mister Major." It amazed me how the farm was run in a purely business-like fashion. Dru said that as soon as he had earned enough from this farm he would buy a bigger one; he already had one in mind and we went to look at it together. In all the plans the high taxes played a significant role. "You see, I don't pay any rent here; and the car is part of the business equipment." This close link between farming, business, writing and family life with dogs and cats all over the place led to an exceedingly colorful variety in the daily routine and to enormously relaxed social intercourse. While I was shaving in the mornings in the bathroom, the daughters came and chatted with me while they themselves went about their own little affairs. Twenty years later one of the girls, Mary, was to correct the botched translation of one of my books, but it was then admittedly never printed. At the table the conversation very quickly turned to politics. Again and again, decades before Bonn's "East Politics," there was talk about the worry which Western powers had that Germany might come to an agreement with Russia — something which seemed completely absurd to me. For a whole evening we would go through the proofs of the *Day and Night Books* by Theodor Haecker which Alick Dru had translated into English; it was unbelievable how many mistakes and errors of understanding could be made by someone so confident in German; besides, it appeared that our language had nuances which simply could not be translated. Again Alick Dru said that he was willing to translate *Leisure and Ritual* and *What is Philosophizing?* as soon as a publisher could be found. It was another year before that happened. As a translator he had a strange way of proceeding. His first principle, he tried to explain to me, was to distance himself as far as possible from the original text in order to then, in a second act, approach it again. When I saw the first draft of his manuscript I was quite dismayed; it read quite well, but often enough I found that my thoughts were either suppressed or distorted. So there was endless correspondence; and one day Alick Dru explained to me in a friendly way that from now on he would only translate dead authors; and I was never able to dissuade him from that decision.

At this point, however, at the beginning of June 1949, with the cats rubbing themselves against my legs in the library of this remarkable farm run by an intellectual, we were discussing the ongoing organization of my trip to England. Dru felt he shared responsibility for it, as he had been asked for advice beforehand. Because of his protest, an official reception with the Papal Delegate was not included in the programme. And now it was annoying him that I was to visit the city of Sheffield. "Would I travel to somewhere like Wanne-Eikkel in Germany?" After some phone calls to the British Council, a longer stay in London instead of Sheffield was planned. Before that there was just a visit to Liverpool; Dru thought that that was not too bad. "You will get the smell of the Irish clergy there"; nine out of ten Catholic priests in the west of England were Irish. So for the first time I was to meet the much spoken-of "barbaric" Irish Catholicism. — In Liverpool I was actually accommodated in a presbytery; as a welcome, there was a huge bunch of yellow and blue irises on the table; in the room beside it someone was playing Bach excellently. The priest, an educated and, in practice, a clearly successful man, had studied in Rome. The beginning was not unpleasant. But the aggressive lack of taste in lifestyle and in the decor of the church almost made me sick. In the toilet there were embarrassing inscriptions on the wall; for that, above the wash hand basin stood: *Lavabo inter innocentes manus meas.* The students' chaplain had been writing a book for years about Satan; in his opinion he was in supreme command of the material. — It was very nice to be awakened by the bull roar of the ships' sirens coming from the port. At Mass there was an unexpected number of black Africans and Malayans. At breakfast the priest explained that his protégés came from thirteen countries; in Liverpool alone there were eight thousand black Africans; "they are all British subjects; that's why we cannot send them home." But, to the annoyance of American visitors, they were living quite well together; even the Church of England had some black priests here. A much more serious problem was the Italian women whom the soldiers had brought home from the war; every second marriage was a tragedy.

The priest had booked me in for lunch at the Atlantic House. That was apparently one establishment I had to see: a Catholic seamen's home, restaurant, hotel, shop, dance-hall and retreat house all in one. Three agile young clerics were the management team; we had a cheerful time during the meal. We ate à la carte, served by a heavily made-up waitress. There was dancing every evening for the seamen — until the dot of ten o'clock. Then the music stopped; one of the walls of the room became divided and then you could see directly behind it an altar lit with candles, and there was a monstrance with the Blessed Sacrament. The organ started a hymn and it all ended with Benediction. They showed me the monstrance; it was constructed out of symbols of the sea; you could make out a lighthouse and a steering wheel, and the host was framed in a lifesaving ring made of amethyst. The priests said that this dance-hall, whose special features were, of course, well known, was hardly big enough for all the visitors. "And where do the girls come from?" "From the congregations of the parishes, that is the whole point! Why should seamen only go to bad pubs?" The girls were specifically trained to say no.

There was something literally unique about Liverpool: in this city two cathedrals were being built, not churches, no, actual cathedrals. One of them, the Anglican one, had been abuilding for almost half a century; the first stone was laid in 1904, the year I was born. Although it had only been half finished, it was in red sandstone in the traditional pattern of Gothic English buildings and extremely impressive. As I know meanwhile from the travel guides, the building, today the largest church in England, was completed in 1970, a good twenty years after my visit. Clearly this undertaking did nothing to calm the ambition of the 270,000 Catholics of Liverpool. They planned to build a huge cathedral modeled on St. Peter's in Rome. They started building it in 1933. When the war caused work to be stopped, the crypt, at least, had been completed. A walk through the reverberating subterranean rooms was really spine-chilling. In the office of the cathedral works a Canon told me that they hoped to resume work the following year, 1950. To my question about when it would be finished the relaxed answer came: "Let's say in a hundred years." In actual fact the cathedral was finished by 1967 and thankfully was not modeled on St. Peter's.

On the train to London — one of the last before the planned train strike at Pentecost — a banker asked me, with clearly genuine concern, if the German people were now on the path of moral reform. I doubt that my answer reassured him. Londoners who were not car owners had to stay in London during Pentecost. Droves of them camped in the public parks. There was more than enough material for "ethnological" studies. Compared to the destruction of German cities, London had remained undamaged apart from some suspiciously spacious car parks, for instance near St. Paul's Cathedral. On Pentecost Monday it was the fifth anniversary of D-Day, the day of the Normandy landing. On television, a medium which was still years away for us Germans, the day was well commemorated. In Westminster Abbey there was liturgical pomp and ceremony but minimal public participation; a procession around the grave of the unknown soldier with a wreath of artificial poppies; even Franklin D. Roosevelt's portrait, a relief on the church wall, was decorated; again the problem of having a state church was evident. On the other hand, while I was waiting in the entrance hall of a somewhat extravagant BBC House built with an oval ground plan for T. S. Gregory, who presumably could not come because of the train strike, I noted down the inscription which was hewn into the stone, a Latin inscription from the year 1931, which began as follows: *Deo omnipotenti templum hoc artium et musarum . . . primi dedicant gubernatores precantes ut messem bonam bona proferat sementis ut immunda omnia et inimica paci expellantur.* This would be absolutely unimaginable in a German broadcasting house.

Despite wonderful theater and concert evenings, the most important things of my last days in England were for me some personal meetings, all arranged by the British Council. The conversation with Frank Sheed, the owner of the publishing house Sheed and Ward, an Australian by birth and currently travelling between the USA and Europe, did not have a good start, because I mentioned our common acquaintance Jakob Hegner, who during the war had found refuge with him: "No, let's not talk about Hegner!" I had already heard it said that the relationship between the two men had been quite strained. On the other hand I was treated to an enthusiastic and, as I was soon to find out, excessively exaggerated hymn of praise about American Catholicism; he, Frank Sheed, was ashamed, every time he was there, that he was such a mediocre

Chapter IV

Christian. I asked him if it was true that in America they were discovering contemplation. The answer was a decisive yes; all classes of people were streaming into the Trappist monasteries. The American bishops, however, who were real manager types, knew nothing about these occurrences at all; of course, they would have nothing against it but they didn't seem to notice it. He thought I should accept the offer from Notre Dame; it was the only Catholic University in the USA that could afford to pay lay professors, if only — I could not believe my ears — thanks to their famous football team. When I was leaving, Mr. Sheed asked me to send on to him the books which I thought ought to be translated into English. But I had something else in mind.

For the afternoon of the same day, a visit to T. S. Eliot had been arranged. Alick Dru had told me that Eliot, who was the director of a publishing house in civilian life, was impressed with my work. According to Dru, conversation with him was not the easiest thing; one had to take the initiative oneself; he went in for long silences. This had happened since his wife became mentally ill twenty years previously, and he more or less lived alone and avoided company. — My smart companion, a young admirer of last year's winner of the Nobel prize, was deeply upset when I told him on the way to the publishing house Faber and Faber in Russell Square that I wanted to be alone for the conversation with Eliot; but of course he handled this disappointment in impeccable fashion. Eliot worked in an incredibly confined office whose wall of corrugated glass afforded some light to the otherwise completely dark passage. It was clear that any type of middle-class style in the house was renounced. The passages of the old-fashioned building also seemed to serve partly as storerooms; in any case, they were difficult to get through because of the piled up books, some of which were packed for dispatch. Eliot proved not at all disinclined to talk; and when I gave him the invitation from the Münster University for his planned trip to Germany in the autumn, he immediately said yes. He did not even have any objection to the fact that a lecture or anything else of a public nature would be expected of him. However, he did add that a visit without any such obligation and purely for conversation and getting to know one another would be a much better thing. He said that he had told Robert Birley many times that this type of thing should be organized for the Germans, and now he was glad to see that, for example, in my case it had been heeded. Eliot seemed to be well informed about post-war literary life in Germany. I felt I had to tell him about Konrad Wei whom he did not know, of course, but who then seemed to be very akin to him — more akin at least than Rilke, for example, whose decidedly non-Christian stance remained a serious deficit. He found it laudable that there was such a large number of good German periodicals like *Merkur*, *Wandlung*, and *Hochland*; England should feel shamed by the contrast; he was probably thinking of his own periodical *Criterion* and its demise at the beginning of World War II. I said to him that maybe losing a war was not bad in all respects. "Perhaps it is not good in all respects to have won a war — in as far as one can say that England won it." Eliot then spoke of the absurd idea of a *re-education* by occupying forces. The bad thing was, I replied, that whereas we now heard about more or less enlightening theories, particularly in pedagogy, as I now saw with my own eyes, the English way of life — which, as luck would have it, had remained rather conservative — could not be imported as well. When I naturally said I presumed that in England the substance of Christianity still had a stronger and more obvious public presence that in Germany, he shook his head vigorously. He felt that in the long run there would be very few "chosen ones" left. Again the topic of the "end of history" came up. I persisted a little more about the impression I had that there was a more effective presence of the Christian element in modern England. And I asked as an example what the inscription in stone in the BBC broadcasting studio meant. His answer was: nothing but hypocrisy and blasphemy! At the end he brought the conversation around to my books and their translation into English; this matter had to be tackled, and he himself wanted to do something about it. In Faber and Faber, he continued, he was only one of five directors and also was known for suggesting books for publication which would not bring in much money.

For me, meeting Eliot was an exhilarating experience; we were clearly on the same wavelength with regard to fundamental questions. The short but thoughtful essay which he later included in the English edition of *Leisure and Cult* showed that Eliot felt the same way, especially as he was supposed to hate prefaces (Alick Dru: *He hates prefaces*); incidentally the title *Leisure, the Basis of Culture* comes from him. Of course, I do not know — and it will not now be possible to verify — the truth of the claim in a memoir published in 1971 that Eliot felt a similar direct affinity with his German visitor, as, more than a lifetime ago, he did when he encountered the writings of the remarkable poet Jules Laforgue, who died as a young man before Eliot's birth and of whose writings, up to this day, I have never read a line.

On the day after the meeting with Eliot I had to defend England against an enthusiastic overestimation of Germany. This was in a conversation with Stanley Morrison — like Graham Greene and Evelyn Waugh, one of the prominent English converts. Alick Dru had simply decided that we had to meet one another. He called him the "grey eminence" of the London *Times*, where he was responsible for a lot more than the typography. For years he had edited the literature section, *The Literary Supplement*. So Morrison took me to lunch in the famous Garrick Club, from whose darkly paneled stateliness it was not easy to see that it was mainly a place for artists, actors and writers. The polished tables made of cherry wood had no tablecloth on them. Immediately I was asked about Germany with a passionate curiosity. The fire in his eyes and the lively gestures made him look very young despite his snow-white hair. What could Germany learn from England, he began, besides football or horse racing? Intellectually there was much more life in Germany than on the island, which clearly stifled any sense of philosophy and metaphysics. I tried to speak up on behalf of men like, for example, the medieval John of Salisbury, who had brought into European philosophy the typical English "sense of the concrete" when it badly needed it. "Not at all." He did not even let me finish. "The English sense of the concrete" was no more than a sense of business, "the sense for pounds." Because of his career he knew a little about print runs of books; it was true that T. S. Eliot's books had six or seven print runs, but each of them amounted to hardly more than a thousand copies, apart from maybe *Murder in the Cathedral*. In Germany the situation was completely different. He asked about the print run figures for my books and then hit the table resoundingly: these figures would just be impossible in England. We parted hours later, stimulated both by the wine and the conversation.

Before traveling home I made a quick visit to St. Albans to my wife's brother. It was now more than ten years since his emigration. He seemed to feel no yearning for Germany; and his wife even less so, understandably. Their legal practice in London was thriving, as was the big garden at the back of the house. None of his three daughters spoke or understood a word of German.

On the Friday evening after Pentecost I returned home. The children had decorated the door of the house with flowers. What gave the separation and then also the reunion such exceptional intensity? Clearly it was neither the length of time nor the big distance. How often had I been away in the

Sauerland for a few weeks without anything being made of it? And London is not any further away than Munich. Clearly it had to do with the foreign element. — The youngest, who had made his first confession on that day and who, two days later, on Trinity Sunday, would make his First Holy Communion, came trotting towards me, beaming. I had prepared him for the sacrament myself as I had done with Thomas five years previously. So, on the evening before, we went through everything again when he was lying in bed freshly bathed (white inside and out, as he said himself). And again the three of us visited the Bishop on Sunday morning as my father had arranged. But Cardinal von Galen's successor, almost too serious a man, was not able to talk to a child in a natural way. On the obligatory commemorative picture he wrote, for the seven-year-old child, his own Latin heraldic motto.

Under the pile of post on my desk there was a telegram from the Free University of Berlin: I was expected already in the next week; a flight ticket had been booked for me by the American Military Government and was available in Frankfurt. So I had hardly arrived home when I set off again and got to see two European capital cities very quickly one after another. We had planned to destroy one of them and maintained it had been destroyed, while the other, Berlin, in truth had been destroyed to such an extent that my friends there warned me that it was worse than anything I could imagine. Peter Suhrkamp, on the other hand, who was moving with his publishing house from Berlin to Frankfurt and who was spending time in both cities, wrote to me at the end of 1948 saying that he "wanted to go back to Berlin"; he maintained that there were "some alarming things about West Germany." "Berlin is definitely not a happy place to be, but that is the intersection of the flow of people from East and West. Besides, I think that what the people in the East and in Berlin experienced — over and above what happened to people in the West

— is closer to the reality which awaits all of us. I also think that in Berlin we have our finger more on the pulse of developments."

I set off full of curiosity. Of course, there was no ticket ready for me in Frankfurt. In the labyrinthine American headquarters there was charming non-committal chat ("Where did you get your British English from? From London? You know the new slogan: Germans, send CARE parcels to England?"), but a flight ticket was not forthcoming. In the meantime Walter Dirks, who was suffering from migraine and had taken time off from his editing work on the *Frankfurter Hefte*, played Hindemith's *Ludus Tonalis* for me and the piano sonatas of Max Reger, which we both loved. God knows how long I might have had to wait if Cardinal von Preysing had not, for some reason or other, been refused permission to leave Berlin so that his return ticket became available. It was then given to me through the combined efforts of the *Frankfurter Hefte* and the Vatican Mission.

At the airport I felt like a foreigner in my own country; I had to swallow the sandwiches dry which thankfully I had brought with me; you could only buy drinks if you had American dollars. Upon my arrival in Berlin the reporters were pushing towards the airplane with cameras and microphones: behind me Ludwig Erhard, the father of the German "economic miracle" which was just getting underway, was coming down the steps; it is amazing how difficult it can be to read the importance of a man just by looking at his face.

The people around the table at the Dahlem guesthouse of the Free University were remarkable. Besides some Jewish professors who had emigrated to the USA in 1933 and were now for a time guests back at their old University, there was an "emigrant" of a completely different kind, the Germanist Helmut de Boor. As he told us without any embarrassment, having been a full Professor in Bern since 1936 he had been deported from Switzerland in 1945 merely because of his membership of the NSDAP; his wife, children and books were still there. He himself had come to Germany with two suitcases, and in Marburg, without anyone's help, he had written several volumes of a history of German literature working in libraries and seminars among the students, and these volumes were now beginning to appear. Dahlem, with its sprinkling of pine forests, looked like a garden city untouched by the war; it was only if you looked more closely that you noticed the countless boarded-up windows and the magnificent cars which the Americans had in front of the undamaged or restored villas. In the mornings we were awoken by birds singing — that is if the ceaseless noise of the roaring engines of the airlift had let you sleep. You saw many stressed-looking faces, which clearly even the Berlin sense of humour could not cheer up. "That's a piece of red flag. It should bring us some culture," the shoe-polisher said, and then he got a bright red rag and polished my shoes until they shone; perhaps, I thought, it is part of a swastika flag.

The situation in the Free University, which was still in its infancy, was somewhat complicated. Not all anti-communists among the professors of the "Linden University" had taken part in the secession. Some, for the moment, understood the bad things as "one-off occurrences" and spoke of the "encroachment of minor authorities." This was all vocabulary which we had heard before. One of those who had remained behind, a well-known legal expert, who was also about to go to the West, had no recourse but to call the new establishment illegal when he was asked for his assessment; after all, the Dahlem Institutes into which the Free University was now moving had until this point clearly belonged to the one Berlin University. But they were already talking about having two Universities; the division between East and West was inexorably running its course. Students whose families lived in the

Russian occupied zone did not dare, for fear of retaliatory measures, to register in the Free University. And the professors in the new establishment did not risk visiting the Eastern Sector any more, even though the movement between East and West in both directions was still possible. When I returned from my trips there, they all asked me about them with curiosity, as if I had returned from a distant, unknown country. And, in fact, that is what it was for me. The Sing Academy which I had known from my student days had now become a Soviet "House of Culture," and it resounded with optical and acoustic propaganda. Cut violently into the scenery of the Treptower Park was the pseudo-cultural memorial for the fallen of the Red Army. It was monumental in its size, expensive — and at the same time unutterably cheap. Or, coming out of the theatre into the summer evening completely enchanted after a rapturing performance in the East Berlin German Theater, one was taken aback to see the glaring lights of the Russian State Police prison; the windows were walled in halfway up, the top half was covered by a light shaft made of planks, so that the prisoner literally could neither see anything of sky or the earth below it. I could understand the people who, because of this sight alone, refused to go to the Deutsches Theater.

At the same time, life in East Berlin was quite bearable because it was being watched by the eyes of the whole world, while Jena, for example, actually seemed to be a completely foreign country. The philosopher Hans Leisegang, who had just got out of there, told me about it in such a fury that I almost regretted having inquired. Every University teacher had to hand in a written piece to the occupying force in which he had to report about his intellectual background, his publications up the present, and the position he took on "dialectical materialism"; heading: "My World View"; length: at least one hundred typed pages. All the lectures which had been offered had to be handed in to administration fully written out before the beginning of the term. "After that I packed my cases and traveled to Berlin."

The horrors of the destruction in the center of the city, of course, went beyond the sector boundary. Whether one was going out of the underground station Potsdamer Platz into the light in the British or American or Russian sector, in every case one found oneself in a no-man's-land overgrown with bushes and thriving weeds. And where formerly because of traffic you were taking your life into your hands to cross the street, now you could, if you had an urgent need, "disappear" behind a shrub the height of a man. Taken aback, I wandered into the former government area on a narrow, worn path under the portal of the halfway intact Reichs President Palace through to the park at the back; it had been divided into dozens of little gardens, each one fenced off from the next with pieces of rusty metal. A handwritten notice invited the leaseholders to a meeting: "War on the potato beetle! It is compulsory for everyone to turn up!" In the zoo, where the trees had literally been burned up by Berlin residents for heating purposes, here and there above the pea and potato-planted borders the high plinth of a heroic marble monument loomed up. On Unter den Linden Rausch's statue of Frederick the Great on horseback, which had already been walled in before the war, was now covered with communist slogans in garish colours. Still, there were fresh flowers in the barred door of the completely run-down memorial. In front of the Anhalter Station, whose huge dimensions were only now really noticeable because of everything else around lying in ruins, there was an announcement, as if in mockery, written in chalk on a wooden board: "No trains." And yet unbelievably there are people living in the basements under the ruins; and in the crypts of the destroyed cathedral the former court chaplain Bruno Doehring, now seventy years old, was said to speak each Sunday to a small community of Berliners of the Prussian Wilhelmian tradition, who still observed the custom that young girls kissed the hands of older ladies.

Wolf S, my wife's cousin, was my indispensable and always helpful companion on such trips to the Eastern area. He was an editor at the RIAS, the American radio in Berlin. For example he made sure that, when I was crossing the sector border, I didn't have a "western" newspaper in my pocket. Sometimes after the theater, when we were in a planned economy "HO-Restaurant" drinking Bulgarian wine, his face would become rigid during a moment of shock when someone was scrutinizing him too intensely. Once a communist colleague had invited him to the pubs around the Alexanderplatz. "And if the police do a raid?" "Then I'll say you are on the quiet list!" "Quiet list?" "Well, they are the secret sympathizers, who would have given in their names in any case."

The students of the Free University were absolutely delightful. Their stimulating attention exceeded all expectations; particularly the otherwise rarely visited no-man's-land between philosophy and theology seemed to fascinate them. Three times we had to move to a bigger lecture theatre, the last one with an attic full of chairs, the largest auditorium which the Free University had at its disposal at the time. There was a special reason for the rush of people, which I found out by chance: a few students had stuck the advertisement about my lectures on the blackboard of the "Linden University"; of course the place was only made known by the street and house number. What was difficult to keep pace with were the invitations to give public lectures, which were mostly held in cinemas or emergency churches. I was brought there by car from quite a distance away. "They are coming for me in a minute," I once innocently said at an afternoon meeting in the Suhrkamp publishing house, to which someone replied that that expression still sounded ominous in Berlin. What was unforgettable after such lectures was the period when a circle of old and new friends sat together, mostly until after midnight. Shortly before leaving Berlin, Johannes Pinsk, one of the most spiritual priests and at the same time one of the most pleasure-loving people I have ever met, held a banquet. Only a few friends were invited, among them the actor and director Wolfgang Kühne and his pretty, quiet and very clever wife. The Kühnes were regular attendants at my Dahlem lectures; to my embarrassment they always walked there from more than an hour away. Until now there had not been more than fleeting greetings; and it was only on this evening that I learned a little about their lives. Wolfgang Kühne told us that they both had been interested in the history of religion for a long time; for example, in the mid-thirties through Leopold Ziegler's book "Deliverance" they made their first acquaintance with the Jakob Hegner publishing house and also with individual writings by J. P. which appeared there. These in turn brought Thomas Aquinas into their field of vision, so that they became familiar with the Catholic view of the world. Shortly before the war they converted to Catholicism; their baptism was arranged by Johannes Pinsk, our host. One thing was not told by the narrator of the story. That Wolfgang Kühne had spent several months as a political prisoner in the Moabiter prison I heard only in 1972, two years after his death, by way of the wonderful letters that completely fed off liturgy and Thomas Aquinas. He had sent these letters to his wife during this prison term. My friend Hermann Volk had written an epilogue. The title "A time not lost," which captured the incomprehensible hope of these letters very exactly, almost certainly came from their addressee, his wife.

The final Berlin days were the most moving. At a type of tea party to which the faculty had invited us, the Rector Edwin Redslob, an unusually knowledgeable man who gave himself the airs of a genius, led me to the table with a charming gesture as if I were his lady dinner partner, and when he noticed that I was a little at home with the older Goethe, it poured out of him: anecdotes about Weimar and quotations from unknown letters in the possession of his wife, who was a granddaughter of the Grand Duke's Forest Master. More topical was what Emil Dovifat, Professor for Journalism, co-founder of the CDU, and licensee of one of the first Berlin newspapers, was able to tell me about the time following the end of the war. Very much in contrast to the Western powers, the Soviets had sent their *best* people to Berlin; among the Russian officers he had met some of the most educated men you could wish to talk to. The other side of the coin was the brutality of the censorship; in his editorial office there were three intelligent Komsomol girls who were responsible for the political vetting of every article. Under this burden they sometimes broke down and had fits of crying as a result of fear.

For the evening meal, my friend Hermann Kunisch, the Germanist, brought me to his house again amongst the pines of Grunewald where I had often been a guest. Suddenly this last evening together turned into a Konrad Wei evening; we could not stop reciting our favorite poems to one another.

To my surprise Werner Becker appeared for my last lecture on Aquinas. He had been a companion in the Rothenfels days and during our time as students in Berlin. First, like me a law student (he graduated with *summa cum laude*, under Carl Schmitt), now an Oratorian and chaplain to students in Leipzig, he was by chance in Berlin for six hours. I looked with apprehension at his face, which had become very thin; but he said that material need was not really the worst thing, not even for his students. What weighed much more heavily on them was that they were constantly under pressure to do espionage work. Then a report about the Corpus Christi procession where he was not so much concerned about the fact that there were 20,000 participants, but about the outspoken speech made afterwards by the bishop of Mei en, Petrus Legge, to priests of the city and the Catholic students. For the first time, this man, who was hunted out of office by the National Socialists on the usual charge of currency offenses, spoke to free himself of the burden: for him it was incomparably more distressing than all other chicanery from those in power to feel that he was abandoned by his fellow bishops and above all by the Papal Nuncio Orsenigo. By his action, according to Werner Becker, the bishop had freed himself from a type of trauma; in any case he was going to withdraw his former refusal to take part in the Bishops Conference in Fulda. — To my question about how West Germany looked from Leipzig's perspective came, without hesitation, the answer "bourgeois." It was clear that this word now had a completely different meaning from the one it had in our Wandervogel jargon of earlier years. "Do you think 'proletariat' is an unrestrictedly positive concept?" He did not want to answer that, and was looking for the appropriate word. "No, do you know, the West is just too . . . differentiated!" At the end we spoke about our plans. He wanted to demonstrate in a new biography of Newman how active this man had been despite all his contemplation. "But you don't want to make him out to be an 'activist,' do you?" This was followed by a warm but somewhat sad parting.

On the trip home, in Frankfurt I saw Peter Suhrkamp again, whom I had constantly been missing; since our last meeting, more than six years had elapsed. I found him cheerful and unexpectedly lively; however, when I said that to him, he waved it off sadly, saying: "Appearances can be deceiving!" And he spoke, almost embarrassed and clearly understating things, about his time in the concentration camp. They had shattered his spinal column; for a time he was lame in both legs. "I won't live much longer." In reality spent nearly another ten years planning and working intensively. We were sitting in the office of his publishing house; Mr. Bermann-Fischer looked in; Suhrkamp introduced us; the conversation faltered. The difficult relationship between the two men would soon be sorted out. The idea of publishing cheap paperbacks for mass consumption was foreign to Suhrkamp; he called it absurd. Instead of that, he was planning thousand-copy books which would just have one print run of a thousand copies. For one of these strangely esoteric publications (1956), which contained Boethius's Latin poems and their translation by Konrad Wei , I would later write an epilogue. When I told him about my plan to travel in the following spring to America, he told me about his author Thornton Wilder, who had recently visited him. The idea of the "humane," this reaching out to the other person, was clearly something American. For example, Wilder had just sent him a handwritten letter in which he had written in bigger print to make it easier to read. "Who would do something like that over here?" He had wandered through the destroyed Frankfurt with Wilder a few times; Wilder particularly loved the German idea of "wandering" through the city — and also doing it — taking two hours to do a twenty-minute walk. On such a walk ("Bummel") on the last day, Suhrkamp asked him what impression he had of Germany. Wilder stood still, and after a long silence said very seriously: "I have to change my life." Suhrkamp had waited for an explanation and then, when it did not come, he laughed, and then Wilder laughed and in a completely different tone said: "Yes, of course I cannot change myself so much that I give up 'Bummeln.'" This appearance of lightness Suhrkamp felt was typical; basically Wilder somehow lived in despair. I looked at him questioningly. "So, just as everyone lives in despair today! Happiness has no role to play anymore!" I asked him: "Maybe not happiness, but bliss?"

The talk then turned to the *Frankfurter Hefte*, among whose editors I had some friends with whom I was constantly arguing about the "direction" of the periodical. What was I objecting to? I said: "Too little identification with the German people; basically too much distrust of tradition; a romantic overestimation of labor; a frivolous involvement with radical ideas; a fascination with the merely 'finely expressed.' Above all, however: if there were among the German periodicals a conservative opponent, then perhaps everything would be alright; but opposition could not be voiced in the current political situation." To my surprise Suhrkamp agreed with me without reservation; in astonishment I even heard him say: "I am nothing if not conservative. But that is perhaps more revolutionary than being progressive." When I was leaving I was given a stapled edition of T. S. Eliot's *Family Day*, which had been translated by him and Rudolf Alexander Schröder.

It was only rarely that we saw one another after that. We exchanged some letters; his were characterized by a special mixture of tranquility and intensity. This man from northern Germany was only himself when conversing in small groups. Even as a correspondent he apparently needed the feeling of spatial intimacy. At least he began a letter which he sent to me in 1956 when I was a guest lecturer in California with this sentence, which was remarkable for a man who was otherwise so cosmopolitan: "Writing a letter to America is always an effort, and where possible, I try to avoid it."

Two days after my arrival home from Berlin, Waldemar Gurian arrived at the house unexpectedly and unannounced. Months previously the University of Notre Dame had asked if I would be prepared to work there as a guest professor for a whole year. I could not decide to be away from the family for that long, so I asked if a semester would be long enough. The answer was a long time in coming, so that I was afraid this pleasant opportunity had been lost. However, in the end they were agreeable; they were expecting me on 1 February

1950 for four months. Gurian found that my English, which he immediately openly tested, was now sufficiently fluent.

Before that, in November 1949, T. S. Eliot came for a visit to Münster. This German tour with receptions, after-dinner speeches, eulogies, and sightseeing tours must have been completely stressful for him, although his own lectures, which were enthusiastically received in overflowing lecture theaters, seemed to energize him. But when it was suggested to him that he should climb ladders and scaffolding up to the former University observatory to look at the city, half of which still lay in ruins, he refused; and I noticed how tired he was. Since he wanted to spend the afternoon with me, I stole away from the celebratory meal being held by my friend, the rector Franz Beckmann, and ordered a hotel room for a couple of hours in the neighborhood. Eliot accepted, at once surprised and delighted. When I then collected him and brought him some soap which was not normally available in German hotels, he was hardly able, snug as a child on its mother's lap, to come out of his deep sleep. Later Joachim Ritter came for tea to my office. When he brought the conversation around to Bertrand Russell in a polemic way and wanted to force Eliot to take a stand, we did not yet know what only became known through Russell's autobiography of 1968: that actually thirty years earlier the somewhat lost young Eliot and his extravagant wife had found in the older man a generous helper and host. "It is really remarkable that I learned to love him like a son," Russell wrote in a letter in 1916. Luckily our children brought our talking shop to an end: they gave the shyly greeted guest a ten-minute concert on their recorders. Eliot praised the musicians to excess: "For the first time, music in the land of Bach!" A long time after that in New York I heard from Kurt Wolff, who had meantime become my American publisher, that Eliot had praised the "Pieper trio" to him.

V

Old-fashioned flight over the Atlantic — The man whom I should make a note of: J. F. Kennedy — Suspect *philosophia negativa* — A Russian in America — The "great books" — Late news about my father

A German person's visit into what was formerly "enemy" territory was a process beset with many obstacles and was also something that happened quite rarely. Before I could be given my visa in the American Consulate in Bremen not only had I to give my thumb-prints to be filed — which was the usual thing — but also the tips of all ten fingers had to be dipped into the black stamp ink and printed on paper. Still, I was then traveling to Frankfurt by the end of January 1950. It was the only German airport from which one could travel overseas. The flight lasted a whole night and, with the time difference, a few hours more. All the same, people said triumphantly at that time: "Imagine, in the afternoon you drink your tea in Frankfurt and the next morning you have breakfast in New York!" Today we laugh about the four-motor propeller airplane *Constellation*; I suppose tomorrow we'll be laughing about the *Caravelle*. In Goethe's journey to Italy he lamented: "Traveling through interesting places at horrifying speed: the coachmen traveled in such a way that you often lost all sense of sight and sound!" "Over there," on the connecting flight from New York to Chicago, I bravely had a first English conversation with the stewardess, but soon found I did not know the word for the northern light which had fascinated me on the night flight. Surprisingly this American girl came out with the Latin: "Oh, you mean the *aurora borealis?*" At the same time she comforted me by saying: "This country is famous for its bad English." Waldemar Gurian, who straightaway fished me out of the crowd in Chicago, to test me let me buy the tickets to South Bend instead of him, something which he admitted directly; and when the official at the counter understood me on the spot, he breathed a sigh of relief: "Your English is perfect."

Immediately after my arrival, the colorful Commencement Day, the start of the semester, was celebrated at Notre Dame. A solemn High Mass in the former Navy gymnasium; the organ music was being transmitted from the University Church which could not accommodate the thousands of people. On the gospel side of the altar was the stars and stripes flag, which, to my surprise, I would then see in every American church. With my beret and my dark blue former German Air Force coat on, I was hesitant about joining the Academic Procession of the teaching body. But I had belonged to them for the past two days! The other professors wore, depending on the their particular discipline or where they had received their doctorate, a blue, red or green stole thrown back over the shoulder of their black academic gowns, and of course a mortar board, from whose square platform a tassel was suspended. This mortar board, so called in the printed brochure of the event, only had to be taken off at Mass during the consecration. Gurian was particularly colorfully dressed, which was most unusual for this man, who otherwise was not one to conform. When I asked him about the meaning of the colors, he answered with his arms opened in a gesture of surrender: "I've no idea." At the afternoon celebration, apart from several hundred students who received their parchment and mortar board there were three who received newly awarded honorary doctorates, one of whom was a young delegate from

Chapter V

Massachusetts who had to make the official speech: the Commencement Address. I wrote in my diary: "He looks almost like Charles Lindbergh." His handshake when being congratulated was noticeably firm. Gurian whispered to me: "That man will be talked about in the future." His name was John F. Kennedy.

My teaching began with a row. I wanted to have some time to look around the country and had decided to put my three-day week of lectures on in the early part of the week each week; but I had made this decision without taking into account the administrative system or, to be precise, the punch-card system. For each course and for all the students taking part in that course there was a blue or a red punch-card provided, one for the Monday, Wednesday, Friday series and one for the Tuesday, Thursday, Saturday series. The Director of Studies, a hard-headed Irishman, insisted that I comply with this system — which meant a semester-long banishment to the godforsaken South Bend, in the "biggest small town of the continent" as the students called it. I was almost in despair. Gurian, who had hastily and without authority conceded everything that I wanted, was dismayed. He spoke with the "authorities" and with some experienced colleagues and then he took me aside: "Choose the Monday, Wednesday, Friday series; and then arrange with your students that the Friday lecture is held on Tuesday." I then followed this good advice; everyone knew about it and the students said that this was quite common. I got a batch of punch cards for use until the end of the semester. I think they were the red ones, on which, at an exact spot and using an electromagnetically pre-programmed pencil, I had to fill in a three-digit number to record the achievement rating. The "system" had then been satisfied.

Scarcely two weeks after the beginning of the semester Gurian flew to Europe to a guest lectureship in Paris. The next time I saw him was in 1953 at the Hamburg "Congress for cultural freedom" to which he had traveled in order to see Germany and his friends once more, as he knew he was dying. In the following spring he died at fifty-two years of age. An unusual and very strange person. Hannah Arendt had tried to characterize him in the memorial copy *Review of Politics* dedicated to him. It was his particular gift that he could analyze a political situation or a social setup instantaneously. He was devoid of vanity and always simple and clear in his diction, and brilliant in discussion. He worked day and night with an almost murderous conscientiousness. For an essay about Toynbee which he had promised to *Hochland* he wanted to read his whole six-volume *opus* for the second time. He clearly did not seem to take any notice of nature around him; presumably he simply never knew whether there was snow on the ground outside. Also it did not seem to matter to him what he ate or drank; he just stuffed or poured it quickly into himself. But he had a very keen eye for the suffering of other people and a sympathetic heart for those in pain. On the other hand, it was hard to have a warm friendship with him. He had had dozens of discussion partners all over the world. But had he any friends? Often enough people who had known him for years had warned me about his unrestrained curiosity, tactlessness and indiscretion; but I myself never noticed him being like that. Also he had never said a word to me about some of his own bad experiences. And so I knew only through his wife about the difficulties of the incomprehensible delay with his naturalization in the USA; anonymous neighbors had informed some FBI agents, who also remained anonymous, that Gurian had been visited by a German — therefore National Socialist — consul; in truth it was the chancellor Joseph Wirth who was also living in exile. If this confusion had not been cleared up at last by a complete coincidence, Gurian would have lost the right to stay and work. For me it was an important lesson in studying the difficult subject called "America."

Chapter V

Conversation with Mrs. Gurian, as with almost all immigrants, became really difficult as soon as I, the European foreigner, criticized *this country* in any way. It so happened that, after the planned temporary arrangement of staying in Gurian's house, I was invited to stay there for the whole semester. I paid the black cleaning woman who came to the house. I looked after my own meals; the refrigerator was available for a small amount of storage. One day, a colleague at the faculty made the pointed comment in passing that in Louvain a professor who was staying in a small house alone with the wife of another would be summoned before the Rector. This colleague would really have been very surprised if he, let's say, had seen our "communal" midday meal, which really was a little strange. I sat with cornflakes, fruit and a book at one end of the table, and she had possibly exactly the same food at the other end; and she also read while eating. There was hardly any conversation. Madame was used to being alone, and she liked it like that. She was the same age as me and wore Quickborn-style plaits around her head, and I would not have been surprised if this pious woman who went to Mass early each morning had taken a vow to wear an earth-colored dress cut like a sack and presumably made by herself. In any case, I have never seen her dressed otherwise even when she had guests. I knew about her charitable activities and also, despite the sparseness of her conversation, she was very pleasant to me. She washed my handkerchiefs, shopped for me and in bad weather drove me to the campus.

After the first laborious weeks of language difficulty were overcome, the students had ceremoniously approved my release from the "broken English department." The time of long journeys began. Sometimes I flew off on Wednesday evenings and returned only on Mondays just in time for my lecture. I had soon already seen more than the average American ever sees of his own country.

While the contact with the students, with whom I had started having an informal evening meal once a week in the cafeteria, was excellent, my inclusion in the Philosophy Department was not going so well. Gurian had already warned me: "Theology, above all, is missing at this University; there is hardly any real philosophizing, and there is nothing of the muses at all." All three of these were my main interests. But was that not too harsh a judgement? Had Charles du Bos not held the lectures "What is poetry?" which had just been published in Germany, in Notre Dame? "Yes, in Notre Dame, but not on this campus; it was in St. Mary's, where, of course, another wind blows!"

The President of St. Mary's, who completely characterized the spirit of this women's college, Sister Madeleva (Wolff) — an outstanding poet, a student of Oxford and a Doctor of Philosophy of the University of California — was one of the most brilliant women I have ever met. I noted in my diary: "Since my arrival the first objective serious conversation which went anywhere beneath the surface." Clearly Sister Madeleva had noted the advice of her friend C. S. Lewis, who, as I read almost forty years later in his letters, wrote to her in 1934: "Be wary of people whose hobby is what they call 'New Scholasticism.'" Not only did the teaching at the University of Notre Dame seem to me to be influenced by such rationalistic schoolbook Thomism, but, to a large extent, discussions among colleagues in the subject area were as well. I encountered a lot of historical scholarship, which has always impressed me. Again and again I was asked what "school" I came from; and they expected that I would say: from Louvain, from Freiburg in Switzerland, from "Laval" in Quebec. But I came from nowhere; and orthodoxy of the schools in the area of philosophy was a completely unfamiliar to me. In Chicago I was once introduced as a "Catholic existentialist"; however the chairman doubted immediately whether I myself would accept that characterization — which, of course, I denied with a vigorous shake of the head, to the amusement of the audience. Above all, it was almost heresy for some of my faculty colleagues, when I stubbornly spoke about the element of *philosophia negativa,* without which, as I maintained, understanding Thomas Aquinas (for example) was not possible. "The essence of things is unknown to us" — this sentence could not really be found in any "Thomist" compendium; but in Thomas himself it comes up dozens of times. Finally, they wanted me to put this outlandish idea forward for discussion at a specially planned meeting of the faculty. I felt a little like someone in the dock in front of a type of court of Inquisition; but they listened to me with respect; then they argued keenly and fairly, and no conclusions were reached. "Typically American?"

More than half of the colleagues who sat with me for the debate were priests — at that time, of course, all were wearing clerical dress, most of them in soutanes. If I think back on that now, something hardly believable comes to mind, something which I found out only years later: that the expert in Scholasticism, Maurice de Wulf from Louvain, invited to Harvard in 1915 as a guest professor, was the first Catholic layman to have taught philosophy at an American university, and that also among the Protestants of the USA before 1850 there was no philosopher who was not also a theologian.

When in my bewilderment I asked why in Notre Dame as in almost all "Catholic" universities of America there was no Theology faculty, I was given what at first seemed an illuminating answer: that training for the priesthood did not take place at the University, but in the Diocesan Seminary. But is a university without theology really a university? School Thomism, supervision of dormitories by priests, obligatory Sunday Mass, the Lourdes Grotto on the campus, the beginning of every lecture with a prayer — all that was not enough to constitute a Catholic university. The almost lethal crisis of American Catholicism after the Second Vatican Council, I was convinced, consisted mainly in the absence of a living theology in the universities.

Again and again the guest from Europe, the *old country*, was the cause of more or less tempestuous debates. There was, for example, the notion of a catastrophic end of time within history, about which I did not hold back in my history of philosophy lecture. This attack on belief in progress, of course, hit a specifically American sensitive nerve. But there was one thing I had not expected. Just in the period from 1948 to 1950 — of course only until the middle of the year — up to the outbreak of the Korean War, the American intellectuals were fascinated by the idea of a politically "one world," as they saw in this a guarantee of "eternal peace"; and the propagandists of this World Government movement, among them the Germanist Professor G. A. Borgese, a son-in-law of Thomas Mann, had their headquarters in a neighborhood directly beside us, at the University of Chicago. So the provocation of my topic was even more explosive; and, understandably, the students and also my colleagues wanted a public discussion. I agreed, but then saw, with some trepidation, the huge letters on all notice-boards announcing my lecture: "Antichrist, World Government and Christian Hope." To my surprise there was more agreement than contradiction in the full auditorium; I felt that there was a touch of general reflectiveness in the air, but I may have been deceiving myself. The Russian Professor Elias Denissoff at least, who grasped my arm while we were in a crowd near the exit and forced me to get into his car, burst out: "These Americans do not understand anything about the Antichrist! But we Russians!" In a small tavern to which he drove me and where he immediately ordered my favorite drink, Bloody Mary, he began to talk. "In the year 1917 we celebrated a seventieth birthday with parents and children, an aunt's birthday. Two years after that, as an exile in Turkey, I met a cousin who had also been at that party and he told me the fate of the others: the two of us are the only ones who are still alive." Denissoff and I had had, since the first days of the semester, a remarkable understanding. Clearly he felt the need to tell me, the European, about his huge disappointment with America and his pride in his daughter who refused ever to marry an American. However, he only spoke about that when whisky or gin loosened his tongue; otherwise he almost always expressed the opposite opinion. During an evening faculty party which made me totally miserable (singing ten-verse songs, drinking Coca-Cola out of the bottle), he kept saying to me: "Europe is lost. Come over here, if not for your own sake, then for your children's sake." Denissoff liked to see himself as a descendant of the Cossack Chief Waska Denissoff from Tolstoy's *War and Peace*, but he had little in common with him. There was nothing of the sturdy vitality, the flashing black eyes, the short-fingered fists and the unkempt jungle hair; instead of that, an educated man with a particularly vulnerable sensitivity. The twenty-four-year-old son of a Petersburg noble class captain had advanced to become secretary to the Prime Minister Kerensky for a short time after the collapse of the Tsarist monarchy. Then he fled from the Bolsheviks over the Turkish border; the next stop was Persia; clearly money was no object. He studied in Frankfurt and was married there. He was friends with Jacques Maritain; under his influence he converted to Catholicism. Finally he did his Doctorate and then Habilitation in 1945 at the University of Louvain. Then, however, two to three years after the end of the war, when the first acute tensions between Russia and the West developed, fear overcame the refugee as he looked at the map of Europe; for him the Soviets were not far enough away. From one day to the next he decided to go to America. The family was horrified; the three children felt completely at home in Belgium, particularly with the French language; but, for better or worse, they followed their father. Jacqueline, the eldest, was giving French classes at a small college near Chicago.

On the trip home from there I was told this whole story, while outside a powerful spring storm was descending. Our car was called "Maxime," after the Greek-Russian monk Maximos, about whom Denissoff had written a very learned book which was awarded a prize by the *Académie Française*. As soon as you entered the prefabricated terraced house in which, for the time being, the immigrant still lived without his wife, you forgot where in the world you were because of the icons, carpets and "Kremlin" furniture. The "Caucasian" beefsteak which he tried to make for me one evening became an adventurous failure; still we drank Burgundy wine with the steak. What French-Russian cuisine had to offer was proven by Jacqueline, who had come over for the time being to honor, with a convivial meal, her godfather Jacques Maritain, after whom she called herself and who was giving some guest lectures in Notre Dame. The very sight of the laid table was a celebration. The loveliest feast for the eyes was, of course, the youthful lady of the house herself, whom I openly courted a little. Not very long after that she did marry an American who was of south Slavonic extraction; and when I visited her two decades later in New Mexico she was running a large household with four adopted children. Her English, colored by her French, had remained unchanged; but precisely that was what her husband found especially attractive.

Elias Denissoff, her father, whom I saw only once again, looked for and found a way of escaping America, which was becoming more and more intolerable for him. His recourse was to the religious culture of eastern Christianity, and the nurturing environment of his origin. Five years after our meeting he was ordained a priest at Nazareth in Israel and appointed as a pastor of the Melkite Catholic Community in

Chicago. He ended our last telephone conversation in the spring of 1968 with the words: "I embrace you in Christ." As I am writing this (1972), his death notice is in front of me; on it his photograph, which shows him in the garb of the Great Archimandrite of Jerusalem.

At the meal in honor of Jacques Maritain, thankfully English was spoken; he himself spoke it with such a pronounced French accent that I immediately understood what had been reported from Princeton: his very full auditorium had been very quickly reduced to a small group, because they simply could not understand him. He wanted news of Peter Wust from me and I told him about the last weeks of his life. Maritain complained about the growing and, as he said, destructive influence of logical positivism in America and then spoke very much at length about the role of Judaism in history. He was a man with an unusual ability to listen; he was always inspiring and clever, although never "lively." He seemed to be very tired and, although hardly at retirement age, since he had snow-white hair and was stooped he seemed like a completely old man. But then twenty years later I received a letter written in very clear handwriting from the meantime eighty-seven-year-old man, from Toulouse, where he, in his own words, lived as a "lay hermit" with the Little Brothers of Jesus. I had asked him if would consider talking to a German TV team, which was planning a documentary about Christian philosophy between the two World Wars. The answer was, not surprisingly, "no"! Yet he reminded himself and me of our first meeting in the Denissoff household, which was also our last.

On a bleak March morning during that first semester in America I traveled by tram through the sleet of Chicago to Kurt Wolff, who was lying in bed with a light flu. We were to talk about the English edition of my books. Kurt Wolff had been watching my output for a long time, without my realizing it, and he wanted, as Gurian told me, to wait until the series about fundamental virtues was finally available; but when he then — again through Gurian — found out that it would still be some time before they would be ready, he decided to do something immediately. When he mentioned the collaborative work which he hoped he would be doing with Faber and Faber in London, I was able to show him a letter which had just arrived from Alick Dru, which reported that T. S. Eliot had read some of my books while on holiday in South Africa and also wanted to publish them. Alick Dru was immediately accepted as the translator; his translation of Haecker's *Journal in the Night* had just been published with Pantheon Books, which was Kurt Wolff's publishing house in New York. Later, after Alick Dru's surprising decision only to translate dead authors, there was a lot of trouble with unsuccessful translations, which even had T. S. Eliot up in arms, while Helen Wolff, the publisher's wife and head editor, felt justified in her complaint: Should I die young, please put on my headstone: *Killed by translators.* — Of course the topic of Germany very soon came into the conversation with Kurt Wolff. The publisher, and often enough also the discoverer of almost all significant writers of the 1920s (Kafka, Sternheim, Trakl, Konrad Wei !), looked disappointed about the sparseness of German literature; Kasack (*The city beyond the river*) Langgässer (*The Indelible Seal*), Stefan Andres (*The Deluge*) — that was all nothing. "How should one expect language culture in a country in which a man like Alfred Weber is seen as someone?" For me he had compliments; however, he feared at the same time that the sober clarity of my language could easily become shallow banality in English translation.

By chance I was in Chicago on the same weekend as the young publisher Henry Regnery. He also spoke of my books, which he wanted to publish because they represented what was for this country a completely new point of view. When I indicated that there might be other interested parties in the

USA, he decided to send a telegram immediately to Dr. Wild. But Regnery was irresolute. Six years later, on Saint Patrick's Day, I was to sit with him again in order to celebrate, at a festive meal, his charming but very quiet daughter's fifteenth birthday in his exclusive club; and now he had to say resignedly: "At that time if I had only . . ." At our first meeting there was something completely different about Regnery which interested me: that he was the publisher of the "great books." On my first free evening in the USA I had come across an English edition of Aristotle's *Poetics*, with the question printed on the cover: "Why see sad movies?" This was, according to the text, one of the questions to which one could find an answer in this book. To my amusement and astonishment, Gurian then told me about the financial attempt through banks, department stores and industry, but also through private contributions, to make the "great books" of the Western tradition accessible to as many people as possible; throughout the whole country there were already thousands of people of all levels of education who discussed such texts — the prior reading of which was taken for granted — in small groups which met regularly. Among the texts were the Platonic dialogues, the *Quaestiones* of Thomas Aquinas, the songs from Dante's *Divine Comedy*. "Where is the average American to see a tragedy, if not in the cinema?" said Gurian. "And so firstly you speak about the *sad movies*!" But the engine room and the intellectual management of the running of the Great Books Movement was again this incredibly lively University of Chicago. Strictly speaking, however, the whole thing was organized by two people: Robert M. Hutchins, the Chancellor of the University, and the philosophy professor Mortimer Adler.

If you were wandering across the campus of the University of Chicago and the clock tower of the University Chapel was just striking the hour, you could for a moment believe you were in Oxford. In the entrance hall of this church, which is more like a cathedral than a "chapel," I was amazed at the bronze plate with the inscription from 1910 in which the Baptist founder of the University, John D. Rockefeller, defined the meaning of the sacred building in the following way: "Because the spirit of religion should penetrate and dominate the university, in the same way the building which represents the religion should be central to and dominant among the university buildings. In such a way it should be proclaimed that the ideal university is dominated by the spirit of religion, that all its Faculties are inspired by religious sentiment and that all their works should be aimed at the highest goals."

And so it was with some curiosity that I visited the Chancellor of the university on an appointment arranged by Henry Regnery. Meantime, I had heard quite a few things about Robert Maynard Hutchins: for example, that year after year he received sixty million dollars in private donations for the university because of his management ability and his personal charm; that, in opposition to the closed front of public opinion, he had banned football from the university; that he was involved in becoming a Catholic, but that he could not take this step without losing his post as Chancellor, because ultimately this university, although meantime completely secularist, was a Baptist establishment. One of his declared opponents, a sociologist, expressed it to me in this way: "This man is trying to lay a Catholic egg in a Protestant nest; this is a Protestant country." Hutchins had made himself into the best-hated university president of the United States — for example, through his definition of the American average college as an establishment which served to make life pleasant for young people who did not belong there. The art historian Otto von Simson, Managing Editor of the periodical *Measure* published by Hutchins, held the view that the attempt to win back a European basis for the American university, in spite of certain partial successes, was hopeless. Above all, Hutchins himself was lacking in basic clarity. Formerly he had declared that theology was the basis of all true education; then metaphysics; and today the magic formula was called *Summa Dialectica,* with which a type of dialogical combination of all, even the most contradictory philosophies was meant.

As I knew that Hutchins had been Chancellor of this big university for twenty years; I was expecting to see an older administrator type; instead of that, a tanned sportsman with a spring in his step came towards me. Like everywhere in America, all the doors of his office were open; but there was absolute silence; the secretary, who brought us the coffee, seemed to float in. Hutchins was clearly enjoying the aggressiveness of my questions and he listened with attention. And then he had fun in forcing me to declare that the problems were unsolvable. "What is a 'great book'"? What's the difference between that and a merely successful book? How does one manage to develop space for contemplation in a world dominated by business? Hutchins answered by referring to the Committee on Social Thought. I had already heard this nebulous name in Notre Dame and asked what it was about. He laughed; the opaqueness was on purpose; it was only by doing this that the undertaking could be protected from the public at large and from that of the university. "But what kind of an undertaking is it?" "A type of Collège de France, a group of chosen researchers who are to research what they think is important and who are the only people who understand what they are doing." Hutchins told me a little about his philosophical studies at Yale University; he had never heard the name Thomas Aquinas there. At the end he asked me directly: "What is to be done against specialization at the university?" I said that you could happily expect more of it and absorb it, as long as the subjects were pursued in a really academic and therefore philosophical way.

I was invited by the Committee on Social Thought to give a lecture, and when on a May evening I climbed the stairs to the lecture theatre and read the name "Swift Hall" above the portal I was finding it quite acceptable to speak under the aegis of Jonathan Swift; but then my companion, the chairman, laughingly destroyed the illusion for me: this Swift was unfortunately a different one, namely the lard king of Chicago, who had funded the construction of the building.

In Chicago I always found accommodation in the International House of the university, a skyscraper residence for students and guest lecturers. It was remarkable that, in an otherwise rather libertine atmosphere, it was still almost technically impossible for a male to enter the living area of the females and vice versa. On the blackboard, which I always studied extensively, mindful of Meister Plenge (for social occasions it was regularly mentioned whether dress was to be formal, semi-formal or informal), I found among other things a notice about a prayer-meeting of Quakers which immediately interested me. I took a seat silently in the quite large circle of similarly silent people, who remained in this programmed silence for a long time, which to my mind seemed somewhat forced, until at last some individuals arose and made short utterances confessing faith. One said: "Are we really candles of the Lord?" But then the so-called ritualistic part was declared finished and, to my surprise, a lecture to be given by Carl Friedrich von Weizsäcker was announced; he reported, with a quiet objectivity and with pleasant sympathy for his home country, about the situation in Germany and in particular the intellectual situation of students. I had been in correspondence with Weizsäcker for some time. This had come about through our mutual friend, the harpsichordist Edith Picht-Axenfeld, who had visited us many times in the years after the war. Weizsäcker, with whom the conversation soon flowed, told me about his American experiences, and again I realized that you are never finished learning here. That his university lectures were dismissed as "medieval" here in liberal Chicago for his use of metaphysical categories was less surprising to me than it seemed to be to him. But that someone could be attacked by the students of a Protestant College because he casually remarked that the world was, of course, older than six thousand years — that bordered on the unbelievable. The worst of it, said Weizsäcker, was that the head of the College, instead of supporting him, had remained silent, and, as later became clear, this was because he was afraid he might lose his job for having opinions that were too liberal.

Some time later I met Weizsäcker again in a discussion group at Georgetown University in Washington; in my paper I was defending the contemplative nature of philosophy. The Chairman of the evening was Rudolf Allers, who had been enthusiastically discovered and published by Jakob Hegner as "his" author and who, just like his publisher, had fled shortly after from an Austria occupied by Hitler. On this occasion he asked me officially if I would accept an appointment in Georgetown, which I politely and guardedly declined. On the way home, Weizsäcker warned me that an American would find such a refusal difficult to understand and would tend to suspect sinister motives behind it, such as a politically difficult past.

But you have hardly started to shake your head about this strange country when you stop and admire it and wonder at it. For example, I had yet to visit Ann Arbor in the state of Michigan; I had to call on a benefactor to say thank you from our family. We had formed a completely false picture of him, as would become clear in rather drastic fashion. A Mr. William Barnds had got our address from somewhere, perhaps from Gurian's list, and had sent us a food parcel every now and then and with it every time a somewhat old-fashioned and tortuous letter. He said that God had blessed him with possessions and he was sharing them with us just as he was sure we would have done if we were in his position and he in ours. There was never a word about his circumstances or his profession. We had a clear picture of him as a well-to-do, not uneducated, but still an ordinary older person, presumably a businessman — a money-maker with a soul. In his last letter he said that he would take care of my overnight stay. But then there followed one surprise after another. The taxi brought me to the house of a student fraternity; and instead of an older businessman I was greeted by a student who was admittedly older than the average; military service in the Far East, he said, had cost him a few years. He was not at all prosperous. In the holidays he worked in a factory, and during the semester he was a daily dishwasher in a restaurant in exchange for a free lunch and dinner. So this was what he meant by God having blessed him with possessions? With regard to my accommodation, he assigned me, without inhibition, the lower bunk of a military bed; his room-mate had been encouraged to visit his family. For dinner there were sandwiches with peanut butter, as much as I'd like; with that, Coca-Cola. When we went to bed, I was looking at a silver chain on his chest; it was a medal of Our Lady; he noticed me and said that he was vice-President of the Newman Club.

In the month of May the semester was at an end. I went to the authorities to bid them farewell. There was nothing but sunshine everywhere; even the Director of Studies said: "If you ever want to come back, the door is open." Well. — Mrs. Gurian brought me to South Bend airport. There was a short but warm farewell. She went home immediately. What was there to talk about? I had time to sit in the blazing sunshine and reflect on the four months which had passed like a dream. Suddenly a young beauty wearing a long summer dress and a fashionable Florentine hat came over to me. What a charming sight, I thought to myself; and only when she said in her

French English that she had come to wish me a good trip home did I recognize Jacqueline Denissoff. I was really astonished, but I only just had time to thank her when the call came to board. Through the narrow window I saw her waving after me with her Russian-French style farewell.

Friends in Clifton, New Jersey, also a friendship which had developed through CARE parcels, had offered me their house as a base for the stopover in New York. From their garden you could see the skyscrapers of Manhattan in the haze; and with the amazing Lincoln tunnel under the Hudson it took only about an hour's drive to get there. At Pantheon Books, at this stage "my" publishing house, I met Kurt Wolff's wife Helen. On her editor's desk lay Heidegger's *Holzwege*; but along with this, overburdened like most of the women over there, she had responsibility for the household. The apartment on Washington Square, eleven stories high above the noise of the street, was more like a library, with old furniture and a few glorious paintings. At dinner Kurt Wolff said: "We are living like an average American couple; from nine until five publishing work; on the way home shopping for the meal; and, of course, I help with the washing up. After that we have visits from authors and friends. One evening a week we have to ourselves." "So, also a complete 'world of work'?" With relish Kurt Wolff latched onto the keyword from *Leisure and Culture* which I had half seriously thrown out; he said there was no real wealth here despite the abundance of material goods; the millionaire was just as much in harness as the worker. "Henry Ford came to his office, year in year out, wearing the same old hat, and worked from nine until five." That was also how the many donations could be explained; they did not know what to do with the money; people's own puritanism prevented them from keeping a mistress or from traveling around the world in a yacht. So they collected, for example, old Brussels masters of a certain era — not because of the joy they brought, but because they had been told that they were needed in some museum to complete the collection; and one day there would be a *Mrs. Dorothy Babbit Collection* to be admired. I asked about the book trade and found out that New York's biggest bookshop was a department in Macy's store and the manager just a businessman; he did not need to know anything about books; instead, he read prospectuses and advertisements and particularly those "prognoses" through which bestsellers were made. As for the rest, Kurt Wolff's verdict on America was somewhat differentiated. What Europeans missed, of course, was the assured sense for quality and style. Only a few years previously Adolf Busch had played the Beethoven violin concerto with only a piano accompaniment. But today you could not hear better music anywhere in the world than in New York. Then Kurt Wolff told me a sad story about Adolf Busch, whom I had heard play many times and greatly admired during my students days; the sixty-year-old's playing of the violin had so incomprehensibly disimproved that he was rarely in demand; but Rudolf Serkin, his piano accompanist whose fame was constantly growing, regularly made it a condition of his performance that his friend Adolf Busch would also be engaged. The Wolffs did not just know immigrants. They casually mentioned the Lindberghs, who had just returned from a big trip and saw the world situation in an alarmingly pessimistic light; they were convinced that war could break out again at any moment (1950!), "perhaps even tomorrow morning"!

For my last evening in New York, Kurt Wolff insisted on getting me a ticket to Eliot's *Cocktail Party,* which was hardly possible in the normal way. But then it happened that two tickets had been bought by mistake. So I quickly rang my friends in Clifton; and a few minutes before the curtain went up the eldest daughter arrived, out of breath but carried away with enthusiasm. Afterwards we did not want to go home so early, so we decided on a *night-tour* through Chinatown. In the temple, on the cultic drum you could let heaven know your requests; one beat meant: health; two meant: wealth; three: a happy marriage. Marianna immediately made three resounding beats. Her marriage, which took place shortly after, has in the meantime ended in divorce; she is battling to cope with rearing her four children. Of course, on this lively evening, after which we arrived home well after midnight, nobody could suspect anything about that. On the following morning we drank "sacred tea" from the bowls purchased in Chinatown; I wrote to Eliot, to congratulate him on his *opus* and its wonderful performance, and with pride the twenty-year-old added a postscript.

Heinrich Brüning, who had invited me to visit Harvard, was himself in Münster at this time, so I tried to meet another Harvard Professor, Werner Jaeger, the author of *Paideia* and, as they say, America's best paid university teacher (which clearly did not put him in the position of having a housekeeper, as I was to find out). He seemed at first not very impressed with the idea of being disturbed by a visitor he did not know, but he named a specific amount of time for which he could make himself available. But when we then quickly got into lively conversation in his quite European-looking house out in Watertown, at the end of the time he had allotted to me he put a bottle of Burgundy on the table and began to talk. In Harvard, he said, the old Oxford traditions were still adhered to; Aristotle was "not central enough" in comparison to Plato. John Dewey, the Columbia philosopher, did not of course have the least influence. The visiting groups of Germans officially brought into the country were led with such a sure hand that they only saw the Dewey America. Of course, the professors of philosophy in Harvard were long since not "philosophizing." They were proud of being experts; the "logisticians" were admired the most. I asked if he did not want to publish his Aristotle book from 1923 in a new version. Jaeger shook his head. "I am really only interested in the Church Fathers now; it is my ambition to bring out the first critical edition of the work of Gregory of Nyssa." He did not say a word about his own bitter experiences which Brüning had related to me two years previously in Münster, that, for example, there was hardly any student with knowledge of Greek to be found.

In June 1955 I was to see Werner Jaeger again in Florence at the annual Congress for Peace and Christian Culture organized by Giorgio La Pira. Dieter Sattler, who was then still Cultural Attaché at the German Embassy in Rome, took us to a country hotel in the area of Fiesole for a lively celebratory meal at a stone table under old trees to celebrate an academic honor which had just been bestowed on the great Classics scholar in Rome.

On 7 June 1950 I traveled back to Germany. When, during the customs procedure, my wife appeared, beaming with the joy of seeing me again, the official placed the expensive nylons back in the suitcase and generously let me go. With some surprise I read today, 1972, a comment in the travel diary: "The ruins in Frankfurt depress me a lot, the change is coming too quickly." We traveled home through the Rhine countryside in blazing sunshine through villages which were decorated for Corpus Christi. At home I listened to the table music of the Pieper trio, which was now venturing to play Telemann and Handel. And amongst the post which was piled high on the desk lay the first copies of my history of philosophy meditation about the end of time.

A few days after I arrived home, a Germanist from Stanford University visited me. He had just published the Stuttgart Middle High German translation of selections from Saint Thomas's *Summa* in a critical edition, with the publishing house of his Californian university. To his question about whether I could and would like to come to Stanford and take part in a Humanities Program he was planning, I pointed to the mountain of post which had not yet been dealt with. "I haven't really got back yet!" And then, as he was leaving, and almost too casually, he confided in me that he was considering becoming a Catholic. In this respect, I said, Thomas was really a dangerous author; he had already induced a few people to think this way.

A person traveling to America was at that time still a rarity. So the editor of the *Westfälische Nachrichten*, the same newspaper — though now under a different name — for which I had written my film critiques twenty years before, asked me to report to his colleagues about the trip. The Feuilleton editor who came to collect me entered the house in excitement, and without a greeting said: "It's starting again. There's war in Korea." At a stroke, life can change; everyone thought in fright about a third world war. They bought crazy amounts of food. My bookseller complained that his shop was deathly quiet. Into this atmosphere came an official request from Notre Dame about whether I would take up a permanent position in the Philosophy Department. Immediately I thought of Denissoff and his warnings. Were my children to experience yet another war? I needed time to give an answer; so, expressing my gratitude, I asked for more information about this important invitation. But this time the answer was not long in coming; the invitation was repeated a little bit more urgently. I took the letter with me on a cycling trip on the Rhine-Main which I had been promising my son Thomas; he had just turned fourteen. Imagine if someone had said to him (or me) that half of his lifetime was already over and that he would die in the country in which they were sending for me? But "at that moment" I was thinking about the danger of war in the world and particularly about the letter from Notre Dame, which was burning a hole in my pocket. Suddenly I made the decision. It was Saturday; you had to search early for a place for the night; in Ingelheim we found the right guest house. So I was sitting in the late afternoon on a summer patio, in front of me in a tankard a quarter-liter of the red wine produced there; Thomas was swimming in a branch of the Rhine (or in the Selz, I don't know any more); while I was watching him, the bells which heralded Sunday rang out all over the Rhine valley. And at that moment it became clear to me: I will never leave this country of my own free will! Fate giving me a sign? Instinct? Sentimentality? In any case, my letter of refusal was sent that same evening to Notre Dame.

In December of this same year, 1950, my father died. In the summer, the German Institute for Pedagogical Science, which had been closed down by the National Socialists and deprived of its bookshop, was formally reopened. It was planned that I would give a lecture entitled: "Thomas Aquinas as a teacher." My father, who had been involved in no small way in the foundation of the Institute in the 1920s, had sat in the back row of the auditorium near the exit. While I was speaking I saw him getting up. He went to the door with uncertain footsteps. An old man's illness was making things very difficult for him. A few days later he traveled to Fulda to be operated on by my brother. On the way there, he spoke to my wife, with whom he got on particularly well, about nothing but his childhood. When she told me this I knew that he wouldn't be coming back. Maybe death did not even take him by surprise. The simple desire, about which he spoke every now and then, to sit one more time on the couch with my mother, had an almost unreal sound. When his speech failed he gave out a slurping sound from time to time which only the night nurse understood; it said: Please help me! Sometimes he counted out all the fingers of his right hand, one after the other, and held them in front of his eyes — he was calling his five children to mind.

During the administrative formalities of moving him to Münster, the question of the unknown father of the deceased came up again; it would now remain unanswered. However, in 1972, more than twenty years later, in a very unexpected way information about his mother and some early living circumstances found their way to me. I was traveling home with some university colleagues from an academic meeting in Düsseldorf. On the way we missed a train connection; during the long wait we chatted about this and that. A young historian whom I hardly knew who had been invited to the meeting as a guest brought the conversation around to the German Brukterer tribe from the Paderborn area where he had lived. I mentioned in passing that my father had also come from there; to which he replied, now turning towards me confidentially, and said that he had already known that; because if he wasn't mistaken, his great-grandparents had reared my father. A few questions went back and forth between us and quickly it became clear that it really was my father. But he recommended that I see his mother who lived in Münster and knew more about it than he did. This old widow of a civil servant whom I contacted the very next day immediately put a small leather-bound prayer book in front of me on the table; I remembered the title "Bread of Angels" from my childhood; on the first page there was a dedication on the First Sunday after Easter 1911, written in my father's handwriting. Many of my questions remain unanswered; the woman was only able to tell me what she had heard in her family. Even so, I found out things about my grandmother: she was a serving girl in the family of an aristocratic Hussar officer; the son of the house became the father of her child; after that she lost her job; in her parents' house there is no room for the new-born child; her father had died early and her mother had remarried; there were children from the second marriage there; there was no home there for her anymore. The foster mother, however, who was the wife of a master builder, took on the child and loved the boy as much as her own children. When she was dying and received news that he had passed his teaching examination, she said that now she could die in peace; and actually by the time the traveler had rushed home she was already laid out in her coffin. The working mother, whom her son had thought was the widow of his natural father, refused many offers of marriage because of the boy. When my father took up his first position as a teacher she was promoted to being a housekeeper of a women's clinic at forty-eight years of age and enjoyed the greatest of respect everywhere. In the house of the woman who was giving me all this information, the good china was put on the table whenever my grandmother was there as a guest.

Losing your father has a deeper impact on your life than you expect. It is unexpected because, without much reflection, you have experienced and practiced the old wisdom that your wife and children are closer to you and belong to you more directly. But suddenly you realize how much your life was related to that of your father, how much you owed him and how much you remained in his debt. The unusual modesty of his life style, for example, was, when you look back, nothing but the reverse side of his concern for the future of his sons and daughters. When he returned from a visit they made together to a colleague who maybe had a particularly nice house, he used to say to my mother comfortingly: "Our possessions are not dead things. They are alive." After the death of my father the thought came to me with a new intensity, and perhaps for the first time, about what I may have meant to him, in terms of both joys and sorrows.

VI

"Colleague" of Gerhard Marcks —
An unnoticed listener: Teilhard de Chardin —
Jean Daniélou: an intellectual and a cardinal —
What does it mean to have been in Chartres? —
Spain and death

The early fifties held some unexpected encounters for us. The Cologne sculptor Hildegard Domizlaff wanted to paint a portrait of me, and from that a lasting friendship developed, spiced by very direct and two-way criticism. Through that, a first contact with Gerhard Marcks also developed; the city of Cologne had just built him a very fine house in close proximity to the "Domizlawa." Above the door were the not very inviting but nonetheless, in my view, appealing words: "Go 'way and let me sleep"; and actually he was not really interested in meeting new people. My wife, who was an enthusiastic devotee of the potter's art and who had begun to decorate the house and garden with colorful dishes, jugs, and tiles, was instantaneously greeted with chivalrous exaggeration as a "colleague." And I myself was allowed to enter the studio; and so I could watch the master as he drew with big strokes, from memory, a lioness that was about to spring. The master always wrote his letters by hand and they were all, in themselves, small graphic works of art into which the not so unusual Greek quotations were incorporated like a special ornament. But with time, at least this is what I suspect, our correspondence, at first quite lively, and which was often ignited by my work, approached too dangerously close to the question of fundamental convictions, and so it dried up completely — apart from more conventional New Year's greetings. What answer could I have given to the question: "Can you imagine at eighty years of age being glad to die soon, even without having any Christian hope?"

Strangely the most exciting meeting of those years had not, strictly speaking, taken place. The Paris *Semaine des Intellectuels Catholiques* which took place every year at Pentecost had as its theme in 1951 *Espoir Humain et Espérance Chrétienne* — a formulation which was difficult to put into German, as our language only possesses one word for the concept "hope." On one evening of this "week" there were four presentations on the programme, which did not, however, prevent everything from being be finished in an hour and a half. Clearly this had to do with that fact that the French learned in the subject "rhetoric" at school, among other things, that they should deal with the subject matter in an exactly measured length of time. Here the papers were twenty minutes long. With Olivier Lacombe in the chair, Gabriel Marcel started off; he was followed by Jean Daniélou and Yves Congar; and I was last to speak. I never dreamt that amongst the almost fifteen hundred listeners who filled the crypt of the St. Odile church that Pierre Teilhard de Chardin was sitting "at my feet." Only a decade later, when Teilhard was already dead more than five years, did I discover this from the biography of Claude Cuénot. In it there is a letter, written on the spur of the moment with spontaneous vehemence, in which this prominent listener passionately rejected the thesis which I was putting forward at the time. So there was some form of a "meeting." My topic was "The Hope of Martyrs," and it was my intention to make one thing clear: that you would do better not speak of human hope at all if there is no hope for the person who is willing to be killed for the sake of truth and justice and who, in any case — locked up, isolated, ridiculed and, above all, silenced — finds himself in a "hopeless" situation. Besides, I did not fail to mention that it is written nowhere that human history, in its temporal aspect, will simply end with the victory of reason or justice. Teilhard de Chardin said in that letter that my approach to the issue was "defeatist"; the determining factor was something completely different, namely the future potential of the young human race seen from the point of view of its "biocosmic" possibilities. As one could see, the confusion of evolution with history, which was characteristic of Teilhard's whole thinking, was again at work. Naturally, blood witness can only be spoken of meaningfully in the realm of history, while evolution knows no martyrs.

During my lecture, Jean Daniélou had sat directly in front of me in the first row, and with his stimulating response and his constantly and dramatically changing facial expressions had almost distracted me from my manuscript, which friends had translated into excellent French for me. A few days later we met in his editorial office which was filled with books. Daniélou was all agog to hear about my experiences in America. And we soon actually only spoke English together after it turned out to my chagrin that a single term as a guest lecturer in America kept interfering with my French, which had been quite good up until then. Of course, I reported among other things about the debates I had conducted in Notre Dame about the "negative" element in the world view of Thomas Aquinas, after which he immediately asked for my essay about this topic, which had not yet been published in Germany, for his journal *Dieu Vivant* which was regarded as quite revolutionary. He immediately promised to take responsibility for the good French translation of my history of philosophy book *About the End of Time*. I am sad that, up to the present day, this is the only one of my books on which such an honor was bestowed.

Daniélou was not completely in agreement with the thesis

either of this book or of my Parisian lecture; in any case, he said a few years later that the emphasis on the eschatological aspect was possibly an alibi for the lack of active love, which also has to share earthly hopes — particularly those of the poor — and to work at their realization. In that I agreed with him, but I also had concerns that it was un-Christian to think that no hope remained if there was nothing more we could do. This debate between us which developed, as I said, only a few years later, was nevertheless held publicly — at the Congress for Peace and Christian Culture which I mentioned before, for which in June 1955 the Lord Mayor of Florence, Giorgio La Pira, had settled on the topic "hope." As in Italian *Germania* comes directly after *Francia* alphabetically, we greeted one another in the ballroom of the *Palazzo Vecchio* unexpectedly as neighbors; I sat down in the empty seat between us which was meant for François Mauriac, and immediately we were involved in the liveliest of discussions.

I have never experienced a Congress which, although organized by La Pira who was living with Franciscan frugality, displayed such splendor as would make you think of the princely courts of the Renaissance. The sessions began in the mornings to a fanfare played by heralds, dressed magnificently in the colors of the city. And at the official summer evening reception on the roof of the *Loggia dei Lanzi,* which you could only get to through the Uffizi, they had fitted flaming torches to the external walls and the tower of the *Palazzo.* During this unusual cocktail party I chatted with Bruce Marshall. As a Scotsman, he had reluctantly taken his place under the sign "*Inghilterra*" and happened to be sitting behind me. He noticed my lively discussion with Daniélou as well as the splendid name plate which was hanging in front of me; and so he revealed to me how surprised he had been to see François Mauriac laughing; that just simply was not possible; and, as he now knew, he had not been wrong. On the following day,

Mauriac himself appeared and took his place. And I saw with great respect, and hopefully Bruce Marshall did too, a face which, though seldom laughing, was characterized by a human, benevolent smile.

Many years later, Jean Daniélou, with whom I had always felt a remarkably strong link although we had never corresponded, arrived at the house unexpectedly. Meantime, quite surprisingly the simple priest had been made a cardinal — for which reason the intellectuals no longer saw him as one of them; now he was suddenly seen as "conservative." Incidentally, it amused me for the moment that he wore purple socks with his simple chaplain's uniform. But then his firmly advocated opinion that the fate of the church depended on the activity of the really small groups struck me as quite revolutionary. This last meeting occurred only a few years before his sudden and puzzling death, which aroused public curiosity and, certainly with injustice, was interpreted in a very negative light.

In that year 1951, with countless celebrations the city of Paris celebrated its 2000th birthday — however problematic the exact dating might have been. And we were happy to let the Semaine continue and made some of our own arrangements.

There was a concert every night in the Sainte Chapelle. With wonderment and curiosity we stepped into the almost complete darkness. We were led by the narrow beam of a torch to our places and we waited in suspense for the beginning. Suddenly, from outside, the flame of beaming lights lit up, in glorious color, the windows whose glass constitutes nearly the whole structure of the building. At the same moment the choir, which remained hidden, filled the room with an almost unearthly music; it was a Mass by Guillaume de Machaut. — In Notre Dame Cathedral, when the *Lauda Sion* sounded at the Pentecost High Mass, the thought suddenly came to me that this hymn by none other than Thomas Aquinas, a professor of the University of Paris, had been composed and perhaps first performed in this cathedral. It was also a surprise to discover Descartes's grave in St. Germain des Prés; almost more unexpected were, I thought, the celebratory words which were hewn into the stone: that Descartes was "the first to proclaim and defend the right of human reason regardless of the authority of Christian belief." I made a note of this questionable formulation.[1]

Also in the Cathedral of Chartres, which we had visited once before, we were confronted by something unknown to us or just something we had never thought of, when we joined a small group of pilgrims from Beauce and so ended up in a small side chapel we had scarcely noticed. Here the Madonna was enthroned and honored as Notre Dame de Chartres. And these simple people confronted us with the question about what way one could physically take part in something. Until now the "viewing" had been enough for us to be able to say: We've been to Chartres. The pilgrims, however, were completely convinced that they had only really been there if they had touched the pillar in front the image of Mary with their hands and kissed it with their lips. In Versailles, which we visited also not for the first time, my attention, perhaps to my shame, was almost completely fixed on the huge boxwood hedges of Trianon Park; I had got it into my head that, with my pocket knife, I could make off with one or two thick sticks for my potter; inexplicably, one needs precisely this kind of wood for modeling clay.

Almost exactly a year after the remarkable "meeting" with Teilhard de Chardin, in the same city another one-sided meeting happened to us with another Frenchman whom we had

1   "Bene qui latuit, bene vixit" seems to be what is on the gravestone. (from the translator)

revered. My wife and I had interrupted a trip to Spain to spend two or three days in Paris, and we had noticed huge posters advertising a "Gala" in honor of Don Bosco, at which only the speaker interested us: it was Paul Claudel. The public had clearly not expected to gain much from the event. The wonderful Salle Pleyel was scarcely half full, and the celebration organized by the community of a religious order was of a really pathetic standard. Claudel, who was then eighty-four years old, trudged with heavy steps — and obvious bad humor — to the speaker's podium to read his short address in a monotone and almost with indifference, which presumably was not much to the liking of the organizers. Don Bosco did not belong to the "professional" saints, the festival speaker said; and it was certainly not his fault that he was canonized. For us, it was as depressing as it was moving that the lion's paw did not like to be shown in this way. Still we were happy to have seen and to have heard in person, for the first and probably the last time, the writer of *Satin Slipper* and *The Five Great Odes*. Like himself, we left the dreary "Gala" after the address. At the exit, like a young student, I lay in wait for the man I still admired, and walked all the way to his car, keeping close to his side and not letting him out of my sight. Naturally, the thought of addressing him never entered my head.

In Paris also our first trip to Spain was given a completely unplanned "introduction." This was a remarkable country and, despite all its fascination, a country which was very strange to us. The introduction came through the Spanish dancer Carmen Amayo and the large exhibition of Mexican art which had come to Europe for the first time. Because of the impossibility of transport there were, of course, only a few enormous works to be seen, almost eerily impressive monuments from the time before Columbus; most of it went back to the colonial era. But even that proved to be a particularly thorough introduction to the specific Spanish theme "death."

We stood somewhat dismayed in the rooms with old and new folk art in front of the display cases full of skulls made of wax (or of sugar?) and bridal-pair dolls which were clearly standard productions, in complete wedding garb, but with a bare death-head instead of the human face. (Twenty years later I was to see, in America's New Mexico, death, a female creature, *la muerte,* as a church cult figure on a coach driver's seat, swinging a whip and driving invisible horses.) And so we were not completely unprepared for the sight of Spanish passion figures which are regularly to be seen — covered in blood and with faces distorted in pain — in the side chapels of the churches, which were mostly harshly lit by a hidden source of light. And where else would you find a grave inscription like the one in big metal letters without any name or date, placed in the stone floor in the cathedral of Toledo: "Here lies dust and ash and nothing"? Death and the fleeting nature of earthly life are forcefully kept in mind — and not only inside churches. When you open a popular daily newspaper you see the huge death notices with black borders filling half a page, in which someone who died two decades ago is remembered. On the street now and then we saw women who were wearing a high-necked, violet, apparently woollen dress in the heat of the summer days with a gold cord as a belt; it was, as we later heard, a penitential gown which people themselves had chosen to wear for a period of time as a method self-chastisement. For a woman this meant nothing less than complete renunciation of any womanly charm. Beauty, grace, loving charm: all that is vain! — And the famous Spanish dance? That it should not simply be taken as an expression of joy in living was already made clear to us in Paris at the sight of the young Carmen Amayo; in the newspapers they compared her to a wild horse coming over the plain, which aroused not so much delight as fright and fear. And we came across this element of angry displeasure again and again — despite all the lightness and erotic grace of the dance. In Seville, the city of my informed boyhood dreams, during the siesta time in one of the big restaurants we asked for permission to watch a dance group rehearsing for an evening performance. In the middle of an empty room, when we went in on tiptoe, the dancers — two young men and about ten girls, some of them still children — were already working. Now and then a man whom we could not see gave directions with a hard, domineering voice which had to be followed without contradiction. After an unusually sharp reprimand which drew no reaction, a rotund dwarf with a limp stamped angrily out from behind a column, took off his jacket, threw it on the floor, had castanets handed to him, danced the figure he wanted — in a manner that was as grotesque as it was precise — and disappeared again back to his place, which was out of our sight. It was like a scene from Goya. The dancer, however, to whom the correction had been directed, began obediently and docilely to learn his part again with the precise grace and unmitigated seriousness of a bullfighter.

Vicente Marrero Suarez, an established expert, introduced us to the death metaphysics of the bullfight, which, although apparently merely crowd-pleasing, is, of course, anything but a happy game. His book *Picasso and the Bull* had only recently been published. In a ministerial capacity he also accompanied us, as an indispensable commentator, to the Corpus Christi celebration. Through him we received the text of a law just pronounced by the Head of State, containing just one single paragraph, which is in honor of the *Virgen de Toledo:* "To the wonderful picture of the Most Holy Virgin of Hope in Toledo the highest military honors, *los maximos honores militares,* are to be shown. 31 May 1952. Francisco Franco." Despite all love for the Mother of the Lord, the Catholic Christian from Northern Europe is reminded by such a gesture of *Don Quichote,* with all the ambivalence of feeling which is characteristic of the tragic rider. — We have seldom experienced a feast day which combined all the elements of festiveness and realized them so convincingly as that Toledo Corpus Christi: the whole city, with its streets covered in marquees and its house fronts decorated with carpets, was one single festive space; the rosemary and lavender branches which covered the street pavement emitted their strong fragrance the more the people walked on them. The procession flowing out of the cathedral after the pontifical High Mass was, of course, mainly the accompaniment of the Blessed Sacrament; at the same time there was a military parade led by the almost mythical defender of the Alcazar, General Moscardo; and if anyone were to have called the celebratory parade a social representation of the community he would have been right. But also the bullfight in the afternoon belonged to it as well; that the particularly sought-after fighters, upon their entrance into the arena, made the sign of the cross was clearly nothing special, as they did that before every fight; the whole thing was like a secular event; still, it was the *Corrida del Corpus*. In Toledo we did not just see the defenders of the Alcazar but, of course, also the huge building itself. At that time it had been only partly restored but was long since a place of pilgrimage for patriots as well as tourists.

We heard surprisingly little about the civil war itself, although traces of its black smoke were evident in several famous churches: on the seats, on the organ or in the roof beams; clearly people did not like talking about it. Still, Calvo Serer, a young professor of the history of philosophy at the University of Madrid and one of the leading lights in Opus Dei, gave me, in reply to some of my questions during an intimate midnight meal we shared, quite significant information. We sat under the starry sky in the roof garden of a hotel as if we were on an island to which the street noise came as a distant rustling. As my discussion partner, whose *Restoration*

Chapter VI

Theory had just appeared, said: Spain had been living in a civil war for one hundred and fifty years; perhaps twenty-five years of peace would be enough to lead to unity at least through the education of the younger generation. He spoke, however, with a skepticism you could feel, as if he were more convinced that one day the murders would begin again. "Nowhere in the world did anarchy, the simple denial of all political authority, of whatever type, hold such power. The Spanish anarchist denies every form of order." The real difficulty lay not in the "Social," even though the "social question" in the European meaning of this word was hardly solvable. — I asked about the fate of the people who had been on the "other" side during the civil war. "There are three hundred thousand emigrants; they are shaping opinion about Spain throughout the world." "What will happen if Franco becomes the victim of an attack tomorrow?" "Then the churches will burn again throughout Spain the day after tomorrow." Calvo Serer was not a supporter of Franco, but he said that there was, at that time, no other solution. Today (1975), more than twenty years after our night discussion, he lives in exile himself, in Paris.

I am speaking lastly about the actual reason for this Spanish trip — and not particularly fondly. I had been invited somewhat "officially" to hold a lecture in Madrid and Barcelona in the "Ateneo" in each place about "The relevance of Thomism." The success was, however, as I feared, really disappointing for my hosts. Probably I had taken too literally the assurance, given with generosity, that I could speak in German; there was no plan to provide a translation. And so most of the guests who had been invited to the cocktail reception left before ever going into the lecture theatre. Whether those in the small group who were left were all able to understand German was not apparent to me. And the few who were really in a position to follow the lecture were presumably not exactly impressed by my thesis that the relevance of Saint Thomas, to a large extent, was that there could not legitimately be a "Thomism." Still, the polite applause lasted a long time. And in the same year the text of the lecture appeared in Spanish translation and printed in an exemplary manner by a Madrid publisher.

VII

Joyless start to a trip to Canada — Strange Rendezvous — Karl Stern and the "fire pillars" — Frightening instruction in the "America" lesson

Seldom have I so reluctantly gone on a journey as on my first trip to Canada in August 1952. The fact alone that I was to be taking part in the World Congress of the Mouvement International des Intellectuels Catholiques as the delegate of an association did not particularly appeal to me; I have never seen it as my thing to "represent" any group. And then the — to my mind — sinister name of that organization: *Pax Romana*! The possible confusion with something pacifist; the striking emphasis on confessionality; the reminder — clearly not sufficiently considered — of the military establishment of peace campaigns in Ancient Rome — all of those things were not to my taste. In fact, it was particularly because of this name, which I saw as completely wrong, that I declined when some time later I was offered the honor of becoming the first postwar German President of the World Association. For the boat trip, my first since the trip to Iceland in 1923, I was supposed to share a cabin with the legal historian Hermann Conrad, whom I found a decidedly boring bachelor. The boat was the "Groote Beer," a converted transporter of military troops. I realized later with dismay how wrong you can be about a person. To my amazement, my travel companion proved himself shortly after that, in the Rhine-Westphalian Academy of Sciences of which in the meantime we had both become members, to be exceedingly lively and interesting in discussion; and when I discovered more than a decade later, when he died suddenly, that he had decided after his retirement to become ordained a priest, I felt very ashamed. It has puzzled me up to now why on that trip together we had never engaged in a conversation of any significance. Anyhow, I found I was able to engross myself for the whole day in Thomas Aquinas, in the treatise on justice in his *Summa* about which I was planning to give a lecture the following winter semester. I was also to put a shape on a short essay about "Philosophy and the common good" which I had promised to Henry Kissinger — who was at that time still a Harvard Professor — for his periodical *Confluence*.

Then, however, one bright morning the sea, which until then had been a dark slate grey color, almost from one moment to the next became bottle green, and we were greeted by whales blowing fountains of water from their nostrils as we entered the mighty St. Lawrence river. The intoxication of travel poured over me; I found it absolutely wonderful to be landing again in a part of this earth which was still unknown to me.

The Congress, designed to run for several weeks, was to begin deep inland, starting in Toronto, continuing in Montreal, and finishing in Quebec, and so would lead us through almost the whole of east Canada. And in fact we did see quite a lot of this huge country, which stretches from the magnetic North Pole to the latitude of the Italian Riviera, and about which it was said that there was still not a fully complete and exact map of it. One day we traveled northwards in the "bush" past the last police station, which made a note of all our details, including the car registration, and would start searching if we had not returned by a certain time. Or we arrived in a town which two or three years ago had not yet existed. The same was true of the aluminum mine, a few kilometers away, to which the town belonged and which was the biggest in the world, we were told. In the school yard little girls dressed in white aprons were sitting on a swing pushed by a nun; it could have been Tours or Poitiers; but the year 1950 was on the foundation stone of the church. In the fields, which we looked out at during an hour-long train trip, I was surprised and amazed to recognize, in the white-blooming vegetation, the buckwheat of home. The varied landscape of this unbelievable country was almost overpowering; it extended from the white tourist ships which you saw at night on Lake Ontario like fairy-tale characters floating out of the light, to the northern tents of the Indians who could not get used to the stone houses which had been specially built for them. And then again you read on an advertisement boarding at the entrance to a middle-sized city: "Praised be the Blessed Heart of Jesus!" In Montreal, though it was about one thousand kilometers from the Atlantic Coast, you could hear early in the mornings the noise of the ocean liners which had docked in the middle of the city. And in Quebec, the fortress built on high steep rocks — the only one on the continent — you were awakened by the far-reaching sound of the horns of the castle guard.

About the Congress ("The mission — *la Mission* — of the university") there were, as was to be expected, many talks, discussions and "resolutions." I was asked to chair one session dealing with the problem "The University and Researching Truth." I wanted to explain to this thoroughly experienced group that there could neither be a true university, nor research about truth, without "a free area" being separated out from the "world of work." Against this, some American academics who were fixated on the terrible experience of the Korean War posed the question whether the university could be allowed to withdraw from the duties of defending their country. At the end, the "secretaries" who had been assigned to me

— both Jesuits — gave me a text which had clearly been drawn up beforehand and which had very little to do with the discussion in which we were actually engaged. It was to be put before the closing plenum of the Congress and voted on by us. This raised such a decided protest that the prefabricated "resolution" soon disappeared back into the briefcase of its authors. If one were to look back on what has happened to both the European and the American universities in the last twenty-five years, one would ask with some skepticism, what has, in fact, been achieved by such declarations, no matter how they have been formulated.

But here the rule was confirmed that what happens outside the program is the most important — as unexpected as it is unplanned. At least for me there were again some really remarkable encounters. In Toronto there was the obligatory toast to the Queen, which later would be followed by another dozen, during which a glass of fruit juice was raised. It was not just the French who found this *impossible*. On that evening, when the series of long welcoming speeches was beginning to seem endless, a young professor brought me to his apartment away from the official boredom of the opening banquet, where he immediately openly admitted to me that he had purchased my book about leisure because of the introduction by Eliot. Still, he did want to meet the author and put some provocative questions to him. The name of the man has come back to me only now (1977) upon re-reading the diary about the trip: it was Marshall McLuhan. At that time he had already published his book about the folklore of industrial society, with the aggressive title *The Mechanical Bride*, but I did not know that, and its meteoric rise in the international best-seller lists still lay ahead. Curiously, on our meeting a second time more than twenty years later, again in Toronto, neither of us remembered that first conversation; we had completely forgotten it and shook hands like two strangers — with due respect for the work which each had in the meantime had published.

Even stranger was another meeting about which it could be said that it occupied my imagination but in reality did not happen at all. A year earlier I was invited to a tea party near Essen, completely unexpectedly, in order to meet a quite famous German scientist who had migrated to the USA and remained as good as unknown to me personally. I hardly saw a face I knew among any of the gathering. They had placed me beside the second wife of that migrant, a woman who was still young and breathtakingly beautiful. Out of the blue, she asked me whether she could translate some of my books into English. She paid me particularly flattering compliments about them and she named some titles. She was clearly familiar with the material. The gathering left us to this conversation, with the result that afterwards I was suspicious that the whole thing may have been arranged with this in mind. My news, that we were in fact looking for a good translator, was immediately greeted with enthusiasm; however, I did have to add that the author did not have the deciding word but the publisher — actually the American publisher. My neighbor thought this was wonderful too. Because I would soon be flying back to New York I should contact her there. I therefore wrote to Kurt Wolff, whose sensitivity to female beauty was not unknown to me, and told him he had better be prepared. A short time after that he confirmed that he had seldom met such a beautiful woman; but he then asked her to translate a chapter from my book about hope and send it to him. The result of the test was — whatever about charm and beauty — an almost cutting definitive rejection, a copy of which I was given to read. You cannot really reply to that, I thought. However, the woman who had been rejected did contact the publisher again in a disarmingly charming letter, promising renewed effort and, if necessary, a planned course of study. But Kurt Wolff still declined.

And so nothing ever happened about the matter, and strangely that little book about hope did not find an English translator at all. A year later in Montreal, where the *Pax Romana* Congress had meantime migrated, a university colleague from Washington confessed that he had had a letter to give me from that beautiful woman, but despite looking for it for days, he could not find it; the whole thing was clearly jinxed. On the other hand, it was not too bad, as he knew exactly what was in the letter: the writer was spending her holidays in a country house not far from Quebec and was inviting me to go there and stay for as long as I liked. To the address I had been given I hesitantly wrote to the woman about the strange disappearance of the letter and let her know when and where I would be in Quebec to receive any messages. Days later, the Washington colleague rushed towards me waving the letter, which he had now found, high in the air. It contained friendly greetings but not a word about an invitation.

The third actual meeting, to do with my *opusculum About Hope*, has continued right down to the present. I am indebted to the persistence of a woman attending the Congress who thought it scandalous that I should be in Montreal without having met the psychiatrist Karl Stern. The autobiography of his conversion, *The Pillar of Fire*, published in New York a year earlier, had been sent to me through a friend; later it also appeared in German with the nonsensical title *The Cloud of Fire* (Feuerwolke) — nonsensical because the author understood his remarkable "return" to the Catholic church as the strict consequence of religious Judaism, as an act of obedience to the Old Testament God of Israel who showed himself nightly in the pillar of fire. A chapter of this moving report carried the heading "About hope"; and the author said in it that my book of the same title, which he was reading on a park bench in London when he was already a refugee, revealed to him, "as through a narrow crack, a glimpse of the great

Christian anthropology." Of course, we did not talk about this at the lively meal around the family table, although we spoke about a whole variety of other things. Afterwards Karl Stern played off by heart the great posthumous sonatas of Franz Schubert; for me it was as if I were hearing them for the first time. When I was leaving, the lady of the house did put the little well-worn book in front of me to sign; her husband had brought it with him into their marriage, she said. As my accommodation was at the other end of the city I was only brought to the bus station by car. There we stayed for another hour chatting in the car while one bus after another departed. Karl Stern had told me during the short trip about his decision to give up his position in the famous McGill University and instead to go to the not exactly significant Catholic University in Ottawa. I could not understand it and asked him about his reasoning. And then he began a long drawn-out defense of his decision as if he were not altogether sure of it himself — he was so unexpectedly serious and there was such an undercurrent of despair that I almost regretted having brought up the matter so spontaneously. He said that it was no longer possible for him to work in the atmosphere of a fully secular psychiatry which was more or less expressly characterized by the conviction that the ultimate reason for all spiritual disorders was religion, which had to be eliminated as a "complex." The idea that some time, from this North American continent, the radical nihilistic revolution would begin with the declared goal of the social psychoanalytical therapeutic provision of general happiness came between him and his sleep. Depressed as we took leave of one another we said: "Until we meet again in Munich" — something which was quite feasible; but, in fact, fifteen years were to pass before our next and also final meeting, again in Montreal, where Karl Stern had returned, but not, of course, to his former university. When I rang him from Toronto in 1967, the year of the Canadian centenary celebrations, and told him of my intention to visit the world exhibition in Montreal, he immediately gave me a very warm invitation to his home, as there was an enormous amount to discuss. When I got out of the night train I met a restless and exhausted-looking man. We spoke to one another about what had happened in the intervening years; when I mentioned the sudden death of our eldest son, he confided in me, almost with the gesture of one betraying a secret, that the same had happened to him, but that his son had committed suicide. Some hours later, his daughter-in-law, who as a European did not feel happy in this country, brought me by car to the World Exhibition. Conversation was difficult, so we talked about the underground strike and the wonderful September day. On the following morning, after a night spent mostly in conversation, as I set off for Toronto I was given his last book published in 1965, *Flight From Woman*. Upon our farewell, which again was a sad one, I was quite sure that a life led with still undiminished intellectual passion, but saddled with such burdens, would not last very long. And when a few years later the news came of a physical breakdown I was not surprised. His wife wrote that the most difficult thing for him was that the stroke had made it impossible for him to play the piano.

The *Pax Romana* Congress ended in celebratory fashion with the *Magnificat* prayed together in Latin (and the question comes to mind as I write this, twenty-five years later, whether it would be possible today for a thousand Christians from all over the world to recite a text in one language — spontaneously, off by heart, *par coeur*). This happened in Quebec, doubtless one of the most beautiful cities in the world, high over the St. Lawrence River. The ship which was to bring the European participants home, again a former transporter of military troops, set off, contrary to plan, not from Quebec but from Hoboken. And so there was a stopover of almost a week in New York which was very welcome. Kurt Wolff, who himself was on a trip to Europe, generously offered me his room in the apartment on Washington Square. With his son Christian, who was at that time eighteen years old, a Harvard student and keen player of Bach and today a well-known composer of electronic music — and, like his teacher John Cage, an advocate of the "chance method" — I wandered for hours through shops known for their long-playing records, shops which at that time were still attractive to Europeans. That you could take a catalog of several hundred pages from the pile was to me quite unbelievable. The most important lesson in my education about America, which had just begun again, was given to me by his mother, Helen Wolff. A friend of the family had invited me to his house about seventy miles from New York. We drove out on a hot late summer's day, bathed in the sea on the way and only arrived towards evening. Before we went to the table we went for a quick walk around the dark forest where you could hear the sound of the cicadas. The forest, like the tennis court, belonged to the property. It was only a few steps to their private beach and a small boat harbor. I could not resist the invitation to stay the night. The late hours were passed with Californian wine and good conversation. The next day I chatted about this "paradise," full of enthusiasm and still stunned by such an unexpected place, secluded from the world, and yet so near to New York. Helen Wolff listened for a while and said that this "paradise" had its own horrors, which I could not discern. That friend, whose wife had died a few years previously, had remarried; his second wife, however, whom I knew, was Jewish. Hardly anyone knew that until now; but both of them were constantly in fear that the neighbors might find out some day. For the time being, I did not understand what she meant. "What would happen if the neighbors found out?" "That would be the end of the 'paradise'!" Then followed, out of the authoritative mouth of the wife of a Jew, though she herself was not Jewish, the elementary lesson about such simple facts as that in this free country there were areas — beaches and hotels — which counted as *restricted* or even *highly restricted*, and others also which were more or less discreetly identifiable as only "with limited access": so, for example, not accessible to Jews. She told me (and I still did not believe her), ashamedly, about several experiences which her husband had had on this issue. But then she was suddenly averse to telling me more, and she recommended me to read an early novel, *Focus*, by Arthur Miller who was beginning to dominate the stages of the country. I then read the book at home with profound amazement, but also with fear and anger.

As had almost become a habit with me, on the last Sunday before the ship was to set sail, after the Catholic Mass in which I was treated to a dollar sermon which was without any vestige of religion, I attended the service of a sect, this time the *Ramakrishna Mission*. I had not known until then what a problematic, almost demonic affair this Neo-Hinduism is. Exactly ten years later in Calcutta I really became aware of it in comparison to the traditional Hindu cults. Still, I thought the prayer with which the gathering ended in New York expressed quite an apt theme to accompany me on the trip home: "You, whom the Christians honor, whom the Jews call Jehovah, the Muslims Allah and the Hindus Brahman: lead us from non-reality to true reality, from the dark into the light. Shanti, Shanti, Shanti — Peace, peace, peace!"

VIII
An abruptly ended conversation — Dismissal from the political reservation — The "German Committee" — On lost post — Virgin territory: television

Under the mountain of post which awaited me 0n my return from Canada there was a letter from a reader. I dealt with it out of its turn. Because of its unusual seriousness I could not leave it unanswered, even though the writer had not asked for a reply. So a strange and moving correspondence began, which led to our meeting several times, almost as if we were friends. Then, of course, after a good three years it all ended suddenly. The last letter, a kind of cry for help, came too late for a reply to reach him in time — which for him, I feared, must have been a deep disappointment which he would not have understood. The first letter, which, like all the later ones, was written in a clear, energetic, plain hand, had introduced the writer: he was born in 1892; on the circuitous route of being firstly an officer at sea, next a graduated lawyer, then on to his true profession, that of musician. His *Small Handbook of Music*, which was in its fifth edition in 1949, was enclosed; the author: Karl Gerstberger. The book, in spite of its alphabetical order, only *seemed* to be a reference work. It is, in fact, a collection of sharply focused biographies of musicians and some historical and systematic treatises — with masterly formulation — about melody, meter, and song. In his own compositional work, as he wrote in a later letter, he felt "unexpectedly like a 'resistance fighter' in his opposition to the terrorism of the modernists." Music was almost always our only topic. He loved comparing the art of the composing musician with that of the chess player, both of which were pointless if there were no compulsory rules. In music the main thing was to handle the natural "materials" of melody, harmony, and rhythm in such a way that each of these elements could play its part. Countless possibilities were available and only arbitrariness was excluded. "Anyone can live haphazardly." I could only agree wholeheartedly with this concept, which was reinforced by Goethe's words. We were happy to be in agreement. But then by chance we spoke of Béla Bartók, and it became apparent how fully one can isolate oneself despite one's wide-ranging theories. In our house, Bartók was almost seen as a classical musician; particularly the children loved him. With innocent enthusiasm they put on a record with pieces from *Mikrokosmos*. Then they fell silent and became somewhat confused when they noticed that the visitor simply could not relate to the music. And so I was not too surprised when his own compositions, although approximately thirty of them were published, remained as good as unknown; a large record company answered with a clear rejection, and the head of a radio station, who was personally well-disposed to him, said: "Wonderful, but no future!" Gerstberger himself reported all of this with no suggestion of complaint and quite unmoved. I myself tried to get funding for him from the Deutsche Forschungsgemeinschaft to cover the printing costs of a musically and pedagogically wonderful commentary on the complete *Well-tempered Clavier*; but then my suspicions were confirmed that they could do nothing because it was not "scientific research," which was true. Perhaps Gerstberger was never really aware of the formal rejection, which was sent to him only later. A pernicious illness, which was diagnosed only late and which must have weakened the physical resistance of the North German, who held himself very erect, had already finally killed him. Nevertheless, I cannot rid myself of the idea that this high-minded man was much more affected by something completely different from the lack of success of his works — which was becoming increasingly more evident — and from the invisibly advancing illness: it was the result of the equally unstoppable crisis which more and more unsettled the framework of his hitherto fundamental convictions, and yet at the same time gave him an insight which he was not yet able to formulate but which he was determined to confront. Even in the first of the letters I received he wrote: "As a Protestant and passionate admirer of Luther I found it particularly beneficial to encounter the Catholic way of thinking, and to approach it was for me a joy rather than a labor." I am quite certain that in my reply I did say one word on this point. He clearly had no intention of letting the matter drop, certainly not in his letters, while in personal conversation a kind of awkwardness stopped both of us from discussing such matters. One of his next letters contains the confession: "That I felt the need on New Year's Day, overcoming all opposition to the inadequacy of Protestant formlessness, to attend the service in our little village church, I owe to the embarrassing insight gained from *Leisure and Culture*." Shortly before he went into hospital he stated, like a dispassionate observer, that on the one hand "he had momentarily, at almost sixty-four years of age, a feeling of complete helplessness"; and on the other hand he knew that he was "in completely different hands than those of the best doctors." In his last letter there was then the last appeal, meant directly for me, which, as I already mentioned, only reached me when it was too late: "I am longing, ever more intensely, to grow into that spirit which I find in the writings of J. P. . . . Would you allow me to speak to you about this topic soon? . . . Can I reach you by telephone at home or in the University? Sorry about this question, which is perhaps somewhat surprising for you, but I am assuming that you understand." I did, in fact, believe that I had "understood." The letter was dated 24 October, 1955. At this time I was on a lecture tour in Switzerland. On 30 October I returned; I did not yet know that it was the day of Karl Gerstberger's death. A week after that, the semester began. For the first time my lecture topic was: "Faith as a philosophical problem." Only fifteen years later (1971) did I receive the good news that, through the loyalty of a close friend, all the works of Karl Gerstberger, both musical and literary, were to be entrusted to the care of the Hannover City Library.

In the fifties, the post-war period finally came to an end for us West Germans, and with it also the unregimented and spontaneous unfolding of intellectual vitality, which, when I look back at it, was the real happiness of the "heroic" years of the new beginning. We had been living in a type of reservation, in an open-air enclosure watched over by others, cut off, indeed, from political responsibility but at the same time dispensed from it. And it must be remembered that this — as can be seen from the Adenauer memoirs — meant something entirely different for the actual leaders of the community. In the consciousness of the average citizen, in any case, the fact that the vanquished had no voice promoted the feeling of an almost unreal release from obligation. But with one single blow this uncertain situation then ceased for everyone through the formal end of the war situation and the reinstatement of inner and outer sovereignty. Little by little we started to become aware of the regime of our own State, which now had to secure and organize its own existence.

During the first period of my teaching at the Pedagogical Academy, for example, no administrative authority worried about the fact that I declared attendance at my lectures and seminars was not obligatory; even so the students completely filled the lecture room. For years I could successfully refuse to burden the students with having philosophy as an examination subject; I even defended this refusal in a quasi-official pedagogical periodical with a half-joking scholastic *articulus* written in the context of carnival. As regimentation took hold, however, philosophy and also other disciplines were made compulsory and became examination subjects. — At the University, the *Philosophicum* was introduced as an obligatory interim examination for every student who aspired to be a teacher at higher level. Methods and institutions are to be "scientific" — that was everywhere the battle-cry. Although the most varied impulses were behind this, from social prestige to ideological scientism, it was consistently taken up by the governments of the states or even reinforced. In the Düsseldorf Ministry of Culture it was planned for a time to reduce the philosophy being taught in the framework of teacher training to the "pedagogically relevant," and in that way — against its nature — to make it into a piece of "professional training." I immediately stated my intention that if that were the case I would leave the Pedagogical Academy. It was a curious fact that allowed me to put my opinion to the minister responsible in such a blunt way: a long time previously when I was a student I had helped this clever man — a man of integrity, who was open to every factual argument — by teaching him Latin in preparation for his delayed final school examination. This was something we never mentioned again, not even in private. He accepted my objection immediately, but it was more or less chance.

At that time the number one topic of conversation in the public domain was the question of rearmament and general conscription. "Department Blank," the early form of the Defense Ministry, was working on plans for the organization of the future Armed Forces, and Count Baudissin was developing and propagating the notion of interior "leadership." Discussion groups of lawyers, historians, theologians and philosophers debated under his guidance, for example, the problem of whether and how the abuse of power — above all in the lower echelons — could be prevented from the outset through organized safeguards. Strangely, I was also invited to one of these conferences, presumably as the author of writings about the idea of man, about justice and bravery. However, my contributions must have disappointed the practitioner, something which I was openly given to understand. But, after all, given the optimism which was based on a mere improvement of the right of appeal, I could not suppress the received wisdom that ultimately only one thing can stop the injustice of a person who exercises real power, and that is the justice of the person himself. And also I suggested for discussion the skeptical and realistic question of my teacher Thomas whether perhaps ethically less brave men could be the better soldiers — who need first and foremost a fighting spirit, tenacity, courage and physical strength.

Still this meeting had a special surprise in store for me. I will just mention in passing that in the same discussion group there was a future army General Inspector who many years later would become my youngest son's father-in-law. Of course, we did not know one another, and at the formal greeting neither one of us had taken particular note of the other's name. No, the surprise refers to something else; it had to do with the topic of "reform" in my own area. In a break in the discussion, someone I did not know spoke to me. I had noticed him because, when he was putting forward precise arguments, he had his eyes tightly closed. It was the Ministerial Advisor, Dr. Edo Osterloh, who in 1964, as Minister of Culture in Schleswig-Holstein and not yet fifty-five years old, mysteriously met his death. In an almost casual, matter of fact way he said that I would soon be working with him; and he was very surprised that I did not know what he was talking about at all. It turned out then that a letter had gone astray, in which the Federal Interior Minister and the chairman of the Ministry of Culture Conference had appointed me to the German

Commission for Education and Training. This Commission had the task of compiling, completely independently in the style of a "Royal Commission," recommendations which would then provide the local governments of the federal states with a more unified cultural and educational policy. Highly respectable names were given to me; the whole thing seemed to be a wonderful project. All the same, it was not just my private misgivings about such a form of public involvement which had eventually led me to decline — something I had also done a year and a half previously with regard to the appointment to the German UNESCO Commission. It was more that I had meantime had some experience of both the irrational arbitrariness of administrative decrees and also of the visibly increasing power seen in the proliferation of reforms based on interests approximating to ideologies. Already for this reason I had decided to withdraw my initial engagement in this matter and preferred for the moment to carry on, unperturbed, with my own "thing" — which was teaching and writing. I answered the letter of appointment stating that in my view what was missing was not advisers to the king, but the king himself. I was not particularly happy with this answer; but subsequently it turned out to be the right one. The so-called "German Commission" freely dissolved itself after twelve years of activity, but not without a sense of resignation. The foreword to the impressive volume, which mainly contained expert reports reflecting wonderful commitment and selfless effort, expressly complained about the lack of support from politicians. Above all, on reading many of the recommendations, one becomes aware, with consternation, with what crazed brutality the actual development of things rode roughshod over plans which only a decade previously were considered to be "realistic." Anybody who, around 1970, walked through the entrance hall — of which the walls were papered with newspapers — of what is now a Teacher

Training College cannot help but feel nostalgic when reading the well-formulated expert report (of 5.9.1955), which "particularly recommends the establishment of pedagogical institutions which have the focus of a religious denomination or of another fundamental conviction," "characterizing the life of the institution and, in Christian institutions, including the religious service." In fact North Rhine-Westphalia had made the "religious denomination teacher training" the state norm during those years which, though not so long ago, seemed, because of a silently opening abyss, to be unutterably far away in time. Despite the undoubtedly sinister terminology, the homogeneity in the teaching staff that was to some extent guaranteed in this way never appeared to me as a restriction of student freedom, but rather as a special chance to achieve real personal education. In the end, the aim is none other than, by combining knowledge and belief, to give a deeper dimension to the students' image of the world and of existence — an image which, of course, remained highly fragmentary. This chance, of course — and this is intrinsic to the concept — can either be utilized or lost. And the latter, I fear, is what actually happened. In any case, it is a concern and a deeply problematic fact that, under the slogan "make the training of teachers more scientific," the declared aim of providing the foundation for understanding the world has been replaced by a much less obvious susceptibility to ideologies of any type.

If my information was, as I said, disappointing for officials in "Department Blank," I have never felt myself to be fighting a losing battle as much as at two international conferences in Hamburg and Berlin, both of which were organized at great expense by the "Congress for the Freedom of Culture," an institution which was mainly financed by Americans — clearly anti-totalitarian and anti-communist, but in no way "conservative." When I traveled light-heartedly with my wife to Hamburg, I did not yet know what awaited me; it was all the more drastically brought home to me. The Congress in the Hanseatic City organized under the title "Knowledge and Freedom" took place in the last week of July 1953 in which the half-rebuilt Hamburg was marking the tenth anniversary of its destruction. The English historian J. C. Fuller called it a "terrible slaughter," which "even Attila would have considered a disgrace." But from a purely military point of view, they say that even today it counts as a brilliant attack carried out by the British bombers under the macabre codename "Gomorrah." At the time the dreadful event took place, very few of those taking part in the Congress had been in Germany. Even the Lord Mayor of Hamburg had not been there. And so it was just mentioned in passing and in conversation; however, the atmosphere of the gathering was, under the surface, affected by that gruesome event. In this city you could not get out of your head the thought of the thirty thousand people who died mainly by fire. In the Town Hall, however, at the public ceremony with which the Congress started, the great hall had recovered its former splendor. When the opening speeches went on too long as usual, in a whisper I asked Michael Polanyi, the chairman of the organizing committee, whether it would not be better to drop my own forty-minute lecture about "Recognition and Freedom." But he insisted that not a single sentence should be omitted. I did not know that it was Polanyi who had expressly wanted me to speak in this circle: as I later noticed, he was particularly definite about it. I had never met this remarkable man before. He was born in Hungary in 1933 and had then worked for ten years as a teacher of chemistry at Berlin's Kaiser-Wilhelm Institute and then, having been in exile in England, moved from science, through sociology to philosophy, and to a very precisely formulated and at the same time completely personal metaphysics, which was focused on the religious dimension. With some discomfort I went to the lectern. The very fact that

Nicolas Nabokow, who was introducing the speakers, referred to me as a theologian made me, for the first time, feel this as a type of disqualification. It was deliberately relegating to the expressly "non-scientific" field. But my thesis would, in any case, probably have met with resistance among most of the participants at the conference. ("Against the decline of freedom of science, as it is found in the totalitarian worker state, nothing of substance can be done in the field of intellectual debate, if at the same time some fundamental insights formulated in the pre-modern Western tradition are not brought into play.") Even as people were slowly streaming out of the packed hall I was told that quite a few people had reacted to my provocation with bitterness and anger; particularly the temperamental Sidney Hook, professor of philosophy at the University of New York, appeared to be infuriated. When we met one another a few hours later with cocktail glasses in our hands before sitting down to the festival meal given by the city of Hamburg for the lecturers and some prominent guests, I asked him if he was carrying a hidden dagger. He answered me curtly with: "My dagger is my logic." "Oh, I have that type of dagger too," I said. And then a lively debate ensued which only really developed when, unexpectedly, we ended up being placed beside one another at table. The host's exquisite and abundant wine played its part. Interestingly enough, the atmosphere of the discussion changed in my favor when, by chance, I mentioned my semester as guest lecturer in America. From the beginning, our topic was the philosophy of religion; and it amused me to see how stubbornly my partner reacted to my admission — natural to me — that we are not in a position to name God adequately. He loudly insisted that we had more right to call him father than cousin or brother-in-law. We separated very amicably. And years later, when I telephoned Sidney Hook, who was living for a time in California as a scholar in the Ford Foundation, he almost enthusiastically invited me for a meal like an old friend; when we parted he wrote me a dedication in the collection of essays he had published: *Religious Experience and Truth;* I was quite amazed.

At that meal in Hamburg we had become so involved in our debate that I had not really profited from what the other people at the table had been talking about; after all, there were some world famous scientists there. In my copy of the "Hamburg Guest Book" which everyone at the table had to sign for one another, are the names of Lise Meitner, James Franck, Max von Laue, Salvador de Madariaga, Arthur Compton, Ernst Reuter. The two last-named remained particularly clear in my memory. Ernst Reuter, who, as Lord Mayor of Berlin, was always greeted with abundant applause, seemed to me not without declamatory exuberance when he, for example, celebrated the rebellion of 17 June in Central Germany, which had taken place a good month ago, as "a new hope for the world." ("The German workers, who were wearing black-red-gold flags on their shoulders, are marching from the East to the West through the Brandenburg Gate.") Even though I did not doubt in the least that this unusually gifted man, who at that time was already dying, had done everything humanly possible for the freedom of his city, I could still hear in my head the wild outburst of anger of an old German-Russian winegrower, who meantime was producing a famous Riesling in the vineyards of New York State: If there was ever a person he and his friends had ever hated and would have "torn limb from limb while he was still alive" it would have been this Ernst Reuter, whom Lenin himself had named as the political commissar of the Volga German Republic.

I think of the atomic physicist and Nobel Prize winner Arthur Compton with particular respect; and I am still pleased today that I had a few short conversations with him. You were not surprised, seeing the radiating clarity and the somewhat old-fashioned sincerity expressed in his face, about what he, as the only one among the "fathers of the atom bomb," had done: he permanently renounced his science the very moment it became clear what results it would lead to.

Waldemar Gurian also appeared unexpectedly at the Congress, though expressly as a non-participant. Suddenly he was sitting amongst us in the hotel foyer; his sick, somewhat bloated face was pale; and his suit looked as if he had slept in it somewhere overnight. Now and then he picked some potato crisps from a torn plastic bag. With a friendly air he wandered quietly from one conversation group to the other. His wife told me later that he had flown to Germany one last time for no other reason than to say goodbye to his friends and also to the country; and in fact he only had less than a year to live.

After a few months, the Hamburg Congress Report was published in a stately volume of almost three hundred pages. I had not expected that my lecture would simply be missing from it, despite everything; I was quite disappointed. Still, there was the small consolation that the text could be read in the English edition, slightly abbreviated, but including the final sentence which had had the most impact, quoted from Boethius's *The Consolation of Philosophy*, written while he was awaiting a horrible execution: "The soul of a person is most free when it preserves itself in the contemplation of the divine spirit." Clearly the English publisher did not want to leave it out; he was none other than Michael Polanyi.

I had him to thank for the invitation to Berlin, where a much smaller group of intellectuals from all over the world gathered in June 1960, again to discuss the "freedom of culture." It began with a public event with speeches by Robert Oppenheimer and Ignazio Silone given to very large audiences. The Congress itself was divided up into small work groups. This seemed to contribute even more to the intensity of the debate. At Polanyi's suggestion, I went into the section which he was leading; their topic "religion and freedom" would have

Chapter VIII

interested me the most. For two days I listened without saying anything; but then Polanyi rang me in my hotel room and encouraged me, with some energy, not to hold back with my opinions. In actual fact, I had built up some resistance to what I had been hearing up until now. On the next day, the chairman gave me the floor without any signal from me. I began by examining the fact highlighted in the program of the congress that one must "examine all ideas from the point of view of what guarantees or dangers they mean for freedom," and then posed in exaggerated form the question of whether the very *idea* of freedom could stand in the way of the realization of freedom. Were there not goods which were only "added" to one who primarily and expressly wanted something completely different, truth, for example, or justice? What religion achieves, however, consists perhaps in keeping present to our consciousness those values to whose realization freedom would then be "added." My contribution was hardly finished when all the misdeeds committed in the name of religion came up for vehement debate, particularly, of course, the Inquisition, which was seen to be worse than any totalitarian campaign of annihilation. I defended myself with the proposition that nobody would find justification for the Inquisition in the New Testament, whereas the atrocities of violent regimes, whether Nazi or Bolshevik, were nothing other than the consequence of their formulated program. My idea had only one defender: the atomic physicist Robert Oppenheimer. Although he was almost sitting beside me during the debate, we still had never spoken a word to one another. This remarkable man, though his face in those years absolutely everyone knew in every detail, was always alone. Even in the small bus which brought us in the mornings from the hotel to the Congress Hall, he always stayed in apparently deliberate isolation, as if he accepted as his fate that he was to be pilloried naked in front of the whole world.

The daily report about what was discussed in the individual groups never contained a syllable of my contribution; the author clearly existed as little as did his argument; yet again I felt that I was out of place.

Also Carl Linfert, leader of the "night programs" in North Western Germany Radio, whom I felt I knew well, greeted me in a friendly way but was then silent. He was the only one who actually had something in mind with my contribution to the debate. But I did not know that; and he himself had never told me. Only a long time afterwards had I suspected what the reason for this persistent silence might have been. At the Ruhr Festival Games in 1953 we had met him and his particularly charming wife, a former dancer; and I had, in a highly stimulating discussion, replied to his very discreetly put question about my opinion of his programs, given the robust if completely accurate answer: "Night program? You'll laugh, but I sleep at night!" Since then Carl Linfert had been silent; and, I admit, quite understandably. Some months after the Berlin Congress I came across a casual postscript in the letter of a former student that he had been, "by the way," very interested in my lecture about religion and freedom which had recently been broadcast in the "night program." So I wrote to Carl Linfert and asked repentantly if by way of exception he could send me, for one or two days, the recording of this program which I had again slept through. Then came the prompt reply that, although contrary to regulations, the recording was already on its way. And so, on a tape recorder borrowed from friends, the family listened to the lecture introduced intelligently and with unveiled sympathy by Carl Linfert, together with the discussion, cleanly extracted as if with a scalpel, the improvised details of which had already slipped my mind. Even my children, gradually becoming more critical, found the whole thing "not so bad."

From that day on, my relationship with Carl Linfert changed; it became the way it might have been from the start.

He showed his interest in my work quite openly. He answered my letter of sympathy on the death of his wife with a moving reply. And in the following years it happened regularly enough that I found the recording car from the radio station already parked and installed when I was lecturing somewhere around the country. In the meantime, Carl Linfert, who was a few years older than me, having been honored with the title of professor, withdrew into private life. Since then there has no longer been a "night program" in Cologne. And, at the same time my participation at the West German Radio was virtually finished; and so it has remained down to this day. I had experienced here for the first and, of course, not the last time how much program design and choice of collaborators was a personal matter and to that extent "chance." The form of utterance geared especially to radio and therefore expressly to listeners appealed to me more and more; I had meantime "gotten the bug." I had no difficulty, when speaking alone in the studio through the microphone, in "seeing" an auditorium of living people; often enough the radio technicians were amused by my insistent gesticulations. "By chance" there was always someone sitting in the radio station who found my work desirable. In the Munich broadcasting station, for example, my friend was for years running the "culture" department, having taken an adventurous and circuitous professional route to get there — the same friend to whom I had whistled the Aida march decades ago in his doctoral laboratory in Münster, and who missed the beginning of the Third Reich with me in Italy and whose cousin had meantime become my wife: his name was Clemens Münster. After his doctorate in the field of physical optics, absolved with *magna cum laude,* he went first to Jena, to Carl Zei , where he was later promoted to Head of Department. When in the last year of the war the air attacks on west German cities became more and more threatening, he gave us the advice which we fortunately did not follow, that my wife should move with the children into the country near Jena; it would remain fairly quiet there and also, not as in the case of Silesia, at the end of the war you would be west of a particular border. Like all the uninitiated people he was wrong about this. This became clear to him the moment an American officer said that if he wanted they would bring him, with all his family and whatever personal belongings he could gather in a few hours, in a military lorry to the West — directly before the Russians marched in. In this way he saw himself from one day to the next moved into the Rhine-Main region, more or less without any means of supporting himself. After having already made some overtures in the publishing world, he did not continue the relationship with the firm that was being newly established. Instead, he co-founded the *Frankfurter Hefte* with Walter Dirks and Eugen Kogon. Not long afterwards he was appointed chief editor of Bavarian Radio. Almost every contribution I offered him in the following years met with a friendly reception. Among the projects which were to be critically discussed there was one day the attempt — sketched from a sudden thought which occurred to me during a train journey — to interpret the biblical report of the healing of the man born blind through the use of a second voice accompanying him and providing an up-to-date, almost political angle: how incredibly real is not just the freedom, but also the weakness of people, and truth is not at all "compelling," no matter how obvious it might seem to be. I was encouraged to tell the story of the "experiment with blindness" in which the New Testament text of John's Gospel was linked with a simple story of the present day. — At that time my publisher decided to bring out a series of records with texts by his authors, including "The experiment with blindness." It was an undertaking which after a while proved quite unsuccessful. For me, however, preparing a speaking text suitable for a record was a completely new experience. But I did have an excellent

teacher for this difficult task: Dr. Lutz Besch, who for a long
time had been my guardian angel at Radio Bremen. After the
actress Helga Roloff and I had repeated our part five times
over, we were close to despair; still, we believed the very experienced *maestro* who encouraged us with endless patience,
saying that the next time it would finally be "good"; and it
was so.

Clemens Münster did not stay long with radio. He was attracted by the new medium of television which was coming
forcefully on the scene, and since he possessed all the technical,
scientific and artistic qualities to give it shape, he was given
exactly this assignment. He brushed aside my belated concerns
about whether he would end up too much in show-business
with the incontrovertible reply that at least he would be at the
front line of what was happening in the world. My friend's
change of job would have significant consequences for me.
Not only did my work at Munich Radio stop overnight; it was
suddenly not sought after at all; the "person" who had requested it was gone. But I gradually began to realize that there
might be, in the new medium which I had still always viewed
with some suspicion, a chance for my own work, which I had
not yet thought about. Even "The experiment with blindness"
had been a first step towards the scenic form of representation.
But had I not also tried for years, in lectures and seminars, to
bring before the students' eyes the figures in the Platonic dialogues — learners, power practitioners, and Sophists above all
— as the actors in a highly dramatic debate which spanned all
those eras right up to the present? Even the sophistic misuse
of words in their exercise of power seemed to me, from the
start, a theme of the most acute topicality. So one day I took
Plato's *Gorgias* with me on holidays and wrote down almost
in one sitting, and as far away as possible from Schleiermacher
— who still remains the best translator of Plato — the first
draft of a television play. I had foreseen the head-shaking

disapproval of some of my university colleagues and had already taken it into account. I had learned this much from the Platonic Socrates: that teaching can never take place unless you meet the learners exactly at the place where they are, whether this is gratifying or not. At the first editorial meeting with the experts, on the other hand, in general I found unexpectedly unanimous agreement, but was nonetheless confronted with objections for which I was not prepared. I could almost have accepted the necessity of brutal abbreviation of the text; I did agree that the average viewer simply could not be expected to cope with Plato for more than an hour. But now the theater people insisted that it was impossible to have a television play without a woman. And so, for better or for worse, I introduced a young woman into the framework of the story through which the Platonic text had to be interpreted. Her function was, through resolute and precise questioning, to elicit information which the normal viewer would need.

Three to four completely new versions of the text had still to be written, and much more than a year passed until finally the rehearsals began. From then on the author had little more to add. And not without a certain trepidation I slipped one afternoon, for the first time, into a world which was completely new to me and fitted with strange equipment. It seemed somewhat surreal. Here I heard in disbelief a clear, austere metallic voice speaking the part of Socrates which I knew so well. Immediately I was freed from all concern. This actor, Heinz Moog from the Viennese Burgtheater, who, in addition, looked like Socrates himself, was the exactly the right man for the crucial role. Besides, he did not even need to have the text with him for the rehearsals, unlike his younger colleagues; he already knew the words of the extensive text. And in the other two Platonic television plays which I wrote during the following five years — always during the holidays — Heinz Moog took on the role of Socrates quite naturally, as if it was made for him. And it came as no surprise to me that, in 1977, for a new production of a play by another company about the death of Socrates, in which naturally there had to be an entirely new casting, it took a full year to search for a new performer in the title role.

During the preparation for the screenplay of the *Symposium* I had an interesting experience. In the speech in honor of Socrates, the drunken Alcibiades compared his cunning and puzzling master, whose school he had finally run away from, with the figures of the squatting Silenus blowing his shepherd's pipe — figures that could be bought at the wood carver's shop. You opened them up and saw inside them the image of a god. "I don't know if anyone else has seen the image of a god hidden in this Silenus: I got to see it." Of course in my play, which was meant for viewers, there was meant to be plenty to *see*. And so I thought that such a Silenus figure — which was presumably a mass-produced work of popular art — ought to be in the house of the *Symposium* and then brought out by one of the drinking partners of Alcibiades and playfully opened and closed. During the search for an antique model I received from all my archaeologically knowledgeable colleagues and friends the surprising information that, because they were made of wood, there was not one of these figures in any museum anywhere in world. This has reinforced my longstanding and cherished distrust of all evolutionistic evaluations of prehistoric cultures based purely on the findings of technical artefacts. If such wooden figures were not detectable after only two thousand years, then how could we know anything about a perhaps brilliant love poem, produced only in language and song, or about a symbolic ornament which may have existed in a perfectly shaped network of Gingko leaves? — "The human being in paradise was doubtless 'wild,' and we would no doubt view him as a completely cultureless being. Only one or two, and indeed the holiest amongst us, would give this naked being a second look; and would then, a few minutes later, fall down at his feet."

These words are from one of the most profound and at the same time most serene books I know. It is a book which has been able to express an amazingly differentiated and comprehensive conception of human existence in completely simple language: C. S. Lewis, *The Problem of Pain*. My wife and I had the joy of translating it into German at that time under the title *Über den Schmerz*.

Naturally, alongside the "fun" of the television plays, the real work went on — teaching at the University and the Pedagogical Institute — and, of course, the laborious work of writing books. With the not inconsiderable fee which I received for the television play, I had had a summer house built, with the outside walls made of Californian redwood. In the architect's catalogue it was entered under the name "refugium." And, in fact, it was to be a refuge in which I intended to escape from the noisy goings-on of my growing children and their visiting friends — in other respects quite joyous sounds. The bookshelves were completely lined with modern literature. Sitting at the table in front of the window, I could see no housing, only the green of the gardens and the splendor of the colorful flowers. And when the phone rang it could truthfully be said that I was "not at home." I did really manage to write a lot in this retreat. Later on it served my wife as a secluded potter's room — until an illness put an abrupt end to her practicing this beautiful art: twenty years after the enthusiastic beginning. Nowadays, the "refugium" remains empty. The children have moved out into their own worlds. And in the spacious house it is, in the meantime, quiet enough.

IX

Trips to France — The posthumous adventures
of Thomas Aquinas — What does
"Montmartre" mean? — The Paris of Saints —
"The last person on the scaffold" —
Saint Antony: a prayer or magic?

"Saint Martin de Boscherville! I don't even know where that
is." This is what the French language assistant, whom I had
not known up until then, said when I got into the car of a
Faculty colleague who wanted to drive me home from the university because of a sudden shower of rain. The Frenchman
was animatedly describing what a plague it was always having to arrange lectures given by professors from his own
country. "And now even a slide lecture about this supposedly
really famous church which nobody knows." At this stage I
tuned into the conversation with deliberate casualness. "Did
you say Saint Martin de Boscherville? That is a wonderful
Romanesque Abbey, from the twelfth century as far as I
know; in the lower Seine Valley not far from Rouen. If you
have a minute I can show you a couple of photographs." The
surprised assistant swung around and stared at me with his
mouth open. With the Michelin map of *Belles Églises de
France* in the glove compartment, my wife and I were driven
through France in the years 1953 to 1955, on each occasion
for almost four weeks, by our medical friend Dr. Schranz.
And there were very few significant churches and monasteries
we had omitted on these trips. Our hunting ground stretched

from the cathedral in Amiens to St. Michel de Cuxa in the Pyrenees. And, in particular, this unusual abbey had a surprise ready for me. After we had, on the way, read a little about the building, which was richly ornamented and had a mighty tower, we were expecting something we had never seen before. But when, in the glistening midday light, it suddenly lay before us in all its glory, I thought: you've seen this once before, particularly the tower and also the cloister with the fantastic animal shapes on the capitals! I know all this! But from where? I did not dream it! Already my friend Schranz was beginning to tease me ironically and good-humoredly about my Münster "lingo," when a monk dressed in black came over to us with an eagle in his hand which, as he said, he had just killed with a stone and whose wings were spread in such a way that they almost touched the ground. It was as if a heraldic figure had just stepped out of the stone sculpture. When, in the ensuing conversation, I told the priest about my sense of "déjà vu" he laughed and solved the mystery immediately: I must have been to New York! The Americans had copied the tower the exactly in *The Cloisters,* the Museum for Medieval Art, whereby with their dollars a large part of the cloisters was bought — with the result that, unbelievably, some of what you saw in St. Michel de Cuxa today was "fake" as it was a copy of the original from New York. It should be mentioned that our itinerary was not exclusively dictated by architectural masterpieces, but, for example, also by the places of French gastronomy which were equally clearly marked in the Michelin Guide. We descended into some of the winegrowers' cellars, and not only did we taste the champagne in Reims, but also in Château-Neuf-du-Pape, drinking the red wine which is named after the ruined castle; we looked down from the terrace on the night lights of Avignon. Neither did we miss out on the pike from the Loire nor the *Langoustines* at the coast of Normandy or the

Bouillabaisse in the port of Sête down from the Cimetière Marin, in which Paul Valéry is buried.

Quite often, even with the very famous buildings, we were not concerned in the first instance with the architecture. In Le Bec-Hellouin, for example, which was also in the Seine Valley, I hoped above all to come across visible traces of Anselm of Canterbury, for many years the Abbot of this well-known Benedictine monastery which was famous in his time and because of him. One hundred and eighty monks entered the monastery during his fifteen years as Abbot; "and almost all of you entered because of me," as was said by Anselm himself in his farewell letter. But from the monk who, with annoying lack of interest, led this group of tourists through the building, no information was forthcoming about his wonderful Benedictine colleague. Much more important for me, of course, was the pilgrimage to Toulouse, to the grave of my teacher Thomas Aquinas, or much more to the casket which contains his relics; for you cannot really say that he was buried there. The shameful and almost criminal events during the first fifty years after his death were well known to me; I knew that almost a century had passed before the casket could finally be brought to Toulouse — still not yet to this present place, but at least to the city where the Dominican Order had its origin. A fact which was at that time difficult to accept for the Dominicans was that on the way from Naples to Rome and then on to Lyon, to the Council, Thomas had not just died in a Cistercian Abbey but had also been buried there. For the Dominicans at the time this was intolerable. And the Cistercians from Fossanova justifiably feared that the corpse would not be safe with them; it might be stolen or worse still, a pope, if he, as twice happened, came from the Dominican Order, could order it to be handed over to the Order of the dead person. So the corpse which was firstly solemnly buried in front of the high altar of the Abbey was shortly afterwards secretly moved to another grave, but still in the same year — because of the terrifying dreams of the Abbot — was brought back to its first grave. A year later, because of the acute danger of a papal order to hand it over, the head was cut off the corpse, so that at least it would be secretly retained. The fact that in the meantime a relative asked for the saint's right hand and was given it was only mentioned to us in passing; it hardly counted, compared with what happened thirty years later. When again a Dominican was elected pope, the monks of Fossanova formed the monstrous plan of boiling the body, so that in this way the "corpse" could be hidden in a relatively small casket, which they then hid in a secret, now the third grave. But then, ninety-five years after the death of Saint Thomas, the long-feared order from the Pope was actually issued; and the corpse was brought, presumably in triumphal procession, to Toulouse, into the first Dominican Priory which had been founded in 1216. This was clearly not yet the "last resting place." At the onset of the French Revolution there was clearly good reason to prepare for and expect the ravaging of their Abbey. So they brought the Thomas coffin into the parish church St. Sernin, the biggest in the city.

Completely alone — it happened in this way, but it "had to" happen in this way — one late September afternoon I was thinking about all this and walking through the huge Basilica with its unexpectedly rich decorations. I found the central nave occupied by a group of pilgrims, who were holding devotions with a bishop, and I ended up diverted to the ring of chapels surrounding the chancel — and suddenly found myself standing in the chapel of the central apse in front of a golden casket with the inscription: *Corpus Sti. Thomae Aquinatis*! — Outside I met my companions who were still looking for a suitable hotel. I first suggested, and then insisted, that we should take a simple guesthouse whose windows looked directly onto the chapel in the apse with the Thomas casket. That, too "had" to be, although the house was way below our level; still, on our request, the bed linen — "mistakenly" used already — was exchanged for fresh linen. On the following morning the Crypt of St. Sernin was opened, with its innumerable relics which were clearly systematically "collected." In all innocence a canon showed us the small reliquary with the skull of Saint Thomas — as if it was the most natural thing in the world that the head did not belong with the body; I did not ask any questions and kept my own thoughts to myself. But the remark did slip out that the right hand was in Paris as far as I knew — to which *Monsieur le Chanoine,* very excitedly and exasperatedly replied, pointing to the small tip of his finger: that much might be in Paris, maybe!

The danger, on this journey, of us losing ourselves in simple history or in the delights of gastronomy was slim. All too drastically we were reminded again and again about what was happening in the world in which we were living. We were standing in front of a placard in this city, which was visited by travelers from all over the world, which stated: "Why do you not see Russian tourists in our country? It is because they are prisoners in their own country!" Or at the beginning of September 1954 we found in St. Denis whole house fronts covered in Communist Party banners celebrating the parliamentary collapse of the contract about European Defense Community brought about by the Party in collaboration with the Nationalist Right.

Although St. Denis is virtually a suburb of Paris, we carefully drove around the city itself on these car trips; the doctor did not relish the idea of getting embroiled in the traffic of the world city, with the result that I feared he never experienced this metropolis of the Western world. To my wife and me, on the other hand, it was quite familiar; admittedly we knew very well its many facets. In the spring of 1954 I also traveled there with Thomas, my son, not yet eighteen, and Monica, my daughter, almost sixteen years old. There is no need to go into much detail; naturally we visited the Louvre, the Eiffel Tower, the Opera House and even the Grand Guignol. One particular day has stayed with me as particularly memorable. In my mind I file it under the heading "memory and forgetting." On the way to our hotel, Thomas, while squashed in the overcrowded metro, had been reading the individual stations shown at head level and, in a loud voice, expressed his surprise at how many were named after saints: St. Michel, St. Germain, St. Placide, St. Marcel, St. Jacques, etc. I had then posed the prize question to him about the original meaning of the word "Montmartre," and the answer they had half-guessed had surprised him and my daughter: "martyrs' mountain"? Not far from the place where once the St. Jacques Monastery had stood — where the preacher monk Thomas Aquinas had lived — we discovered in the church St. Etienne-du-Mont, in which I just wanted to visit Pascal's grave, the coffin of Genevieve, the patron saint of Paris; she did not just save her city from the Huns almost fifteen hundred years ago, but as an amazingly official-looking marble plaque testified, also at the beginning of the First World War brought about the puzzling retreat of the German troops, who up until then had been victoriously pressing forward. On this day we now decided to set off in search of the hidden Paris of the saints. It is indeed hidden, but a vigilant person could find it at every turn. For example, you found out that, in the Rue Vaugirard, whose name you knew from the Balzac novel, under one of these dark-looking buildings there was a type of crypt with the remains of a martyr, beatified in 1926, who was massacred at this very spot on 2 September 1792; and you might be told in addition to this about the descendant of one of those who died here, an officer who was expelled from the army, later became a Trappist, and was himself murdered in the Sahara as a hermit — Charles de Foucauld. He had once celebrated Mass above this mass grave. Or, only a few of the thousands who poured through the *Rue du Bac* day after day knew that under house number 140 in an insignificant nuns' convent there is a chapel in which two holy women are buried: Louise de Marillac, who founded the Order of *Filles de la Charité* with Vincent de Paul; and Catherine Labouré, a Burgundian farmer's daughter, later a Parisian bar girl and finally a doorkeeper in this convent. She was privy to mystical experiences and instructions and said nothing about it except to her father confessor until her death (1876). The father confessor, however, a thirty-year-old Order priest, was apparently, to begin with, not overly impressed when the twenty-four-year-old novice confided in him that, on behalf of the Mother of God she was to tell him not to be worried about giving asylum to a bishop. But it was shortly before 27 June 1830 that he received a message — the day before the July Revolution broke out — and the Minister for Culture of the overthrown king, a bishop, was asking for asylum at the gate of the monastery. Unbelievably, we saw both of the saints in person; in the middle of Paris they are lying, like Snow White, in a glass coffin. Where in the world would you find a city like this? It occurred to me to ask one of the Sisters of the Order whether it was known where, in the time of the revolution, the murdered Carmelite sisters from Compiègne were buried. "Oh yes." Clearly excited and amazed about this certainly unusual question, the Sister gave us very exact information. We climbed back down into the Metro and traveled far out to the east to the "Picpus Cemetery." This proved again to be a hidden and, to a large extent unknown and forgotten place. Three or four times we had already asked people on the *Rue de Picpus;* no one had the faintest idea. But then I saw a man in shirt-sleeves coming across the street towards us. It was clear that he lived in the area. "A cemetery? There's no cemetery here." He shook his head as if to emphasize his conviction. "But there *must* be a cemetery, the Picpus Cemetery!" The man now almost became angry. "My dear sir, I've been living here for thirty years, and I've never either seen or heard anything about a cemetery!" Suddenly a Sister from a religious Order came along; she seemed to have simply stepped out of a long high wall. Of course she knew about it; she pointed back at the barely noticeable gate, which would be opened if we rang the bell. And that is what happened. Astonished, we entered a broad paved yard with several buildings and a church. The attendant told us, with a broad gesture, to go past the buildings and cross the yard and then we would already see the cemetery. What we then saw was in fact a cemetery, but not the one that we were looking for. On the gravestones we read famous names like La Rochefoucauld and Noailles; but the dates of death only began in the 19th century and went right up to the present; a memorial stone recalled the memory of a person who had died at the concentration camp in Dachau. From the attendant, who had in the meantime joined us, we found out that the families of those executed in the years of the Revolution have their dead buried here, even today; but the victims of the guillotine itself were lying in a big mass grave behind the cemetery, enclosed not by a wall but by a high fence made of iron bars. We silently looked at a completely fenced-in grass field where there were some cypress trees but not a single tombstone. Only on one of the columns of the iron bars does a plaque give the names of the sixteen Carmelite Sisters who were executed by guillotine as "fanatics" on 17 July 1794 while singing the *Salve Regina*. On the way to the small church, the attendant told us that more than three hundred corpses were at that time brought on carts from the nearby *Place de la Nation* and thrown into the pit. "Here nobody is left out and forgotten." And he pointed to the walls on the inside of the church, covered all over with the names of all those victims whom no tombstone had remembered. We fell silent and walked through the gate in the wall back onto the street and went as a matter of course — as if it had been arranged — to the square on which the guillotine had stood one hundred and sixty years previously. But the *Place de la Nation* is occupied by a noisy Luna Park which was just opening with its thousand lights. My son and daughter were immediately excited, and suddenly nothing seemed more important than deciding between the big wheel and the roller coaster. The dead, like the saints, sank back into oblivion.

The following year, in the spring of 1955, I was to be involved with a saint again, this time, however, in a somewhat dubious way. I had promised my son Thomas that to celebrate his final school examination we would go on a trip of at least three weeks — within Europe, of course. He was allowed to choose the destination and the route. So he wanted, as a future student of mathematics and physics, to travel to Syracuse, the city of Archimedes. Curiously he knew about the memorial monument, placed right on the seashore, representing the great technician as he set the attacking ships of the enemy fleet on fire with his invention, the concave mirror. We traveled first, and almost without any overnight stays but with quite a lot of exertion, to Syracuse. However, all we saw of the Archimedes statue was the pedestal. We discovered the figure itself after making some enquiries. It was in a sculptor's workshop being restored. The actual Italy trip, which in a manner of speaking began backwards, passed off not without some dramatic incidents, which were attributable in particular to the third-class accommodation we had booked for reasons of thrift. Still, we saw quite a lot in Palermo, Paestum, Naples, Rome, Orvieto, Siena and Verona. We wanted to start the journey home from Verona and so we had decided, as a triumphal highpoint of the trip, to travel in a sleeper from Munich to Münster, which we had already booked in advance. For Thomas this was the first time in his life and probably also the last. We left our Verona hotel early in the morning after having had an evening with Venetian Soave wine and a lot of laughter during our review of our adventure, and somewhat prematurely we celebrated its happy end. While we dragged our luggage to the tram stop which was not too far away, it suddenly occurred to me that my passport was not in the usual place in my coat pocket; as I then remembered, it had not been returned to me at all. Luckily there was enough time before the departure of the train; and so I went back to the hotel without any particular hurry. There they rummaged about in some drawers and even let me look myself. "No, the passport is no longer here. You definitely received it yesterday!" "But perhaps the woman from Reception, the one with the red hair, put it somewhere else?" "Gina? Yes. She doesn't live here; she's only coming in at nine." Yet again the drawers were opened; but there was no trace of a passport. I said that they would need to look again and went back to Thomas and sent him into the hotel again. Meanwhile I was in no doubt anymore; the passport was definitely *not* going to be found; it was simply not there. I would not be allowed to pass the border without my passport; we would miss our sleeping car; a lecture which was to be held on the day after my return would have to be cancelled — and so on. In short, I urgently needed the passport and immediately! At this moment I thought of Saint Anthony and the fact that simple people turned to him when they had lost something and used to promise to give, in return, an offering to the poor. I had never done that; something like that was beneath the dignity of this highly educated Doctor of the Church and especially below mine, too. But this was a critical situation. It was a case of "man overboard." I began to talk to the saint in the following way: "I don't know how you do it; but clearly you know what you're at. You can see the position I'm in. I will give you twenty marks for the poor if you help me." But it was immediately clear to me that that was not enough. And so I said: "Ok, I will donate fifty marks." Immediately I had the feeling that there would be a good ending to this. And in fact a moment later I saw my son Thomas making his way through the crowds of people waving something high in his hand: my passport! What had happened? We quickly boarded the tram which had just stopped and Thomas, still a little out of breath, told me: the people in the hotel just shook their heads and dismissed him with the consoling idea that it was certain his father had meantime found it in some pocket. After that, he had gone hesitantly to the exit; in the swinging door another guest rushing excitedly from the stairwell almost knocked him over. It was also a German, whom he heard saying: "You gave me someone else's passport last night . . ." Half a second later and he would not have heard the man! Without much thought as to my "dignity" I felt in my coat pocket for the passport which I had had returned to me in such a remarkable way. At home I then searched in several churches of the city for an "Anthony bread" offerings box, but there were no more to be found. Finally, I sent the promised amount to "Caritas" without naming a definite recipient. It was intended for the unknown person who clearly had not seen it as unworthy of him to help me in such a small matter.

X

Suarez Lecture in New York — Interview in Chicago: Boxing match and race issue — Stanford: "Western tradition" — Chinese peculiarities — Farewell evening with Alma Mahler-Werfel

It was almost by chance that I was asked by the New York Fordham University to give the celebrated and well-paid annual *Suarez Lecture*. The celebration began, a little at my expense, with an explosive outburst of merriment. The chairman, a shocking tease, was well versed in the contents of *Who's Who* and spoke the first sentences of his greeting in such an innocent monotone that you would think he intended nothing more than to bore the audience with the usual bibliographical introduction. But then without raising his voice he made a completely accurate remark, but one that surprised me, that I had married after writing my two first books about bravery and hope, and then apparently felt the need to write one about prudence. Then he looked up and gave the audience time for the expected reaction.

After the lecture there was another occasion for me to admire the naturalness of American students; and I tried to imagine the unimaginable, that here a charming female student would give me her hand without coquetry and affectation and say: it was a wonderful experience to meet you!

The invitation to Fordham had materialized through the arrangement of a young Jesuit who, like many of his American Jesuit colleagues, had completed his third year in the novitiate, the Tertianship, in Münster. He was particularly interested in philosophy, and he visited me and heard with amazement that I would be going to Stanford in California for the coming spring term; he then asked me spontaneously if I would give a lecture in "his" university. I did not straightaway decline; and so he soon arrived, bringing me, as he casually announced, the invitation — an unusual distinction — to give the *Suarez Lecture*, to which numerous guests came from the other universities of the city. He also told me of his parents' offer to put me up for a few days in a suburb of villas in New York, not too far from the university. I accepted both invitations gratefully. And already on the first morning, while I was walking through the quiet green area with my friendly host who was a retired lawyer, a new lesson about the inexhaustible subject matter of "America" began. *Keep it clean here* — this is what I heard the old man saying again and again, full of pride. With my eagerness to learn — which did not always lie comfortably with him — I inquired what this *clean* was supposed to mean exactly. So little by little it became clear that here they wanted not only not to have colored people or Jews, which I had already known, but they wanted also, if possible, just moneyed people. "And how do you do that?" I then learned that these small suburbs, which had their own town council, possessed an enormous autonomy and somehow, as in this case, could decide by law that in their area not only could no rental houses be erected but also that there were no bus stops allowed from which people who had no cars could all too easily get to the nearby beach. By contrast, the inhabitants of this happy suburbia of course owned several cars; one was parked at the suburb railway station where the father of the family parked it when he set off to his New York office in the mornings and could drive home immediately in the evening. On the day on which I was moving on, I saw dozens of them filling the car park and afterwards becoming engrossed in their morning newspapers which, extremely practically, were folded long-ways. After a short visit to Helen and Kurt Wolff, with whom again there was a problematic translation to be discussed, I traveled first to Chicago in the luxury night train called the *Twentieth Century Limited*, which was soon to be abolished and for whose passengers an actual red carpet was rolled out all the way along the platform in New York's Central Station. But of course it was not this extravagance for which I was willing to pay the substantial extra fee; rather, I really wanted physically to travel on the same train, in which, almost fifteen years before at night-time, the first secret discussion — which here no one could overhear — took place between the physicists and the military about the possible construction of an atom bomb. Early in the morning I collected, along with my highly polished shoes, the weather forecast: "Snow in Chicago." On the windy platform, I was met by the Dean of the Faculty of Loyola University, also by an editor of the *Chicago Daily News*, and a press photographer. "An interview?" I said, "I haven't even had my breakfast yet." "That's good; then we'll have breakfast together." As it quickly emerged, they had thought out two very concrete questions, which were exactly related to the topic of my lecture. "You will be speaking about the relevance today of Thomas Aquinas. What would Thomas say to professional boxing and also to the problem about black people?" The first question, arising from several life-threatening sports accidents, was a matter for lively debate at the time but one which I did not take too seriously. "Thomas would probably have taken an Aristotelian view and said: an amusement for slaves!" And it was printed exactly like that in the evening edition: "an amusement for slaves." The second problem was, of course, much more acute, more serious and also more difficult. First I attempted to interpret and make plausible the theory represented by Thomas that with any amendment of legal status not only the demands of reason but also *consuetudo* — custom, usual traditional practice — were of importance. This was too abstract for the journalists; they wanted to be told point-blank what Thomas would decide today. "His decision would probably sound like this: integration — yes! But it must be done cautiously, gradually, not all at once!"

As we continued our conversation I inquired about Robert M. Hutchins, about whom I had already been told that he had meanwhile become the most hated man at the University of Chicago; the same was confirmed to me now. "When is your birthday? You can have him as a present from us!"

While ambling through the lobbies of Loyola University, as always I studied the notices on the blackboard. This time there was one which would really surprise European Catholics: for the upcoming Saint Patrick's Day (which was not falling on a Friday) the law of fast and abstinence was suspended, "also for the lucky Non-Irish." That was how things were done in "pre-Council" America, and not just with Catholics. After my lecture, when we sat down to dinner in a restaurant of absolutely world-class standard, we found two menus there, one for the fasting period, the Lenten menu. However, yet again, I did get to see the other side of the coin. In the student residence where they had put me up and which was rather comfortable, there was also a chapel, no bigger than a living room; the eight to ten students who came to the weekday Mass could have almost touched the priest with an outstretched hand. But when he turned around saying the blessing *Dominus vobiscum,* he had to answer it himself; the small community remained silent.

In Californian Stanford, I thought that a completely different atmosphere would await me; and at first I found myself completely confirmed in this. It was a richly endowed university from the time when the first railways were built across the continent; like some of the most famous American universities, for example, Harvard, it was not a state institution. Neither were the University of Chicago and Princeton. Stanford, from what I was told, was in constant competition with the neighboring Berkeley, which is part of the huge State University, and the criterion for judging their performance is the alternating number of Nobel prize winners. Stanford was unmistakeably imbued with the spirit of puritanism and, at the same time, secularism. It is true that the architectural center point was formed by a "church" built on the model of the cathedral of Orvieto and decorated with mosaics on the outside walls; but it is strictly "non-confessional." Then again its wonderfully colorful windows represent only biblical scenes. (Admittedly it is reported that, during a university celebration, the young son of a professor had rapturously pointed at the image of Adam in paradise and shouted at the top of his voice: "Look, Daddy, there is Tarzan!") In any case, the erection on the extensive grounds of a sacred building associated with one particular religious denomination was forbidden by the original constitution, as were the serving and selling of alcoholic drinks within a radius of several miles. Years later, when I was again invited to Stanford and was not enthusiastic about the proposition of having to live in a hotel again for months on end, I enquired about an apartment near the university or even on the campus itself, and something particularly suitable was offered to me again; but the owner, an emeritus professor, had one condition, and that was that I would not drink whisky, beer, or wine in the apartment. Better a hotel, I thought. Even in the hotel there was a curious sign prohibiting gambling! But I was not interested in that anyway.

The title of the course on which I was to lecture and which was to run over two years was *The Western Traditions*. Even the formal structure of this "interdisciplinary" venture contained some amazing aspects. In the lecture catalogue it was called the *Graduate Honors Program in Humanities;* and of course here I had my "candid questions" to ask, as my colleagues soon used to call them in a friendly and ironic tone. The word which puzzled me the most was understandably "honors." "Why an honors program?" But then I was told that the "honor" was not attached to the course of studies but to the students themselves; "honor students" were the students with the highest performance level. And only they were entitled to take this course. In answer to my strange silence, I found out that, not exceptionally, this "program" was highly rated and afforded students an above average number of "points," which is, of course, why they pushed to get on it. The group was to be kept small, however, and that accounts for the barrier: for "honors students" only! I tried to imagine what authority in a German university would attempt to — and want to — define and fix the weight and the "relevance" of a particular course. And, of course, it soon became clear to me that having honors students required an almost continuous assessment, which at our universities would be neither possible nor desirable. Still, this chosen group of almost twenty male and female students was excellent to work with. The methodological principle was that in a colloquium which I was discreetly to guide we would discuss particular texts which were printed or otherwise reproduced, and thus available to the students, and which had to be worked through beforehand. And often I was amazed how thoroughly they knew the material and particularly with what wonderful naturalness these specialist students — who were in the first instance preoccupied with completely different themes — were ready and able to debate the texts which I had specifically chosen from medieval scholasticism and mysticism.

In Stanford there were, of course, some amazing things to see — for example, the windowless tower where the Hoover Library is housed. Being both library and archive it claims to possess all the documents of war and revolution from the time of the First World War onwards. The librarian who was accompanying me said that not one political poster from Nazi Germany was missing. One special item was the original of Joseph Goebbels's diary, of which only the very last part was missing. As we were leaving the reading room, my companion pointed back to an old man who was engrossed in his books, and whispered to me: "Alexander Kerenski! He's been working here for weeks." I could not believe that he was still alive. "He must be almost a hundred years old?" "No, he is seventy-five!" I stepped back into the reading room and went slowly past him. Lenin's predecessor was actually sitting there; and the father of young Jacqueline Denissoff was his secretary.

For the last weeks of the term my wife was to join me; it was her first visit to the American continent. As was to be expected, at first she found it confusing and shocking. Until then I had stayed in the house of the Newman Club, a spacious villa in the Spanish colonial style with a completely separate garden behind it. On the edge of this, Clare Boothe Luce had, after an adventurous life, become a Catholic and was the wife of the owner of *Time* and *Life*; she later became American ambassador to the Vatican. She had had St. Ann's Chapel built as a memorial to her daughter Ann who had died in a car accident while a student at Stanford. Sitting at the foot of the gleaming white bell tower in the spring sunshine I was preparing my colloquium. When it occurred to me at some stage to ask when the tower would get its voice, the students' chaplain laughed at me: "You don't think that in this exclusive area the noise of a bell tolling is allowed?" Of the dozen students who were living with me in the house, nobody was taking my course; there was perhaps no honors student in this pleasant boyish group. In the mornings, when I had made a small space for breakfast in the jungle of cornflake boxes, milk bottles, ashtrays and newspapers, I called out to the group of newspaper readers asking what news there was in the world —

above all, whether war had broken out in Israel, which could happen at any time. The young people hardly even answered. Either they had become fully engrossed in the comics called *Fun* which were delivered every morning; or they were following the development of the affair between the film star Grace Kelly and the Prince of Monaco. This reminded me of the time when, six years ago, I innocently caused an uproar when I arrived at a party for professors and, for fun, reported the news which I had picked up on the way: "Ingrid has a bambino." I was completely taken aback by the reaction at the time. But I was told in all seriousness that a woman might well be divorced three or four times, but to have a child with another man while she was still married, well that was simply scandalous. And in fact a short time later in the Chicago University quarter I saw a poster advertising an Ingrid Bergman film — painted over with the intelligently chosen abusive term "Prostitute."

On her arrival in New York, my wife felt oppressed by the voicelessness of this country — which far outweighed the incredible loudness — and by the almost complete invisibility of the individual. "You saw only cars!" And Helen Wolff admitted to her that often enough during her first time in New York she had got into the shower to give vent to her tears in secret. But after the daylong train trip from Chicago, when I completely unexpectedly boarded the *California Zephyr* train at the second-to-last station and greeted Madame with a bouquet of dark gold yellow eschscholtzia — the official state flower of California — which I had illegally picked from the embankment, all her worries were soon forgotten. We went in brilliant sunshine on the open ferry under the enormous bridge across the bay and approached the city of San Francisco with all its hills.

The stay in the small town of Palo Alto — disappointingly far from the Pacific beach — was not exactly interesting; but mostly we left on Friday mornings and only returned on Monday evenings. It was pure chance that during the first weekend in San Francisco we came across the very colorful parade with which the city remembered the earthquake which had devastated it fifty years previously on 18 April 1906. The "Parade" seemed to have no end. A regiment of fire fighters in strange uniforms from a previous era was followed by a parish mothers' club with the flag of Mother Frances Cabrini, the first Saint of America; *Mr. Earthquake,* a gruesome, masked monster carried along in an enormous cage, was booed from all sides; then there were droves of schoolgirls in short skirts juggling their colorful batons, or a group of respectable female citizens who, in honor of historical truth, raised and swung their frou-frous like ladies from the Moulin Rouge.

Again and again we were surprised, as we wandered through this unique city, by the somehow un-American discreet elegance in the fashionable cut of female clothing. My wife guessed that some influence from the huge Chinese quarter must be at work. And so we welcomed the chance we had at a farewell evening in the Newman Club — where I of course had to give a lecture — when we were brought together with a Chinese student, who had just converted, and her father who was a Confucian philosophy professor, a refugee from the kingdom of Mao. He immediately invited us to a meal which for once would be "really" Chinese, because what was served to us in those American Chinese restaurants which I had so innocently praised was not known in his homeland at all. And in fact his charming daughter Diana had made us a true feast, which started with a wheat soup. Her father, who had studied with Rudolf Eucken and accompanied Hans Driesch through China as an interpreter, insisted every now and then on speaking German with us. That led to me asking a question which had been puzzling me for a long time; luckily I had remembered it so well that an exact formulation came to me. In my treatise about prudence I had quoted the wonderful words of Lao-tse, which in my student days I had taken from a translation of Viktor von Strauss: "Whoever looks at himself does not shine"; but later on I had come across Richard Wilhelm's translation where the same sentence reads like this: "Whoever wants to shine will not be illuminated"; and the excellently commentated edition of Lin Yutang's English translation of Fischer Publishers says: "Whoever unveils himself does not shed light." So I asked the expert who had proved his competence which translation really expressed the essence of the original. And I received the confusing answer that even in Chinese there were the most different ways of reading it, all of which might be deemed "correct." Baffled, I turned to his daughter Diana; but her information was *really* puzzling: she had completed her high school education in China but she knew nowhere near enough Chinese characters to be able even to *read* Lao-tse let alone understand him.

While we were silently drinking the jasmine tea, my host began to speak about Communism, which in his opinion would never come to power in China. "Can you do away with the language or Confucianism?!" When he noticed my silent skepticism he opted for telling us stories not just about Hans Driesch but much more amusingly about Bertrand Russell and his strange partner who was to be addressed *partout* as "Miss Black," for whom he had also for a while acted as interpreter.

Soon, and not at all expectedly, the topic of "China" was to come up for lengthy discussion in Santa Fe — one of the stations of our week-long relaxing trip from the West Coast to New York. Already in Chicago the publisher Henry Regnery had given me the address of an author who was involved in writing for him the biography of one of the most controversial men in recent American history, the former Brigadier General Patrick J. Hurley, who had in turn said he was willing to open up his personal archives. Meanwhile the book was almost ready; the author gave us an appointment. Our visit lasted a little more than an hour; but we ourselves did not need to contribute more than two or three sentences to the "conversation," which the seventy-three-year-old animatedly carried on alone. On the way to his fine country house outside the city we heard a little of his life story. As a shepherd boy he had grown up amongst the Indians, worked his way up to the rank of General in the army, and at the end of his career, by personal order of Roosevelt, had been the last American ambassador in pre-Communist China. So he told us with pride that he had been the only non-Russian officer present for the surrender of Stalingrad. The most outrageous thing was what he had to report — with anger and conviction — about the communist seizure of power in China. He kept on pulling documents out of the steel filing cabinet which covered the full length of the wall of his office. His thesis, in a nutshell, was no less than that the American government had placed Mao Tse-tung in the saddle, systematically misled through its own "left" informants, who had described the Communist Revolution as a moderate democratic land reform movement. "There is no other betrayal as momentous as this in world history!" In great agitation he consulted a file and read us a statement by Senator Robert A. Taft from the beginning of the fifties: "If the government had listened to Pat Hurley in 1945, then the great Chinese nation would not be in Communist hands and the current Korean War would not have happened." Our shocked silence clearly did not surprise the General; he had experienced similar reactions before. What could you say? And so our host began, on a completely different tack while he served us cocktails, to speak to us about the First World War in which he had taken part as a Colonel. In Koblenz, while he had been riding across the Rhine towards the Ehrenbreitstein garrison, he looked at the people on the street and said to his Adjutant: "We have been fighting on the wrong side!" He said farewell to us in great spirits and with a song of praise to Germany. Seven years later, when in Hong Kong and on the island of Formosa, I told some discerning people about this remarkable view of General Hurley and asked their opinion. Some dismissed it immediately: "Rubbish!" Others remembered that American politics had been incomprehensible at the time; but still there were one or two people who felt confirmed in their view: "That is exactly what happened!"

From our base in Santa Fe we visited Jacqueline Denissoff and her young household. We went on some trips to American Indian areas. At the bank of the Rio Grande an early settlement of the Pueblos had been excavated; it looked like a broken up honeycomb. During a relaxed walk through the small museum at the settlement I came across the translation of a prayer which — perhaps even today, centuries after all the missionary activity — was spoken by Indians at dawn, to accompany the offering of corn. As the commentary said, it was, like all Indian prayers, in three parts; it described the occasion, then the offering, and then expressed a petition. I made a note of the text and I wonder if it is not the natural model of all invocations:

"Now, my sun father, now that you have emerged, standing at your holy place:

Through which we received the water of life, here, I give it to you!

Your long life, your great age, your waters, your seeds, your wealth, your power, your strong spirit: grant me all of these!"

As we left, occupied with our thoughts, an old Indian was standing in front of us; he was busy with a wheelbarrow taking away the sand which had blown in in the storm. He did not put down the full barrow while he watched us quietly. "Where are you from?" "From Europe, from Germany!"

"And the others?" He pointed with his head to the river, where our friends were preparing a picnic. "They're Americans!" "No, they're not American! Where are they from?" "Well the woman is from Belgium; and the man's father is Yugoslavian." "You see, we are the only real Americans!" His completely steady hands were still holding onto the heavy barrow; he walked away slowly.

On the same day we were to meet a monk whose "frontier" life I would without hesitation regard as completely American, even though his grandfather was a German farmer. We traveled to a monastery which our companions were clearly supporting. "Monastery" was a completely exaggerated term for the couple of primitive buildings, which had recently been relinquished by the Trappists and taken over by Benedictines. Two to three monks were laboring at making something useful out of it. We asked for the Superior and were directed to the bakery. And then a sturdy man, radiating vitality and dressed in trousers and an undershirt, stepped out the door and said laughingly: "I am the Prior!" He was willing to show us around a little. He had not yet had enough time to walk around the border of the land that belonged to them; he made a broad gesture with his arm. Yes, the Trappists were not able to live by their rules here because they could not grow enough vegetables. For that a thorough irrigation system would be necessary; and he was working at bringing one into operation. We were brought to the narrow Pecos creek and had to inspect the stone wall which was almost able to stop the quick-flowing water. I asked if he, the Prior, had built the dam himself. Again he laughed: "Who else? You borrow a bulldozer for one or two days!" "And where do you get the stones?" "Look around you: there are enough rocks around here. A few explosions and in no time you have more stones than you need. You learn all that very quickly." It then emerged that a couple of weeks previously he knew nothing about baking bread either. "But people have to know when they come to the Lord's table what proper bread looks like and how it tastes. We are supplying the whole area with it." During the trip home we found out that the Prior's father, as he wanted to live near a monastery because of his children, had fifty years previously sold his farm and acquired new land in the neighborhood of the big Benedictine Conception Abbey in Missouri. This, however, had resulted in the majority of his numerous children becoming Sons and Daughters of Saint Benedict, including our Prior. By the time of my next visit to the Pecos monastery, which, by the way, was under the protection of the Indian-Mexican Madonna of Guadalupe, not less than twelve years had passed; and some things had changed in the meantime: for example, a spacious and really comfortable guest house had been built; but there was also a new Prior. The first one, who had not been at all old, had gone about his jobs far too vigorously, was suffering from circulatory disorder and had to live under the younger Superior. Again two years later I was told that the first Prior, this *frontier* man, had been called back by his Abbot to Conception Abbey shortly after my visit; but when the longing for "his" foundation became too strong, he gained permission to return. The joy about this unexpected gift simply overwhelmed him; on that same day, as he was celebrating Mass, he fell down and died at the altar.

When we set off for New Orleans during those days of May 1956 my wife was to have a concrete encounter with the "negro" problem, about which she had only an abstract notion before that. Full of curiosity, setting out from Notre Dame I myself had visited this completely un-American city — as others had described it to me — six years earlier. And it had been an adventure to travel in the early morning in Chicago through the snow drifts and blizzard and to make it just on time to catch the airplane, and then a few hours later to step

out of the airplane into the tropical humid heat of the Missis-
sippi Delta. The most adventurous thing was, however, to
travel up and down by bus through New Orleans. And I
"knew" of course, about the legally required segregation (in
public transport, in restaurants and in schools). But the physical doing and experiencing of it was still like a slap in the face.
I sat down at random in a free seat, still carefully beside a
"white person"; I had already begun, of necessity, to think in
these categories which up to then would have been completely
alien to me. In the back of the bus there were a few "coloreds." But soon my neighbor got out; likewise, little by little,
most of the other "whites," until at last there was only one
other besides me. He was sitting right up the front directly behind the driver, who was actually "colored," while my seat
was situated about in the middle of the bus. Meantime more
and more "coloreds" came on board; they crowded into the
area set aside for them. The "white" man waved to me that I
should move forward to one of the seats nearer the front. Only
then did I notice the sign which was in the back of my seat,
which was now being taken out by one of the "coloreds"; he
carried it in front of him and put it onto the back of the seat
on which I was now sitting, after which the "coloreds" pushed
forward and were now almost occupying the whole front of
the bus. At the terminus from which I intended to travel back,
I looked more closely at the sign which appeared to be completely innocent looking and neutral and discovered the word
"colored" on the back. It was all about the drastically materialized colour line. Another day the ("white") parish priest
of the biggest black community in America told me he had
once, out of pure wilfulness and as an experiment, sat beside
one of his parishioners and begun a conversation with him.
But immediately the bus stopped with a jolt. "Father, you are
sitting in the wrong place!" "No, my place is right; just drive
on!" I asked out of curiosity how that had ended. "So I had

to move into the part of the bus near the front; the law is not just for the blacks!" This, of course, was just one of the more harmless "true stories" which I had asked him to tell me. There was more depressing information when I asked him what the most difficult problem of his parish was. He did not need much time to think about it: "The discrimination of the black people among themselves!" When I did not immediately understand what he meant, he said full of anger: "Those with brighter skin want nothing to do with those with darker skins!" That was 1950, as I said.

Meanwhile things had moved on somewhat. In 1955 the Supreme Court in Washington had declared racial segregation to be illegal — and had, at least in the Southern States, thereby heightened the tension. More than a hundred Southern State members of the House of Representatives and the Senate, in a manifesto, called for passive resistance to this decision. A pastoral letter from the Archbishop of New Orleans, on the other hand, expressly supported the Court's judgement. This succeeded in making the Catholic Christians feel uneasy for the first time, and they asked themselves — and also their confessors — whether or not the racial segregation which had been considered natural up until then was really something unjust. Only a few years previously, a priest said to us, such unrest would have been unthinkable. And also to the Archbishop himself, as I myself could well remember, it had seemed impossible not so long ago to accede to the quite modest request of a civil rights group to oblige his parish priests, once a year on the occasion of the evangelical text of the Good Samaritan ("Who is my neighbor?"), to preach on the topic: "The negro is also my neighbor!"

However, in the reality of everyday life there was not much trace of any type of change in 1956. For example, to my wife's stunned surprise the situation was such that, while our scrambled eggs with mushrooms were prepared and served to us at the bar by a black person, time and again a portion of food was passed over our shoulders to other black people standing behind us, who paid and then went outside because it was forbidden for them to consume it in the presence of us "whites" — this in spite of the recently altered *federal law*. It was still not allowed by the *state law* in Louisiana. I know that these things have changed in recent times; during my next visit in New Orleans, again twelve years later and over a week after the murder of Martin Luther King, you saw black and white people sitting beside one another in the buses and in the restaurants as if it had always been like that. Still, all my informants, white priests and colored association functionaries alike, held the view that deep down nothing had changed; In fact, things had dis-improved; the blacks themselves did not want integration anymore! In Europe we did not have problems which seemed so acute and crying out for resolution.

We were in New York on our last evening at a small party with Kurt Wolff. Almost apologetically and as if he wanted to prepare us for something we might not find acceptable, he had mentioned "as a precaution" that Alma Mahler-Werfel would be there; he knew the widow of his long-time publishing house reader and friend Franz Werfel a little too well. We, however, were looking forward to meeting her for the first time. It was difficult to recognize the Bride of the Wind of the Kokoschka picture in the now seventy-seven-year-old, especially as she was gaudily made up and was wearing a huge amount of extremely expensive jewellery — "for security reasons," as she puzzlingly put it. Kurt Wolff had probably told the old woman, in advance, a little about the guest and author whom she did not know beforehand. When she then greeted me quite enthusiastically with the proclamation: "The first thing you need to know is that I am a fervent Catholic!" words failed me for the moment. But then I took the cue and asked my publisher to explain to me again what he had already written to me about, which was why in America my books need the bishop's *imprimatur* — something which was not the case in Germany or even Italy. It amazed me. Even Henry Regnery, with whom Walter Nigg's successful book about the saints had just appeared, complained to me that the book was plainly dead: "The Protestants are ignoring it because the saints are for them a Catholic matter; and the Catholics do not buy it because the writings of a reformed theologian cannot display a bishop's *imprimatur.*" Kurt Wolff, who was himself a non-Catholic, confirmed to me again that in the USA no Catholic bookshop and no parish library could acquire a book which did not have the church's permission to print. That sounded unbelievable to me; and I particularly did not at all like this categorizing of my books as "religious literature." "If it ever occurred to my German publisher to call me an 'outstanding lay-apostle' as you did once, I would personally strangle him!" At this moment Alma Mahler who, because of her considerable deafness had not understood why we were suddenly laughing so loudly, with disarming naturalness took over running the conversation with the obvious intention of not handing it back to anyone else. She was working on completing the manuscript of her memoirs, the candidness of which bordered on indiscretion; two years later (1958), to the annoyance of many people, they were on the market. And so, on that for us unforgettable evening, through her lively and brilliant storytelling she told us all about the dramatic way in which she and Franz Werfel came from the south of France through Spain and Portugal to America; she gave us a particularly thorough account of their stay in Lourdes. On the last day she could not find Werfel; and then, when he suddenly appeared, he reported about his vow that if they managed to make a successful trip across the Atlantic he would write a book in honor of Bernadette Soubirous. Both of the Wolffs listened to this story — which they must have already heard many times — with the patient attention of perfect hosts. In the same year, 1940, they were not doing any better — worse if anything; Kurt Wolff was imprisoned for several months — something which he never talked about — before he and his wife managed to flee with the help of French friends.

On the following day we began the homeward-bound trip on the Dutch *Maasdam,* which four years previously I had seen in the port of Quebec festively covered in flags for its maiden voyage. When we moored at Southampton for a few hours after a quiet crossing, our fifteen-thousand-ton ship co-incidentally anchored near the huge *Queen Mary,* which loomed above us like a rock face. The ship's newspaper said that T. S. Eliot, who had taken ill, had traveled back from the USA to England on the *Queen Mary.*

XI

"Research working group" — Call to Munich —
The "little wall" — Cultural Minister Werner
Schütz — The Spanish guardian angel — Dieter
Sattler — Stanford for the second time —
Las Vegas and Hawaii

"Since news about University business, particularly when it is
supposed to be a secret in the Faculty, spreads quickly, you may
perhaps already have heard that you are listed as a possible
successor to me." In November 1953 this was the beginning
of a letter from the very learned publisher of Meister Eckhart's
works, the Cologne Professor of Philosophy Josef Koch, who
strangely, in 1947, after my rejection of a post at that time, was
called to Göttingen as my "successor," as it were. Again there
was the request to hand in my curriculum vitae and publication
list to the Cologne faculty. This time, however, I had heard
nothing and I also did not hand in anything. Still it was not a
matter of a nipping in the bud an offer of an appointment; in
fact I could think of something else at work. This, of course,
was attributable to some colleagues and friends, who had spoken to me for a long time — sometimes while tapping their
temples, meaning I ought finally to get used to the generally
practiced custom of letting the "inquiry" of a faculty develop
into a formal "appointment." The focus of my teaching was
still in the Pedagogical Academy of Essen; every week I set off
there for two days. In Münster the University had appointed
me, already during my first semester in America, as an

"Extraordinary Professor"; but this title did not change the fact that fundamentally I was merely a private lecturer. I still considered the work of teacher training to be important work at the coalface. But meanwhile, even in the University, I felt very much at home; it was for me a quite unexpected joy to see how the students, without consideration of any advantage to their exams, filled two to three lecture theaters on a late Saturday morning. Of course, my determination not to give up on the idea of linking work for the Pedagogical Academy with that of the University made everything else somewhat complicated. It was the man who worked in the Ministry of Culture and was responsible for teacher training, my former Latin student, who was urgently advising me not to refuse the next appointment to a chair, as I had just done in Berlin. He calculated that if the *pater familias* were to die in a road traffic accident, my wife would scarcely have the funds to send the children to university — something which not only had to do with the generally small salary, but also with the fact that the bureaucracy had laid down my "length of service" in such a way that, although I was forty-two years old, I was considered to be the same as any young man just "entering on his career." I allowed myself to be persuaded; and so I was able to answer Professor Koch, with whom I later became friends, that clearly he must know, despite faculty confidentiality, that an appointment at the University of Mainz was already at an advanced stage, for which reason there was not much point in speaking to me about succeeding him. It was not completely unexpected that the opportunity in Mainz foundered, firstly because of the impossibility of working in the University and in teaching training at the same time. Also, in the meantime the Cultural Minister in Düsseldorf, who at that time was a woman, had informed me through Robert Grosche, now Professor at Cologne University, that they considered it important for me to stay with the North Rhine-Westphalia Federal State, to which I — perhaps somewhat too cheekily — replied, that up until now I was the only one who was keeping me with the Federal State, and in truth at my own not insignificant cost. Whether on foot of that or not, in any case I was called, during the negotiations about the chair in Mainz, by Prime Minister Karl Arnold — of course on the suggestion of the Cultural Minister — to the "Rhine-Westphalian Academy of Sciences," which at that time was still called the "Research Working Group." That someone less than an Ordinarius was penetrating this "small flock," which saw itself as a republic of scholars, had never happened before and understandably it did not please everyone. And then, to top it all, when I was given the honor of holding the lecture for the next annual festival, in a public celebration of special splendor in the assembly hall of the state parliament, not everyone thought they should be expected to attend. For my part, for the first time dressed with cap and gown of the extraordinary professor, I could not resist the temptation to begin my lecture about Plato's concept of philosophy with the sentence: "I would do a lot to avoid meeting Socrates in this celebratory academic garb — that man through whom Plato most definitively expressed his opinion about the nature of philosophy."

Not much was gained from the Culture Minister's efforts to keep me in the Federal State. They did cherish the notion of establishing an "extraordinary" professorship within the faculty which would be tailor-made for me and would allow me to continue to work the same amount as before at the Pedagogical Academy of Essen — although from now on it would be "part-time." This connection also corresponded to the wishes of the Culture Minister. But, of course, nothing was to happen against the will of the faculty, from whom a suitable application was confidently expected. However, the application was never made. This was no great surprise to me. One of the reasons was that the vociferous demand of the Pedagogical Academies for equal status with the universities was being made in those years and, as one knew, for a variety of reasons was being met with a particularly sharp distancing from the "narrow gauge" discipline. Whatever about that, the Faculty of Philosophy persisted in its silent refusal to recognize my work in teacher training as a legitimate part of my academic teaching.

To me all competing for rank, on both sides, seemed very problematic, and I invariably ended up between the two fronts, without any particular involvement on my part. On the one hand it seemed to me that the difference between a university, which in principle was based on research, and an educational establishment primarily offering a professional training was completely evident. On the other hand, my own experience had strengthened my conviction that the Pedagogical Academy which at that time not only declared itself to be ideologically homogeneous but was also based on the mother tongue, by its very nature possessed the better chance — in comparison with the universities — of providing an academic education for the people, i.e., using the word "academic" in its strictest sense as meaning "philosophical." For example, the task of preparing teachers at primary school for their career involved (and still involves) the obvious necessity of converting the multilingual existence of the Western intellectual heritage into the living form of the German language. The same applies also to the findings of modern research in the natural sciences, which are expressed primarily in abstract formulae. And this constraint seemed to me to be precisely the opposite of a limitation. Only our mother tongue, which has been developed down through history and is influenced above all by dialect and poetic language, normally opens up to us the depths of reality in which we can come to sense the world as a whole and have direct access to insights which determine the course of our lives.

The difficulty of avoiding both foreign language terminological jargon and unacceptable oversimplification has always exercised me. And so I have quite regularly set out to see whether I could make myself comprehensible, in my philosophizing, to the ordinary listener who was not professionally trained — and possibly to "everyman." The ambition which lay behind this was one of the fruits of my dealings with American students, an advantage which I would like some of my eloquent colleagues to have had — even if I was sometimes pushed close to despair through the childish tenacity of the recurring question: *What does it mean?*

I still have gone many times to the radio studios and "to the villages" in order to raise and explain philosophical problems of some complexity to varied and mixed audiences. Whenever there was a complaint about difficulty in understanding me I always saw it as something lacking in me, while I could not think of any better compliment than when occasionally older people sighed and wished they were young and could be my students. After a lecture about a really abstract topic, from among the throng which was leaving, the Rector of a large university called out to me: "People like you don't exist anymore." I felt uneasy, but when I shrugged my shoulders and looked at him in amazement, he added quickly that it was meant as a compliment.

In the autumn of 1958, out of the clear blue sky, the question came to me for the last time, about whether I would perhaps have to tear myself away from my roots in Westphalia. And this time it was not easy to meet the temptation with convincing arguments, as I wanted to with all my heart. Two things made the matter difficult. The first was that as the successor to Alois Dempf in Munich I was, for the first time as full professor at the university, to make the link with a teacher training department at the Pedagogical Academy. The second was as unexpected as it was delicate. Because of the news of the Munich plan, of course, I was immediately summoned to the Düsseldorf Cultural Ministry. And my friends, and I myself, did not doubt that as usual it would be about discussing the possibilities of keeping me in the Federal State. But then it turned out to be completely different. The representative of the Minister, who happened to be absent, a Social Democrat ministerial director surprised me with his enthusiastic congratulations and a thorough description of the advantages of Munich. He spoke for almost half an hour. I thanked him for his good wishes and remained silent for a good length of time. But when he clearly did not wish to say any more I took my leave of him and traveled home feeling quite irritated, and greeted my family with a somewhat forced happy shout: "So, it's off to Munich!" The family reacted with unbelievable surprise and not very much enthusiasm; the children were even in tears, although later they all moved to Munich. In Bavaria I was made generous offers; they even spoke of favorable opportunities for securing a piece of land. And I myself had to start getting used to the idea of a move.

However, a few weeks after the first Düsseldorf conversation the new building of the Pedagogical Academy was inaugurated and I had been asked to give the official speech ("About the impossible and at the same time necessary business of teaching"). Among the guests was the Cultural Minister Werner Schütz from Düsseldorf.

A few years previously we had met in a somewhat complicated situation. A leading CDU politician of the Federal State had asked me by telephone whether I would be willing to be voted onto the radio advisory board, to which I answered recklessly that I would have to think about it. A few days later the daily newspaper published the result of the vote: those who had been voted in were named and my name was amongst them. Shortly after that, the formal invitation came for the inaugural sitting. The answer, which I wrote in a first fit of anger, that I did not see myself as having been voted in and would behave accordingly, was completely ignored. After

Chapter XI

I had persistently stayed away from the meetings, the Cultural Minister came one day personally to my house to put the radio advisory board in a good light. But I had meanwhile informed myself about their especially political function and I stood by my "no": this was not my kind of thing. Whether he liked it or not the Minister made the best of it and asked, suddenly with a more lively interest, what I did consider my thing. After a long "philosophical" conversation about a wide range of subjects we separated almost as friends. Invitations to the meetings continued to be sent to the house, which meant that each of my absences must have been formally explained as resulting from a particular hindrance. Of course, this procedure could not go on indefinitely. And so after my lecture about Plato's concept of philosophy, before I could even take off my gown Prime Minister Arnold invited me into his office in the Düsseldorf State Parliament, and asked me to put my signature to a letter which had already been formulated; it was to do with an application, hastily read to me, for my release from membership of the radio advisory board because of "pressure of work." In this way I withdrew from a committee of which I had never even been a member.

By the time of the inauguration of the Münster Academy this had all long since been forgotten. At drinks after the ceremonial act, a few colleagues cautiously brought up the topic of "Munich." But before I could say anything, a heavy arm was placed around my shoulder from behind; there stood Werner Schütz. He drew me gently into a corner and asked if I would be at home on a particular day the following week. Already in the first minutes of the frank conversation it was clear how much the information of the Ministerial official, which the Minister discreetly passed over, was contrary to his own intention; of course I must in any event stay in the Federal State and maintain the connection between University and teacher training; it would be no problem to create a professorship for me in the Faculty of Philosophy. I reminded him and warned him about the resistance his predecessor had met with for a much less ambitious proposition. Werner Schütz dismissed all concerns with a confident gesture and preferred to chat about my work and my plans, which, of course, led us into philosophizing and even to discussing our favorite poems. The Minister, later President of the German Shakespeare Society, was highly educated in literature and really loved and enjoyed sophisticated conversation. Of course, he was very inclined to underestimate practical difficulties — something which in my case again became clear. Upon his departure he asked again about my wishes, to which I replied, a little elated by the good conversation, that although the money was not at all unimportant to me, the main thing for me was to make the wall a little higher around the *vita contemplativa*. The "little wall" became a type of catchword which he was quick to throw at me at our occasional meetings. Only years after that did I notice, after a coincidental rereading of my own essays about Goethe's *Schweigen* (Silence) that I had unconsciously taken up Goethe's image which he had written to Schiller when he was fifty: "The wall which I have already built around my existence should be heightened by a few feet." At the time I did not yet know that — and in what way — after endless hesitations and complexities, and completely unexpectedly, this would apply to me. Indeed, I was completely correct in my fear that nothing would come of the Minister's negotiations with the Philosophy Faculty. After several weeks of highly annoying experiences, about which I only heard the half, three of us were sitting in the Minister's office, and the secretary, as requested, placed a double gin in front of us. Then the new University Consultant abruptly answered the resigned question of his boss as to what on earth lay behind it: "rivalry."

Finally, after the somewhat adventurous construction of a "senate professorship" was considered and again rejected, the Minister had the idea of offering the Catholic Theology Faculty the affiliation of a Chair for "Philosophical Anthropology" that was to be newly established. Although the chair was to remain available even after my retirement and its creation was not to be to the detriment of other desired full professorships — the Faculty accepted the offer without much enthusiasm.

The official reply contained reservations relating to Canon Law, in which particularly the concept "affiliation" was somewhat curiously defined. The Faculty understood this expression in such a way: "that 1. The new chair was not a chair *in* the Faculty, 2. The holder of the chair a) neither had a seat nor a vote nor a right to promotion in the Faculty, b) nor could he use the title 'Professor of Theology.'" Individual theology professors expressed their regret to me about this decision. It almost sounded like sympathy. For my part, I had to be careful not to trumpet my joy about the solution too loudly — although only years later did it really become clear what a heaven-sent present it was, even just in the fact that as a nondepartmental professor I could not be invited to any faculty meetings. The Faculty of Philosophy at once awarded me *ad personam* the right to award doctorates, but I never made use of it. And on one gloomy February morning the Dean of the Catholic Theology Faculty appeared in my house; I was lying in bed with a slight fever from flu. I got up hastily and went down unshaven to greet the guest whom I had previously never met in person. He solemnly announced to me that, after consultation with some colleagues from the faculty, he could now say that they would mark the inauguration of my professorship with a special emphasis, namely, the long since overdue award of the Honorary Doctorate in Theology. I listened in amazement and with gratitude. However, I never heard another word about it from that moment onward — until, more than fifteen years later, on my seventieth birthday, this honor was conferred, by a meanwhile rejuvenated faculty, of whose members only a few remembered the old "pre-Conciliar" problems. I thought of the words from the bible often cited rather freely by Master Plenge in "immemorial times" and which now could be given a positive slant: "A new Pharaoh came, who knew nothing of Joseph."

It was not just that the theological honor — which in any case I had not been expecting — was delayed far into the future; the whole spring of 1959 seemed, like the preceding winter, to be filled with nothing but waiting, fruitless meetings, dramatic failures, and personal disappointments, with the result that I hardly know, on looking back, how I got through my workload. Among other things I had a university lecture on "Death and Immortality" which I was holding for the first time, and which therefore had to be written out word for word — and as Hermann Volk said: "in blood." There was also a Stalin Seminar at the Essen Academy.

Weakened by the flu and heartily fed up with the goings-on, I began my holidays and spontaneously decided to fly south with Madame. I could not suppress the idea that perhaps I would not return from this trip, but this was, of course, just a sign of exhaustion; in any case, I made my will shortly before the flight. In point of fact it happened that as we, in deep peace, watched Mount Etna from Taormina we had seldom relaxed so quickly and so thoroughly, and defying all the fears which we had now forgotten we came home happy. Meantime my concerns had not been sorted out at all. Only in May, on my fifty-fifth birthday, could I inform the Rector of the University that I had refused the appointment in Munich.

In the summer and autumn of this glorious wine-producing year of 1959, and as I waited for the precious gift of a winter semester free of lectures, I used to work into the night on the patio. I was writing the book about Scholasticism that even permitted me, for example in the chapter on Duns Scotus, imperceptibly to lighten the seriousness of historical scholarship by the introduction of a somewhat frivolous masquerade. And as the *opusculum* was to appear for our twenty-fifth wedding anniversary, the dedication page contained the following: Cujus in hortulo / Hunc conscripsi libellum / Fausta per quinque lustra coniunctae / Conjugi dulci.

While I was trying to get this dedication into the correct form under the critical eye of my "Roman" friend Franz Beckmann, little did I know that a week before the anniversary — the day for which it was meant — we would escape death by a hair's breadth. We had undertaken a car trip to Spain, a little too early in the year, with Hilde Schürk-Frisch, a sculptor with whom we had been friends for years and whose parents' hospitable house had become a refuge for my family during the last months of the war. Finally we had two to three days of sunshine and we played ball on the Catalan strand. At dawn on Palm Sunday we prepared for the journey home. As usual we had sung a morning song and picked a bouquet of fragrant herbs at the side of the road. Then suddenly, as we were driving at speed, a tire burst. "Coincidentally" on the left of the road to the Pyrenees there was no kilometer stone, no tree, no oncoming car, no churchgoer, no sheer drop. So we climbed through the open convertible top of the overturned and completely destroyed car and stood, a little distraught and very relieved, in a freshly sprouting green field. We were completely uninjured. The next day we traveled home by train. On the Tuesday after Easter our friend brought us a bronze angel from her workshop, a present for our silver wedding anniversary, which we were grateful to have reached. Since then it has had its place on the outside wall of my office as a "Spanish Guardian Angel."

Our doctor friend Franz Schranz, whom we had accompanied in his car to see so many nice things in the world, was no longer able to drive. In the early summer of 1960 he was brought to the University Hospital of Münster, with the result that we unexpectedy became neighbors. It was the first serious illness for this man, who was so energetic that you might think that he could only be killed by violence; but it was also his last illness, and he never recovered. After scarcely nine months I was to lose this friend whom I had met when I was thirty and with whom I had remained connected by a hearty but completely unsentimental reciprocal affection. With concern and bewilderment I went to the hospital and into his ward. But as usual we quickly got into conversation about anything and everything; there was no sign that he was a "patient." At that time the writings of Pierre Teilhard de Chardin were becoming known in Germany, particularly his main work, the "Phenomenon of man," of which the German form of the title "Man in the Cosmos" suddenly reminded me of an almost forgotten meeting which had occurred more than thirty years previously. I was occupied with preparing a seminar about this book, and so on the occasion of every visit I read a chapter out of it to my friend who was immediately fascinated by it; and the summaries I wrote down each time on the same evening soon filled a copybook; I absorb nothing more quickly than what I read to someone who is intently listening to me.

The seminar I held in the following winter term turned out to be somewhat strange. While at the beginning the atmosphere was marked by an almost aggressive prejudice in favor of the author who was under church censorship, in the end it was actually the other way around: what seemed to the students to be a scientifically unacceptable inconsistency in his thinking I had to interpret and make plausible for them as a happy inconsistency within a superb hymnic vision which was not to be taken as "scientific."

In November 1960, the Foreign Minister Heinrich von Brentano asked me to join a "Cultural political advisory board of the Department of Foreign Affairs" which was about to be established. The work of the beginning of the semester was completely monopolising my time — not only the unexpectedly multidimensional work of Teilhard de Chardin, but also the university lecture on the topic "Celebration" which was to be offered for the first time although it had been mooted for many years. In this particularly sensitive situation my instinct was to say "no" immediately. After all, what did I have to do with external politics? Besides, I had long since decided not to expose myself to this type of publicity. But then I quickly changed my mind when to my surprise a letter from Dr Dieter Sattler informed me that it was he who had suggested me for this appointment which I simply had to accept; the workload would be minimal and the task very interesting; above all I would find myself in very good company. Even Dieter Sattler himself was a very unusual person. He started off as an architect, and directly after the war he worked for some years in the Bavarian Government as "State Secretary for the Arts," and then he was Cultural Attaché at the German Embassy in Rome. During this time, at the La-Pira-Congress in Florence (1955) I had got to know him as the pleasure-loving organizer of symposia in the antique tradition, at which with his effervescence and under his energetic guidance there was a lot of drinking and much laughter, but also very serious discussion of the topics concerning intellectual and political life. And now he had become the Ministerial Director in the Foreign Office. I found it difficult to imagine this exceedingly unconventional man as a member of a large apparatus of officials. But I was not able to resist his insistent invitation, and I am happy that I accepted it. On the committee, which soon afterwards was set up with a high level of publicity, you did get to meet really unusual people: Theodor Heuss, for example — meantime "former Prime Minister" — Klaus Mehnert, Helmut Becker, and Annedore Leber; of course, there were also some acquaintances among them. In 1950 in Chicago I had already argued with Arnold Bergstraesser about Goethe; the historian Max Braubach and I used to whisper ironic and critical comments in the Düsseldorf Academy of Sciences; Hans von Campenhausen belonged to the Ecumenical work-group as I myself did; and some years earlier I had had a some-what strange encounter with Werner Bergengruen at a conference of the "German Academy for Language and Liter-ature." It was also a particular pleasure to listen to these two people from the Baltic region when, during drinks in the evening, they told stories about home which were sometimes quite spine-chilling. Bergengruen and I had met at the entrance to the Düsseldorf Castle "Jägerhof" and after a short greeting and introduction had walked up to the first floor together in silence. The next day he came up to me with outstretched hand; he said that he had to greet me again, and this time "properly," as the author of some books published twenty years previously, and that I looked far too young to be that author. Six months before his death — it must have been in February 1964 — we met again in the cold wind of the draughty Cologne main train station. I saw him on the plat-form stamping his feet as he walked backwards and forwards near his suitcase; we were both waiting for the same delayed train. He had already withdrawn from the "Cultural political advisory board"; alluding to his deafness, he said that an army had to separate itself from its deserters. He liked that type of military image; and really the seventy-two-year-old still looked like a cavalry captain. When in the meantime the arrival of the train was announced, I wanted to say farewell with the re-mark that he was probably, unlike me, traveling first class. "That's right, but of course now we'll travel together in second class!" "Fine, then I'll carry your suitcase." It was so heavy, however, that I could only barely lift it. "What on earth have you got in it, not gold bars?" "Oh, they're my books! This evening I have to read for people and I need to have my music in front of me!" "And so you carry your books from place to place?" "Yes! I depend on my marginal notes, omission marks etc." On the way I told him, to his obvious joy, about my children's regular request that I read, and with an attempted Baltic intonation, his little Easter story about the "Light Earth." The section about the maid who, full of Easter joy in the kitchen, pours the schnapps, "dear Daddy," down her throat, always caused special merriment. Bergengruen sat opposite me all the time and had placed both hands around his walking stick. As I was admiring its shining, polished round ivory knob he told me with enthusiasm about his much nicer stick which had a screw-off knob under which, in the hollow, there was a hidden glass tube which could hold quite a reasonable amount of drink. — Even today I am glad that I quickly sent a thorough report about this conversation to California to my son Thomas, who was to die some months before Bergengruen. With youthful pleasure he had taken "dear Daddy" into his vocabulary and particularly loved to announce it in broad Baltic tones whenever he saw his father go down into the wine cellar.

Whether anything much ever came out of the conferences of our Committee for the German Cultural External Politics I do not dare judge. In any case, those with responsibility were strongly convinced by us of the need to become financially more involved than they had up until now. Sometimes we were surprised by the frankness with which Dieter Sattler, in the hearing of high-ranking officials on his side of the house, declared what kind of arguments, whether objective or not, were most likely to impress the head of the department. It did not in the least bother this most uninhibited of all the Ministerial Officials I had ever known — in his greeting speech to the Foreign Minister, who from time to time took part in our meetings for a brief period — to inject a powerfully-sung passage from a Wagnerian Opera. And I do not regard it as unthinkable that this certainly not very comfortable *outsider*, who grew up in Diplomatic Service beside the distinguished and discreet State Secretaries Karl Carstens or Rolf Lahr, and seemed like an exotic colorful bird, was removed with praise from the ministry and into the office of Ambassador to the Holy See, which presumably he administered excellently until his early and sudden death in 1968.

One evening, completely unexpectedly and even a little against my will, I was given the nicest present deriving from my years in the "Cultural Political Advisory Council" and one which was most important for my future life. Our group had gathered in the Hessian town of Hirschhorn on the Neckar, and we were sitting together socially after the somewhat official meal to which the Foreign Minister had invited us. It was not entirely easy to chat with Heinrich von Brentano, a nervous chain-smoker, who, after a few puffs, put out his cigarette and immediately lit another one; besides, in conversation he seemed to be speaking to himself rather than to me, with the result that it was difficult to catch what he said. I had just seen the two Baltic men Campenhausen and Bergengruen sitting together and was just about to go and sit with them, when the Minister drew me into a conversation. He started with a compliment about my USA Reports and asked quite directly — and clearly not without forethought — what I would think about going to India. "India is a place one *must* have seen, and as soon as possible, before it changes too much!" I had an intake of breath and had to make an effort to speak with composure of my long cherished wish to get to know a culture which was *not* Western; America was not in principle "different" from Europe, mainly ahead of it in technical aspects of civilization. "But how am I ever to get to India?!" That would be no problem, according to the Minister. But at this exact moment we were interrupted and there was not another word about it. Another day, however, in a break in a meeting Dieter Sattler remarked almost in passing that he would try to organize an India trip for me. Clearly his boss, who had just left, had not forgotten the matter. And so, without any effort on my part, the plan for my trip to the East took shape.

In the 1977 August editions of the newspapers there were half-page advertisements by *Air France*: "Now daily: departure from Paris at 20.00. Arrival in Washington 17.55." Arrive a good two hours before the departure: that borders on the fantastic. But in the spring of 1962 it still did not sound too bad to hear: "You are departing from Cologne at exactly 13.00 and landing in New York at 16.30; from there, after a two-hour break, you will travel on to San Francisco on a non-stop flight arriving in the evening." Such information is, of course, correct, but at the same time it is incorrect. On 31 March when I left the house at about 8 o'clock in the morning to travel for a second time to Stanford to work again on the two-year course *The Western Traditions,* I took no notice of the friendly stewardess's suggestion that I should put my watch back to the respective local time. Long before my arrival in New York my stomach was impatiently awaiting the dinner; and "Lufthansa" at least served a small cold snack. On landing it was 21.45 according to my watch; but in New York everyone was correctly of the view that it was 16.45. When the plane to San Francisco took off, delayed considerably because of rush hour, my longing for dinner had become a veritable pain in the belly. But they had newly adjusted the time difference and were in no hurry. I forced myself to look at my watch again only when the tray with the *dinner* was placed in front of me — which happened at three o'clock in the morning. And when I arrived in San Francisco at 06.45 — almost twenty-four hours after I had left home — and took my suitcase from the luggage belt, my colleague Lawrence V. Ryan from the Humanities Program stood in front of me beaming.

He opened his briefcase, with a look full of promise, to let me see a bottle of Rhine wine — packed carefully in a cellophane bag with ice — which we were to empty in celebration of my return. However, it was more than my physical strength could cope with. I slept like a dead man that night and all the following day.

But then I was again charmed by the blooming Californian spring with its colors and scents. This time I was given an office of my own to work in at the University. But when I noticed that it was considered very strange, not to say impolite, to close the door to the hall, I looked for a quiet area in a park near the city's Children's Library of Palo Alto, where, undisturbed, I could study the texts I was less familiar with — for example, Abelard's foreword to *Sic et Non*. Again I was surprised about how much was available in English translation.

The student group, Professor Ryan had warned me on the way from the airport, was a bit too big; a student had even complained about that to the Dean. I was amazed when I then heard that the number of participants was twenty-five, and I could only think of the overfilled German Universities. The interest of these students was even more intense than when I had given the course the first time; the two-hour discussions were always over in a flash; and so we arranged an additional discussion — *colloquium on the grass* — ending with lunch together, to which a dozen participants came each time. The definition of the "mythical" or Augustine's differentiation between *fruitio* and *usus,* the things which one enjoyed and those which one used, and the provocative question which I added about whether in the USA and also in the Soviet Union there were increasingly only things to be used — these topics excited their minds. Through these discussions, but also through the campus newspaper which was edited by students and which was regularly brought into my office, I learned more about the situation of the academic youth than six years previously.

Chapter XI

Above all, I found the instability of their mental attitudes and views on the world astonishing. The high suicide rate, for example, was ironically taken for granted in a way which made me feel uneasy. Any "candidates" were informed that the lift to the tower platform of the Hoover Library was closed for repair at the moment, so that they would have to go to the trouble of getting to the Golden Gate Bridge. On the other hand, a student said to me on the way to the colloquium lunch at my hotel that "you already got some converts." That could have implied several things, and I did not inquire about the exact meaning.

The result of a vote, which had been publicized with huge extravagance about a new constitution for the student body, was illuminating and not at all unfamiliar. Through the vote their influence in the administration of the University was to be increased; but not only was the voter turnout a mere fifteen percent but the improvement sought was even rejected.

Again I had planned to make good use the long weekends to see as much as possible of the country between Friday afternoons and Tuesday mornings — although you saw quite a bit of America if, as I often did, you sat in the hotel for a quarter of an hour behind the row of armchairs where people were silently watching the screen, taking in the news — and if you also did not forget a sidelong glance at the audience. Within a few minutes you could not only hear the decree of excommunication of the Archbishop of New Orleans — read aloud by the general vicar personally and with the exact wording — which was directed against three prominent Catholics of the city; you also immediately heard through a personal interview the reaction of one of the affected people. This, of course, occurred only after the speaker drew attention to what, as he assured us, was an "equally very interesting matter," namely the effectiveness of a completely new type of floor polish. But the range of events in the incomparable city of San Francisco was so wide this spring that you would not have had to travel any further than those thirty-five miles from Stanford. There was an unbelievable group of Bali dancers to see, of whom the oldest was seventy-five and the youngest eight years old; the London Old Vic was there with the Zeffirelli production of *Romeo and Juliet* — the most colourful and lively performance of this play which I have ever seen.

Still, I felt inclined to broaden the radius of my weekend trips geographically as well. I had already been to Los Angeles, the Grand Canyon, and Yosemite Park. I was not particularly interested in going to Las Vegas, which in my students' opinion was a "must"; but when my colleague, Professor Ryan, a serious and educated man, said that I should not miss out on this sociologically unusual phenomenon, I in fact included this unique amusement city in my program — unique, because its mere existence and naked survival depended on nothing but its unscrupulous show business ("Girls, Girls"!) and the particularly massive levels of organized gambling, which, outlawed everywhere else because of puritanical laws, here attracted countless numbers of tourists; there are thousands of hotel rooms which are expressly organised for "day sleepers," since the performances occupy the whole night, and only the night. Only at night time, in the glare and disguise of the sophisticated floodlights, does this kilometer-long entertainment street look like anything; my hotel, for example, which was equipped with hundreds of burning flares at the street front, presumably run on oil, reminded me for a moment of the festive congress days in Florence. In the exposed, overbright daylight the whole magnificence could be seen for what it was in reality: a shanty town built in the middle of the dreariest wasteland, fitted with all civilized comforts, in which there was also — because of the practice of giving divorces easily — the "prettiest wedding church of Nevada" masked as the village chapel. (One advertisement board stated that

"full marriage" cost twenty dollars but that "wedding information" was free.) My apartment, which, of course, had
noiseless air conditioning, iced water and a TV, belonged to
the cheaper category, because when you looked out the window you could not see the inner patio with palm trees, swimming pool and colorful garden furniture, but the vast
wilderness which began immediately at the wall of the house
– completely bare, as if uncharted, and shimmering in the sun.
I found the bleary-eyed faces of the fortune seekers at the gaming tables and also in the huge hotel halls almost as dismal,
turning their backs on the world, the ghostly long row of people spellbound in front of the gaming machines, who, right
around the clock, could not be distracted from repeatedly putting a silver dollar into the slot. One surprise: the Mass which
was well attended, even if some of the clothes worn were impossible, was sung by a choir in Latin from beginning to end,
and during communion they sang Thomas Aquinas's *Adoro
Te*. Still, I left the wretched place earlier than planned, sad and
utterly bored, and after my return had a really long sleep.

Holy Week had started. An announcement on the blackboard stated that on Good Friday the lectures would *not* be
canceled; still, students who were absent at the times of Mass
would not be penalized. For good or ill I had to inform my colloquium about my next travel plan, as this time the weekend
could possibly begin as early as Thursday. It was clear that
there would not be the least difficulty in shifting the appointed
day. But *Hawaii* — that was almost as far as New York and
almost halfway to Tokyo! The students found that quite exciting and viewed the trip almost as a shared event. For me it was
again, of course, full of surprises. It began in a small way at
the travel agency. I had innocently signed some piece of paper
with my usual bank signature which indicated that I had a doctorate. The employee who was just about to issue the flight
ticket looked up and asked with emphasis: "Mister or

Doctor?" Up until this moment I had been of the opinion that titles meant almost nothing in America. Now, however, I began to hear it everywhere: "To be a professor — that meant nothing more than having a badly paid job! But *Doctor?* That is something completely different!" In fact, wherever I had to present the ticket it was immediately: *"Hello, Doctor!"* Without embarrassment I often used this weakness to my advantage.

In the airplane the stewardess distributed a brochure about Honolulu in two languages. The second language I found not only incomprehensible but even illegible. It was, as I was told, Japanese; sixty percent of the inhabitants of the island were Japanese. On arrival I saw them greeting one another with deep bows. It went on for minutes. Of course, I had seen many times in pictures the garlands which are placed around your neck by girls wearing hula skirts and giving you a kiss. I experienced this several times. Some things, of course, could not be captured in pictures: not just the welcome greeting "Aloha" which means "love," but also the literally stunning scent which the blooms give off.

I did not miss many of the remarkable things that there were to see, to hear, to smell, and to taste on these truly paradisiacal islands — whereby I did not need, and it was also hardly possible, to differentiate between the original and what was just there for tourists. The natural beauty of the indigenous people was in any case just as genuine as the unbelievable lushness of the vegetation. On the other hand, it was not easy to forget the less paradisiacal reality of the present world. The massive sign with the film title *Judgement at Nuremberg*, for example, could hardly be overlooked. And in the newspaper I found the information that it might be possible to see from Hawaii the reflection of the atom bomb detonated in the South Pacific as an experiment; I do not know if there was really anything to see; I was just not interested. But with considerable curiosity I boarded the boat which traveled daily on a sightseeing tour to Pearl Harbor, which even today is the largest American Marine Base in the Pacific Ocean. Unbelievably, it only became clear to me at the site that this "Pearl Harbor" belonged to the Hawaiian Islands and that it took not much more than half an hour to get there. Ten minutes after the departure, the Captain said almost incidentally that he assumed that all participants had American citizenship. I was the only one to report being non-American and like all the others I had not only to hand over my camera but also to tell them my occupation and sign a form. Then everyone was given a map of Pearl Harbor with a detailed report about the course of events of the Japanese surprise attack of 7 December 1941; the heading reads: "The last moment of peace." Although more than two decades have passed since then, you notice with Americans — and it is always men — how deeply what happened back then still affects them now. In total silence we sailed past the sunken battleship "Arizona," of which part of the tower looms above the water and over which every morning the Stars and Stripes is hoisted and then lowered every evening; the ship still has eleven hundred dead "on board." On the map the position of each individual ship was recorded and also some of the everyday random things which occurred there on that Sunday morning at 7.55 a.m: "Captain Simons, in a blue pair of pyjamas, drinking his coffee"; or: "The bandmaster McMillan is getting ready for the national anthem"; or: "Second lieutenant Ingram orders himself a 'poached egg.'" In the spacious harbor bay there were also brand-new warships of the latest kind; and I could not refrain from saying to the Captain of our boat with whom I came into conversation how surprised I was that everyone could be brought here without concern. "Could I not be a paid Russian spy photographing everything with a camera hidden in my buttonhole?" He shook his head with a superior air and pointed to the police badge hidden under his lapel: "I can immediately arrest anyone who seems suspicious to me." But then he dismissed all that with a gesture and began an exuberant hymn of praise to "Volkswagen," pronouncing the word in a way which defies imitation.

At the next colloquium the students awaited me with faces which all seemed to be asking: "So, how was it?" I greeted them laughingly with only one word: "*Aloha!*"

In the hotel, amongst the post there was a letter from the German Embassy in New Delhi: they were busy organizing a series of lectures for me for the autumn at different Indian universities and at the German Cultural Institutes; everything was progressing very well. India — I had hardly thought of it all this time. Instead of that, I was occupied with planning the details of a trip to Mexico with my wife which would last several weeks. At that time no one had ever heard of airplane hijacking and the taking of hostages; and so, light-heartedly, we arranged the details of our rendezvous: 19 May, 23.00; Mexico City Airport.

Before that, however, I had something else planned, in fact, almost too much. The memory of the Brussels World Exhibition of 1958 and of three to four happy days, on which my children and I did not tire of looking around, had inveigled me into booking accommodation for a weekend in Seattle where a World Fair had opened, with the proud program title: "Twenty-first Century." There was no shortage of surprises on the way there. As usual I departed from San Francisco on the Friday; on the lunch menu we were informed that by popular request fish courses would be served — something which would be unimaginable on European airlines (Lufthansa, Air France, Swiss Air). As I looked out of the Seattle bus from the airport into the almost continual traffic jam a newspaper headline printed in red caught my eye: "A severe earthquake devastates Mexico City," while my neighbor, a young man who insisted on speaking, cheerfully told me how in 1944/45 he had targeted German cities from a bomber. I went directly from the hotel to the exhibition on a monorail which had been specially built by a German company. The exhibition announced with over-optimistic naivete the belief in "the world of tomorrow" and, despite countless technically perfected details — for example, in a type of super planetarium, wonderfully simulated space travel in the Andromeda galaxy — it came across as a cause for concern. The American Library Association had a special show about the role of computers for the book industry under the catchphrase "Nothing will be forgotten anymore." This matter, of course, interested me very much, and I could not refrain from inquiring what I could expect should I ask Mr. Computer for a bibliography on the topic "festival." "Oh, you would get a list of three thousand or perhaps even ten thousand titles!" Of course, I did not manage to convince these technocrats that I would have not the least use for it, as I would not be able to test which essay was good and which was not; and that basically I would have to rely on my own instinct as I had done up until then. I thought of Goethe's "high gift of the gods," the famous "river of forgetfulness" — simple forgetting as an indispensable life function. If "nothing more was forgotten" we would, of necessity, suffocate!

On the return flight to San Francisco, as I am reading now in the travel book that I wrote then, the beautiful summit of Mt. Rainier came into view high above the clouds. I did not yet know that, a good two years later, on a slope of this mountain, my son Thomas would collapse and die days later in the city which I was now just leaving.

At a Stanford farewell party a young colleague offered, indeed he insisted with friendly stubbornness, to drive me to the airport: he wanted to tell me something. Himself a Professor of Philosophy at the Diocesan seminary in San Francisco, he had sometimes taken part in my colloquium as a guest; and we had had some discussions together about this and that. And also on the trip to the airport it was no different at first; we chatted about whatever came up, about students, colleagues, "problems." But shortly before we reached the destination my companion became silent for a while and then he said to me with an almost solemn earnestness that I had to hear this once with my own ears: that never before in his intellectual life had there been such a profound revolution as after his reading of my essay about the negative element in the philosophy of Thomas Aquinas. Of course, as an author you are delighted at such a confession; but on the other hand, what are you to say to it? After a somewhat embarrassing silence it occurred to me to ask my colleague, whose name sounded French and which he also pronounced with a French accent, if he had read the works of André Hayen. He said no, seemed suddenly somewhat embarrassed, and quickly took his leave of me. The short text which was very important to me and to which I had given what my publisher considered the unfortunate title of *Philosophia negativa*, remained fairly unknown in Germany, and the "experts" accepted it only with reservation. The scholar Josef Koch, for example, head of the Cologne Thomas Institute, gave — just like the orthodox Thomists at the University of Notre Dame — a friendly shake of the head about what he considered my strange view that Thomas Aquinas had declared the essence of things unintelligible to us. A good deal later, of course, in the break at a meeting of the Düsseldorf Academy, he took me aside in order to admit to me that meantime he believed that I was right. But already in the 1950s, the philosopher André Hayen from Louvain, in a deliberately entitled *retractatio*, had corrected his previously published theses and thought he could not formulate his newly gained insight any better than through a passage from my little book. And now completely independently of it, and at the other end of the world, this unexpectedly enthusiastic approval! While these remarkable things were going through my head, my airplane was approaching the Mexican border.

And still in the same year 1962, again at the "other end of the world" in India, almost the same thing happened to me again. Jacques-Albert Cuttat, the Swiss Ambassador in New Delhi who was expelled because of his excellently written religious and philosophical essays, confided to me that he had, because of his originally cherished opinion that Western and also Christian thinking was completely rational and positivist in character, was dangerously tempted to succumb to the nihilistic mysticism of the Far East, and only my *Philosophia Negativa*, which he had come across "by chance," had convinced him that the former opinion was completely incorrect. But this meeting was still ahead of me; now I was about to land in the airport of Mexico City.

XII
Mexico: what is different? — Cock fights and
macabre play with death — The trauma of Spain
— Aztec and Mayan Monuments —
Farewell to mother

As always when you go to a new country the question is: What
is different here? You must answer immediately, because after
a few hours already the new is no longer new. What is "different" is, and you feel it in the very first breath, the wonderfully light air. Mexico City is two thousand three hundred
meters above sea level. Also new to me, looking out of the bus,
were the political slogans written in chalk or with a paintbrush
on walls, and also house walls (*Long live Socialist Cuba!*); I
had never seen that type of thing in American cities (or maybe
it had just not impinged?). Also different was that bundles or
baskets were carried on the head instead of in the hand; and
that people who were waiting, not just beggars, sat on the
ground; admittedly it seemed to be only Indians who did that,
whom I realized I had also seen sitting in the now American
"New"— Mexico under the arches of the of Santa Fe Square.
The little Madonna altar which the bus driver had put up on
the dashboard, the Guadalupe Madonna, of course made me
think of Spain; when he stopped in front of one of the big hotels he showed me how it was held in place: by a magnet. At
our hotel bar I had immediately to taste the Mexican drink
tequila which I did not know of and which came from the
heart of the agave plant. The waiter wanted to prepare me, as
he said, a "Tequila Collins"; but then the person beside me

got involved, energetically waving this aside. He believed he had understood better what I wanted; no, I certainly would not want an American cocktail; Mexicans drank the two at once, from one glass the pure clear tequila and from the other one the peppery red sangria. And so I did that too and I immediately liked it. I got into conversation with my advisor and I asked him point blank if there was anything to see here that did not exist anywhere else. He thought for a moment and then named two things with conviction: the cock fights and *Las Catacumbas.* "What's that?" "A type of night club." "No, I was in Las Vegas just recently; I've had enough of that." "You will see that it is exactly the opposite of Las Vegas!" Cock fights were prohibited in the city of Mexico, but they took place on the outskirts of the city; any taxi driver could bring you there in a quarter of an hour. Saturday afternoon was the exact right time. And so, before my wife's arrival, and to put it behind me, I drove out to the cockfighting arena, a squalid wooden shed. About a dozen betting agents filled the small room with an almost unbearable noise; without ceasing, at the top of their voices they shouted up to the rows of onlookers — mostly women — the amounts of the bets placed. I watched two fights; then my curiosity had been satisfied. The first one hardly lasted more than a minute and already the cock had killed his opponent with a little knife which had been attached to his spur. The cocks, each of which was held in the arms of its fight director who was made distinguishable by a green or red shoulder ribbon, were artificially made angry by a third cock brought in for the purpose. The managers also pulled some single feathers out of the aggressively aroused ruff. They let the third cock pick at the rear end of the two fighting cocks, which clearly made them angry, etc. And then the fight began. As soon as one of the cocks fell to the ground and no was longer defending itself, the "winner" left him in peace; clearly he knew what was right. But the managers did *not*; they placed the two animals opposite one another again after the knives were tightened again where necessary; and the shameful show went on. You felt ashamed for humankind.

A few days after that we took a late evening taxi to the "Catacombs." Somewhat curious, we knocked with an old-fashioned door knocker; then a tiny flap opened at face level. A skull appeared and we were asked what we wanted. A waiter dressed in the black cassock of a monk brought us through a dimly lit room to a table, and we sat down. After a while someone tapped you on the shoulder; you looked around and again you were looking at the face of a skull, only a few inches from your nose. Then the waiter took the mask off and we ordered something to drink. Again and again you heard from the other tables more or less joyful-sounding expressions of horror. Suddenly it became pitch dark; macabre xylophone music started and above our heads began a fantastic puppet show, magically illuminated. The actors were skeletons that kept on losing their limbs and getting them back again in ever changing dance figures. You were amazed and laughed at this fun though you felt uneasy. The "catacombs" were indeed the opposite of Las Vegas. And it seemed to me no coincidence that both of them bore a Spanish name.

There was no trace of the earthquake, which we were hardly even thinking about any more. Still, people said to me, not without a trace of malicious glee, on that first evening when I went back to the airport and was waiting for my wife, that it had been "quite something" — as if I had missed one of the country's sights. The same impression was given by a newspaper report in the hotel, a painfully witty attempt to reassure tourists in Acapulco, where six big hotels had been badly damaged and people had had to sleep and eat outdoors. The needle of the seismograph had only broken from old age, they said; all the cinemas continued showing their films, and the people continued with their "bikini" experience.

Chapter XII

Acapulco was not on our programme anyway. Along with some Indian pottery workshops, Madame had to see the monuments of the Aztecs and the Mayans; and we did visit all the monuments within reachable range; we also climbed several of them, and sometimes it was the descent which proved to be the much more dangerous. It was hard to imagine that priests would have gone up and down these huge flights of steps in their religious processions. What interested me in addition to that, and almost more, was the directly spontaneous way the people lived — on the street, in the unbelievably colorful and turbulent markets, and particularly in the religious and ritual sphere where life was lived out with unrestrained ardor, extreme seriousness, unashamedly, and with no sense of embarrassment. In this, the Spanish and the Indian elements seemed mutually to reinforce one another; perhaps older historical forces were here asserting themselves. Certainly there was at work the memory — not easily buried — of the much more than five thousand martyrs of the time of persecution: less than a generation ago. All this produced, it appeared, in the countless churches of the country, the explosive pressure of a seething kettle, and gave religion, which was violently excluded from street and market place, a life of almost frightening vehemence. On the first Sunday when we went into a church near our hotel shortly before eight o'clock, there was a Solemn High Mass still going on, with three priests on the altar; but immediately another began which was no less solemn. The church was full to overflowing; the young men, kneeling all the time on the stone floor, wore around their shoulders scapulars with bright red or golden symbols on them. Afterwards, in the porch we studied the order of Masses: in each of the ten to twelve parish churches of the city listed, up to ten Masses were celebrated every Sunday. And this month there were May devotions every evening. An hour beforehand bells tolled throughout the city. The churches overflowed out onto the street; also, outside, the people prayed uninhibitedly with outstretched arms. Inside there were crowds of girls dressed in white, "angels," and altar boys in festive robes. But then, after such a Mass, which at first glance looked more like a passionate outburst than the performance of an orderly liturgy, you saw, say, in a brown suit with a straw hat in his hand, a "civilian" step onto the altar and open the tabernacle; it was the parish priest, who was getting ready to do his round of visits to the sick. Wearing priestly garb in public was just as forbidden as every ritual act; there were neither processions nor church funeral parades; the "secularized" cemeteries were a dismal sight. Only the honoring of the Madonna of Guadalupe could not be forced into the inside of a church; for no church in Mexico was big enough. This Madonna, as we were told, was a national and not just a purely church symbol; even the anti-church movements gathered under her banner. On the square in front of the "national shrine" at the edge of Mexico City the pilgrims usually spent the night before the veneration began. Then in the morning they crowded into the huge hall as soon as it opened. Many crossed the huge forecourt of stone slabs on their knees. At the entrance we saw a man who, smiling with enthusiasm, tried to convert the quiet surface of the very large holy water font into waves with his hand and into a bubbling spring; only then, he seemed to believe, did the water gain truly salutary power. In the front row of pilgrims, a large Indian family was kneeling; the father, still quite a young man, had taken a gladiolus from the pitchers placed in front of the holy image and he rubbed the blooms across his face and across the faces of his wife and children; you could see it: they had all been transported into another world.

But even during the day it was not easy to find a church in which people were not praying. In the alcoves and side chapels, ghastly representations of the passion and death were to be seen, far surpassing all our Spanish experiences: Christ on the whipping post with pitch-black genuine human hair falling from his forehead into his face — it was black also from dripping blood — or the crucified Christ with his back torn open and the flesh hanging down in bleeding strips. The guide assigned to us by the Cook Travel Agency for a trip to Puebla, a knowledgeable, clever, half-educated person who took pride in his level of enlightenment, encouraged me to put my hand into one of those wounds: "That is 'the Church'!" I did not move my hand and answered him with: "No that is Spain, translated into Mexican!" With that answer I had touched on a particularly sensitive nerve and something akin to a trauma. The public self-consciousness of Mexico again and again became excessively intoxicated with liberation from Spanish colonial rule — an event which had taken place more than a century ago; and "Spain" — that was, in the thinking of the average person here, clearly the same as the Catholic Church.

Through hundreds of garlanded placards hung up on the occasion of a centenary celebration (which had taken place weeks before) of a decisive battle we were accompanied on the whole trip by the huge printed statement of a Mexican General: that the troops had "clothed themselves in glory." The simple parish house of Padre Miguel Hidalgo, a revolutionary who was executed in 1811, was declared a "shrine," and you were asked to bare your head when you entered it. Our tour guide, still always telling tales of battles, naturally led us also into the "secret cloister," one of the tourist attractions of Puebla; with the naïvely triumphal assurance of the anti-church liberals, he amusedly gave us an exact report about the circumstances of the "capture" of the convent in the year 1934, when, after several decades of anonymity, it was betrayed by neighbors. I reminded him of the story of the Jewish girl Anne Frank, whom he seemed to know about, and asked him what freedom meant if it was not freedom for all.

Visibly disappointed, and having become silent, he drove us back to Mexico City. We did not ask any more questions and admired the symmetry of the five thousand-meter Popocatepetl, bathed in sunshine, one of the most beautiful snow peaks in the world.

For the last week of our Mexico trip we went into another world; and since we were of course travelling by airplane, the change came all too soon. With a shock you did not breathe the light air of the elevated plain; instead of that, the tropical dampness of the jungle brought the sweat out of every pore. Suddenly on the peninsula of Yucatan, near the Mayan temples puzzlingly abandoned four thousand years ago, it seemed as if we were cut off from historical time. From Merida we had no direct contact with the hotel we had booked for ourselves, "since it is located in the jungle," as they told us in the travel agency; and, indeed, it did lie in the direct region of the exposed monuments of Chich'en Itzá in the jungle. When "the native bus" set off from Merida to go there, the only available information was that it went early in the morning, around six o'clock. On the previous evening in our hotel, while, under the roof of a portico opening onto the patio, we were eating some chicken — with a lot of chili — steamed in a banana leaf, there was the roar of an enormous shower of rain; as if from gutters, the water streamed down the ribs of the huge-leaved tropical plants within reach of our hands. From the street we could hear the noise of cars, up to their wheel hubs in water. In the morning the rain had stopped. From the bus you could see in the bushes near the street the clean white-washed Mayan huts. There were plenty of obstacles for our old-fashioned vehicle, which was completely filled with sleepy children and their mothers, with traders, with piglets, chickens and other market goods. Once we had to stop because in the middle of the road twenty to thirty vultures crouched over carrion, and were not going to be disturbed.

Chapter XII

The contrast between the fully air-conditioned luxury of the hotel in the jungle and the off-putting sparse austerity of the huge ritual buildings had an almost unreal effect. In front of the hotel's well-kept swimming pool, surrounded with lush plants in bloom, it was hardly one hundred meters to the small circular pond in which a thousand years earlier young girls were drowned as an offering for the divinity of the fountain. Even the festive processions of the priests, who had to go up and down the steps to the altars, which were as high as houses, must have been a life and death adventure. I thought of the walled square for the ritual ball game in the temple square of Tula, where the losing team was immediately killed. Before the tropical rain, while the relentless rays of the sun shone directly on our skin, we could watch everything and explore it; I could constantly see beads of perspiration on the hair on the back of my wife's neck.

After the siesta, which was as if taken in a deep well, the unending flow of rain began again; and the experts said that it would go on until early next morning. And so the hotel tried to entertain the guests with its own people. Not expecting too much, we went to the hall where we came across young people who had either been our chamber maids or waiters. The girls, dressed in their native dress and organized as a "troupe," were waiting for their performance. What we then saw was the unusual grace of the dances and dexterity clearly still in evidence among the Mayans, whose unselfconscious freshness you would rarely see on professional stages. A young chamber maid, feeling the heat after a highly artistic dance in which she had a glass filled with wine balanced on her head, placed herself with complete naturalness near a rubber tree and moved one of its leaves, without taking it off the branch, like a fan back and forth in front of her face.

As soon as it became dusk, the many-voiced elemental sounds of the jungle could be heard, an acoustic tumult of incredible strength. Above the *basso continuo*, the chirping of crickets, as if amplified through powerful loudspeakers, was mixed with the dark call of the bull frog — like the sound of a pruning saw — and with the hissing of a locomotive letting off steam, the shrill sound of a signal whistle, and a human voice which from time to time added to the mix and gave orders. Never before had I heard anything like it — not even later on in India.

Because of the trip to the Orient there had to be a protracted, sometimes quite tricky, correspondence with the "institutions." It was an unexpected and not insignificant burden in this summer semester of 1962, which for me only began at Pentecost and so was somewhat condensed. During this time I had taken on myself not only to lecture for the first time on the Platonic myths, but also to hold a seminar, a repeat, again with a not very satisfactory result, about Heidegger's concept of truth. It is true that the Foreign Office had no difficulties in organizing, through the embassy in New Delhi and the Consulates, lectures in the cultural institutes and in the Indian universities, especially since they were not even required to do what was clearly unimaginable to them, namely, to pay a single rupee in fees. However, the matter had become a little complicated by the fact that the "German Research Association" was willing to take some responsibility for the undertaking as a "research trip" for the study of the festival culture of India; I was still working on the "theory of festivals," which was then published a year later, enriched through the Indian experiences. Now, because of the two-track nature of the finances, as was understandable I was expected to keep an exact account and, where possible, with written records, bills and receipts, showing how much I paid for accommodation, food and drink, when and where I had held my lectures, and so on. The whole thing might have broken down at the last moment because of this. I immediately explained that I was not willing to carry out this level of detailed documentation. In fact, the mere thought of such a constraint was spoiling any desire to make the trip. Of course, it was clear to me that it was not private tourism in my case; but I had meantime often experienced that, precisely where things were not at all organizable, or were "unscheduled" and unrestricted by obligations or pressure of time, a leisurely looking around ("and to seek nothing/that was my goal") would bring to light the really decisive discoveries. In the end, with the help of Dieter Sattler, the agreement was reached that a definite, not particularly lavish lump sum of money would be made available to me and that then all costs would be borne by me. This was fine.

For the following winter semester I had requested the second half of the lecture-free year agreed to by the Minister for Culture; and so I flew on 13 September 1962 from Frankfurt to Bombay with the prospect of not returning until shortly before Christmas. Before the day of departure I went to the clinic again to say farewell to my seventy-eight-year-old mother. It was fairly certain that I would not see her alive again. I held her hand in mine, let us say, a second longer than normally. Naturally she noticed this unusual behavior and afterwards said to my sister: "He said goodbye so peculiarly; does he think he's not coming back?" I myself had this time, differently to the flight to Sicily some years before, the certain feeling — even if there had been no reason for it — that it would *not* be a trip without a return. When I greeted my mother after I returned happily after some months, she was not healthy, but relatively well. I did not know that two much younger people in my close circle would die sooner than she did.

XIII

India's first word: Esso — Divination in Bombay
— Basic/fundamental lesson with Pierre Fallon
— In the Kali Temple of Calcutta —
Contemplation in the Tibetan refugee camp —
The Durga Festival

The Boeing 707, this time an Air India airplane, was already a familiar "home" for me after my many journeys. It now turned gradually and unexpectedly into a strange world. I immediately experimented a little with the fan which I had in the bag in front of my knees since Frankfurt. It was, however, perhaps less suited to India than to the flight destination: Tokyo. After the stopover in Rome we were greeted, when we reboarded, by a smiling Indian air stewardess, her hands joined in front of her in a prayer-like gesture. She wore a sari and had an almond-shaped red mark on her forehead, which, as I was later informed, was nowadays more a cosmetic than a religious symbol.

As the trip over the Red Sea and Arabia suddenly became an overnight flight, I thought about the first word I would hear or see on this Asian continent which I had never visited. Disappointingly, it was the word *Esso* which was written in the night sky above the airport of Bombay. And so in no uncertain terms it was immediately clear to me: I had not completely left the world which was familiar to me. And yet in the following months I was to be confronted with an almost overpowering level of strangeness and confusion. The diary of my trip began with the sentence: "India takes away your breath and your voice; after these first days I do not know where my head is; you don't have any yardstick to help you comprehend the completely foreign nature of this country."

When a good two years later Pope Paul VI traveled to the Eucharistic Congress in Bombay the newspapers reported that countless numbers of people, on the basis of this news, set out from faraway places with their whole families to see the holy miracle worker and to get help or to be given some blessing or other. My friends and acquaintances asked me: I had been to India, and how was it thinkable that thousands would simply leave everything in the vague hope of a gain more desired than could really be hoped for. I was in a position to give an answer: that those thousands literally had nothing that they could — or would have to — leave behind! Of course no one actually counted them, but it was not in the least improbable that in Bombay alone about four hundred thousand people slept on the streets every night. Arthur Koestler's spooky vision was completely realistic: anyone who looked out from his hotel window could be forgiven for thinking for a moment that an enemy had struck down every person on the street. In the light of day you could see them now awake. How could you enjoy your American-style breakfast when a loud clapping of hands drew your attention to a very thin, pitifully dressed young mother who was doing cartwheels in front of the window and finally held up her two-year-old child, with him standing on her outstretched hand, while, begging, she held out the other hand to the rich man! So you went out, half despairing, and gave the woman a few rupees — and at the same time became aware of the hundreds of almost naked people who were washing themselves and their squalid rags at a hydrant and how they stretched out to passers-by the stumps of their arms which had been eaten away by leprosy; how they lay on a few newspapers bent over in pain and perhaps dying; and high above this misery in huge letters you could see the title of the psychoanalytical film *The Couch*, and similarly *American style*. To complete the newcomer's confusion there would perhaps also be the garishly painted invitation to *Read the Soviet-Press!*

The first meeting in the German General Consulate was a little confusing for me. I was welcomed with great warmth; but clearly in Bonn they had not deemed it necessary to give them information about me. Nobody had ever heard of the author J.P., it seemed; and "philosophical anthropology" had been taken to be the discipline of biological ethnology. In any case you did not know, despite the list of possible topics which you had handed in, what kind of people you were going to interest. Still, a function was organized by way of a trial in their in-house lecture theatre. An unexpectedly large group of students streamed in, and, not without a smirk, I became aware of the amazed silence of my hosts when one student thanked them and told, full of enthusiasm, of how she had just been studying *Leisure, the Basis of Culture* for her exam. On the same evening I wrote to Dr Wild in Munich that as soon as possible I needed a publisher's house list of my publications to be sent to all the relevant Consulates and Cultural Institutes in India.

In Baroda, a cultivated Maharaja city with a renowned university, where likewise a lecture had been organized, the speaker introducing me was a scientist educated in Germany. He had searched around in Kürschner's "Scholars Calendar" (Gelehrten-Kalender) and taken note of some book titles; since he had used his "Dictionary for Engineers" for the translation, he told the listeners in his introduction that one of my many books was about *Discipline and Limit*. After the lecture, the head of the Philosophy Faculty asked me in astonishment why I had not been asked to speak to students of philosophy, because, without exception, they were well acquainted with books of mine which had been translated into English. In

Chapter XIII

Baroda, when after lunch I was taking a shortcut with the German lector to get quickly to my siesta in the university guest house, for the first time I encountered a monkey at large; the animal, which was quite big, was sitting on a fence post and "grinning" at me; I have to say the difference from a visit to the zoo is enormous.

On the return trip to Bombay in the air-conditioned sleeping carriage, I got into conversation with a clearly well-to-do businessman; I said that it was admirable that India, despite the differences of so many individual states, had merged into a "Union." He was clearly pleased to hear this and spoke very seriously about the horrors of the first years; the main road between New Delhi and present-day Pakistan had for a long time been barely passable — because of the stench of decay of the innumerable dead bodies of those who had been killed either by Moslems or Hindus and which were too much even for the vultures and hyenas to deal with.

On the following morning, when, with no particular aim in mind, I was walking through the streets with the Director of the German Cultural Institute, an old Sikh, recognizable by his turban, stood in front of me suddenly — clearly not in front of the two of us —: he wanted to tell me my fortune. My companion took my arm: "Don't bother about it; that's all a hoax!" But I was in a good humor and asked how much it was; I liked the man with his quiet gaze fixed on me. So I followed him into a primitive inn, in which he was clearly a welcome guest. Quietly he tore a page out of his notebook, turned away from me, wrote something down and gave me the rolled up piece of paper: "Take it in your closed left hand. And now give me the name of a flower and a number between one and nine!" Well, I had five English names of flowers in mind, so there were forty-five possible answers. So I chose one of them and said it aloud, after which the man asked me to read what was on the piece of paper in my hand: it was my exact answer!

Not bad for a start, I thought. There followed some more or less accurate, if not particularly exciting pieces of information. One was of a quite private nature, and only weeks later, after I had long since left Bombay, I received confirmation: the man had been right. At the end he had also said that I would never again step on Indian soil. I laughed: it was not difficult to predict this; there was nobody around who would pay for such an expensive trip for me. I did not yet know that a few months after my return home a Japanese university would invite me to a lecture trip of several weeks duration. On the trip there, shortly before a stopover landing in Calcutta, I suddenly remembered the words of my fortune teller; either he had prophesied wrongly or . . .? Still, something strange happened: either because of the delay or because of the roaring downpour of the monsoon rain, the stewardess "unfortunately" had to ask the transit passengers to remain on board. So, as a matter of fact I never stood on Indian soil again.

Meantime I was still in this country. My next destination was Calcutta, where already hundreds of people were forming, from the clay mud of the Ganges, images of the Shiva wife Durga and her children for the upcoming Durga Festival, images which would, at the end of the festival period, be dissolved again into the Ganges. Already on the first evening a knowledgeable colleague from the German Cultural Institute brought me to the craftsmen, who formed a caste of their own — a dense population of that part of the city. I immediately felt that here I was in the heart of real India! My companion was anxious not to let a certain fear of contact develop in me, which some shocked Europeans wanted to talk me into in Bombay; anyway, Bombay was seen as "Western" and "Americanized," something I could only comprehend much later. Until well past midnight we walked through the workshops in Calcutta, in which, for weeks, no other work was being done apart from the preparation of the festival. Not only were statues being made for the almost seven hundred open squares of the city and for the countless gardens, school yards and gate entrances, but also colorful decorations for festival marquees; even the six-year-olds hardly looked up from their nightly work on bunches of peacock feathers or glittering braids. Nobody stopped us from wandering around between the half-finished sculptures. Clearly in such a crowd you had to step carefully; not only in the huts but also in the lanes there were people sleeping on the ground; people were crouched at tiny little fires preparing their rice; and now and then you brushed against the damp mouth of a cow. Unexpectedly we found ourselves at a riverbank; on a small funeral pyre the dead were being cremated; silent relatives, huddled in the dark, were visible in the light of the fire. There was otherwise not too much to see, but my clever companion, who was much younger than me, had achieved his aim — resolutely followed — of confronting me immediately with the "whole thing." When we finally made our way back through the sleeping people to his car, he said: "If you were to lie down here in the same way, nothing would happen to you!" I believed it without hesitation and for the first time felt a little at home in this puzzling country.

It would not have been difficult to organize my accommodation with the European Missionaries, but I had expressly not done so and arranged it in the house of the Ramakrishna Mission, therefore at the heart of Hinduism — or so I believed anyway. In reality I found I was mistaken on two counts. Firstly it turned out, as I will explain later, that the modern organized Ramakrishna Mission was absolutely *not* representative of the temple religion and Indian belief in the gods. Secondly, more exact and accurate information about real Hinduism was nowhere to be had — not even from an orthodox Professor of a Sanskrit Department — than from the Belgian Jesuit Pierre Fallon, whom I fortunately got to know quite soon; without his untiring basic instruction I would have understood very little about the Durga Festival and its rituals. Having lived in India for nearly twenty-five years, he had carried out thorough studies. In particular, fired by spiritual impulses, he had a truly charismatic ability to empathize, and had become a living proof — which I found immediately convincing — that the truth hidden and embodied in genuine Adventist paganism could never be interpreted properly from the angle of paganism itself, but only in the light of the Word made Man in Christ. And so nothing better could have happened to me than that, through completely external circumstances, I had to break off my stay in the Ramakrishna Mission after a few days, although it had been planned to last several weeks: the otherwise really comfortable guest rooms did not have air conditioning, and unfortunately I was not able to sleep in a temperature which did not fall below thirty degrees at night.

Strangely, the first day of the Durga Festival, which was not an isolated festival but a period of festivities stretching over two weeks, was celebrated in the temple of Kali, who was another Shiva wife. That was strange, of course, though only for a Western mind, which finds it difficult to accept that the benevolent Durga was identical — not only a sibling, blood-related, no, actually identical — with the murderous Kali, whose gruesome ritual image shows her in her black nakedness, her bright red tongue hanging far out of her open mouth, one hand brandishing a butcher's knife, the other holding a human head dripping with blood, around her neck a chain of skulls, as she stands with both feet on the corpse-like Shiva, who had thrown himself in front of her to bring her rage to an end. While the friendly reigning Durga just stayed a few days in her festival marquees — which were quickly erected on a bamboo scaffold and did not have any permanent dwelling place on this earth — richly endowed and much visited temples were constantly being built to the fearsome Kali, after whom Calcutta was named. I traveled to one of them, the most famous one, at the beginning of the festival and stood spellbound in the middle of the expectant and elated, and — clearly without exception — simple people, who, with hands raised in front of them, carried their gifts of hibiscus blossoms or rice or fruits laid out on leaves. All the men were dressed in gleaming white; and the women, whose charm could always fascinate you afresh, wore saris which shone in all colors of the rainbow. Today some of them had charming little slippers painted on their bare feet with red paint — something which, despite the almost fashionable elegance, originally was certainly not meant as a mere cosmetic ornamentation; in any case, later, when I was at the crematorium of Benares, I sometimes saw the same ritual of shoes given to the dead for their journey, but apparently only to women.

It becomes immediately clear that sacrifices are offered to this Goddess Kali and, of the Indian deities, only to her. And so for the first time in my life, in the presence of the goddess who remained hidden in the temple, I saw the killing of a living being, a kid. With one single stroke of a large sickle-shaped knife, to the dark sound of a drum roll, the head was separated from the body. Immediately the temple servant put his hand into the dripping blood and with it signed the foreheads of those who stood around in a small circle witnessing the moving and dignified process, which, of course — something that some modern theologians do not understand — as a *sacrificium* was qualitatively different from the *oblatio* of blossoms and rice.

When I was still standing there a little stunned and could not see enough of the colorful surging of people, a youngish man coming from inside the temple, which was inaccessible for me, approached and introduced himself to me as a solicitor. "How nice," I said, "at last I'm meeting an educated and at the same time religious and practicing Hindu." He answered with a little embarrassment that he was not very orthodox. "And yet you have come directly from inside the temple!" Yes, today was a special day: he had brought the family's offerings and, when the prayers were spoken over them, he would immediately take some of them home again. He suggested that if I wanted to meet an orthodox and at the same time highly educated Hindu I would have to meet his old teacher, a specialist for the iconography of Hinduism, about which he had written a very learned book. After taking the gifts from the temple he immediately brought me to the teacher. He was sitting behind his desk — which was full of books — his feet pulled under him and the holy cord diagonally over his bare chest, a lively old man who had clearly just performed the household celebration. We immediately got into conversation: while with somewhat forced amusement he bemoaned the fact that the young generation was losing the faith, I asked him a question which I had posed to some others during my trip. "Since a festival is a day of joy, what is the Hindu joyous about during such a festival?" Normally people did not immediately understand this clearly very "Western" question, so I had to explain what I meant. The professor answered after a while: "We celebrate the fact that our deity can hear our prayer and also wants to." Another person said that the reason for joy was the certainty that light would always win out over darkness. The most wonderful answer came later from an artist who had found his way back to Hinduism after a secular phase: it was the joy of being a creature which God had created out of joy. I knew that near the Kali temple, at the entrance of which I spent many more hours, there was a "Hospital for the dying" which a southern Slavonic nun, "Mother Teresa," had set up there. I saw this accommodation which at that time was still quite wretched, but Pierre Fallon said in a tone of regret that it would become the destination of the newspaper people and tourists; the story was told that an American journalist had for a time watched the nun while she tended the wound of a leper and then said he would not do something like that even for a thousand dollars a day, to which he heard the reply from over her shoulder: "I wouldn't either!" I now regret it a little that I did not take the opportunity of meeting that extraordinary woman — although it was definitely right not to "have a look at" her.

Although I had asked to be spared receptions and cocktail parties where possible, I could not resist the curious invitation of the aristocratic old-school cavalier who was Director of the German Cultural Institute. The first part of the reception was to take place, of necessity, in the host's very comfortable, but yet very small, hotel room. There we were to be offered whisky, gin, or vermouth — because the hotel restaurant into which we were then to go to for the evening meal had its legally mandatory alcohol-free day. I was delighted to get to sit beside Günter Eich on the baronial bed. I had read many of his poems and radio plays to my students in Essen. I have seldom experienced such a taciturn person as he; and it was not just the fact that in the general noise of conversation he was hopelessly hard of hearing, which thwarted my efforts to make my meaning plausible to him: namely, that actually hell, about which his radio play "Festianus, Martyr" dealt both at length and inappropriately, in truth was not to be thought of as an area locked from the outside but on the inside. But my esteemed neighbor seemed really to have gone to a place where words did not reach him — and certainly not these ones. And I remembered a sentence from his Büchner Prize speech of only a few years previously: "One could become a Trappist monk; but it doesn't help."

The Durga festival took its course meanwhile; or rather, it gradually got going. The festival marquees were still being worked on; and also sculptures of the gods were for the most part only on the way there on trucks or rickshaws. The actual festival days came only at the end. For the time being not much would happen, and I decided to get away for a few days from the dripping heat of the Ganges Delta — into the high valleys of the Himalayas. Pierre Fallon agreed heartily with my decision and suggested Darjeeling, where he wanted to put me in contact with his friends in the Jesuit College without delay. I would doubtless be made very welcome. Before that, however, as was already planned, I was to witness the daily morning service celebrated by a Brahman who had been asked to perform it in the house of a factory owner. The son of the house, who was a physics student, collected me; he had brought a friend with him for whom, of course, not the familiar cult procedure was of interest but my reaction to it. We were already expected in the house; I took off my shoes and stepped into a bare room; on the walls there were fairly cheap prints representing the gods; on the floor under a canopy there was an altar-like structure. In front of it the "priest" squatted in his orange-colored vestments, quite a young man who seemed inwardly focused and intelligent. Immediately he began carrying out the ritual. Around him there were dishes with fruits, rice, water, and grains of incense. Five or six small bronze figures of gods were washed and anointed, then dressed in the laid-out garments and placed on the altar. This all happened during the constant chanting of the "priest" who had to observe very precisely laid-down gestures and hand positions. Occasionally a gong was struck and a hand bell sounded; incense was put into a receptacle with glowing wooden coals; and eventually the celebrant took a big white shell to his mouth and with it made a loud sound which was repeated three times, after which the woman of the house, who up until now had been hidden, rushed into the room, threw herself down and silently lay for a long time with her forehead touching the floor. The father had from time to time briefly looked in through the door. The two students were clearly only watching me; I was the only one looking at the performance of the ceremony, full of curiosity. When I asked my young companions about the meaning of individual rituals they just laughed in my face: all of that meant nothing, absolutely nothing! And so I turned to the father, a serious, educated man; he shrugged his shoulders: "That has been the tradition with us for years, for a thousand years they've been doing it like this!" As we were leaving the house, the students were complaining angrily: this was the only answer they ever heard. The Brahman, who had disappeared immediately, would certainly not have been able to give me any information. I already knew this from Pierre Fallon. The same thing happened to me several times more, namely, the lack of any interpretation of what was handed down as "holy" — "theology" — and which clearly did not exist in Hinduism.

The trip to Darjeeling — firstly by airplane, from which an unearthly gleaming stretch of snow peaks came into view, then in an overcrowded bus — led to a completely new world. The tortuous and strict passport controls reminded you that it was not very far to the Himalayan border with the Chinese aggressor. You saw women carrying heavy loads — on their backs, but with a strap stretched over their foreheads.

The reception in the Jesuit College was at first a very embarrassing affair. Nothing was known about a letter from Calcutta; Pierre Fallon had probably never given it another thought. The Institute was just celebrating some festival or other; there were competitions between a half dozen north Indian Jesuit Colleges, and the guest rooms were all occupied. Clearly the likeable Canadian Rector, a straightforward down-to-earth man, considered me something of an intellectual vagrant. On the point of taking my leave and going to a dubious "hotel," I adopted the ruse of asking about the house library and its catalog; with some curiosity the suspicious man who was not quite yet my host led the way — and then in surprise read from the index cards eight to ten English titles of my books which were available in his own house; I was amazed myself. So the situation changed in one instant. For the night, all that was available was the untidy room of a student who was on holidays. It was wallpapered with pin-up girls. But for meals I was brought to the table of the guests of honor. There were plenty of unusual things to see. Already during the first walk through an inner yard with noisy boys the Rector pointed to a boy of about thirteen: "That is the brother of the Dalai Lama; a boy like any other, and yet it is sometimes difficult. For example when the Tibetan dignitaries come and the boy is called to the visitors' room they all stand up reverently, and no one dares to sit down again in the presence of this 'incarnation of the Buddha.' Do you think I stand up too?"

In the afternoon a speech competition was held. One by one the participants stepped into the spotlight and, off by heart, spoke a passage from a text of their choice for about five minutes; it could be a piece from Cicero or a Shakespearean monolog. A student who recited the end of John F. Kennedy's 1961 memorial speech for Dag Hammarskjöld at the United Nations was to me by far the best; but he was not the winner. The relaxed and seemingly obvious reply to my surprised and critical question surprised me even more: the Crown Prince of Nepal had already won first prize often enough!

In the early morning, in the sunlight to which we exposed ourselves without hesitation, we took a walk to a Tibetan refugee camp, far outside of Darjeeling. On the way we saw tea plantations which looked like fields of box trees; in the distant haze you could almost make out the eight- thousand-meter mountains. Warned by many television reports I braced myself for something quite desolate, but what I saw was the exact opposite of what I expected. A clearly delighted Tibetan greeted me with a laughing face and endless floods of words;

I did not understand a word; so for my part I spoke Low German; and there was no doubt that we completely shared the same opinion. From the school building in front of which several dozen school children dressed in blue stood waiting to go in in an orderly line, a young Indian teacher saw me; when the children were looked after, he wanted to show me around a little. I went with him into the spacious classroom; the children had taken their places with unbelievable discipline and in loud voices began at once to recite a text in chorus; some held up between their fingers a pencil, which a Tibetan teacher pared with his pocket knife as he went through the rows. The Indian brought me out; this Morning Prayer would last about forty minutes, so he had time. "What are the children praying?" Well it was a constant variation of the petition that God would help them to become good people. The streets of the camp looked as if they had been swept clean; men and women were all at work, at the weaving looms, or engraving gold jewelry, or at the forge from which came the sound of happy laughter. On the huts they lived in I saw from a placard that they were gifts from the American people. All are unlocked ("No one steals here," said my Indian guide); we looked into some of them; it was as if they had just been cleaned. We passed by a sacrificial altar made of bricks on which a flame flickered in the wind, and we went to the spinning room. My companion said as he opened the door that I should watch the lips of the women. They were squatting on the floor, next to the walls of the bare room, in front of their old-fashioned spinning wheels; beside some of them there were babies lying in cardboard boxes. There was a remarkably cheerful quietness which became even deeper through a hardly noticeable humming. Not in the least disturbed by our presence, the women continued saying the words: *Om mani padme hum.* I had just learned that the holy syllable "om," with which the Hindus introduced every festive activity with a long-lasting incantation, actually had no meaning in words, but still meant something wonderful: namely the attempt to integrate themselves into the rhythm of the cosmos. The *mani padme*, however was a praising appeal to Buddha as the "jewel in the lotus." I could not remember anywhere else — apart from possibly during a High Mass with the Benedictines of Solesmes — that I had come across such a dense, physically perceptible atmosphere of contemplative life. In the tiny administration office I wrote my name and origin into the guest book and added: "I admire the Tibetan people"; my school teacher looked curiously over my shoulder and asked: Is Germany in America?

My hosts found it difficult to understand that I did not want to waste my last afternoon in Darjeeling at the students' sports competitions, but instead preferred to go by taxi to one of the Lama cloisters hidden in the hills. A greater problem was my own inability to achieve even the slightest understanding of the religious practice of Lamaism. Completely baffled and alienated, I watched a group of pilgrims, as, with a strong hand-movement, they set in motion the turning cylinders with carved prayer texts, which were embedded in the outer wall of the temple; then, as they ran around the temple many times, each time they brought the now more slowly rotating prayer mills into quicker motion. In the temple itself then the paper spirals, with written prayers on them, were turned by a tallow candle underneath them which burned for days or perhaps for weeks, depending on the mass of candle matter. "It's praying": that was for me a nightmare of a religion.

Of course, when on my return to Calcutta I used this formulation in conversation with Pierre Fallon, he raised his hand in a mild warning: "Oh, behind that there is a very complicated metaphysics!" What irritated me a little about this tolerance which was sometimes difficult to understand, was that it did not exclude or mitigate the critical severity with which the self-same Pierre Fallon used to speak about the

Neo-Hinduism of the Ramakrishna Mission. Of course, he did not say a word against the revered mystic Ramakrishna himself, a monk of the goddess Kali who had died fifty years previously in 1886. On the other hand, he referred to what he considered a highly questionable matter: the Vivekananda in America about which a student had informed him — a teaching system propagated with amazing financial success together with the particularly well calculated formation of a legend around the master. He saw it simply as a fabrication which had nothing to do with Ramakrishna or with original Hinduism.

I myself was to have some odd experiences in this regard. While waiting for a lecture on the "Finding of the eternal self within us" I was sitting in the first row of the large, air-conditioned lecture theatre of the Ramakrishna Mission; they had not taken it as an insult that I had left; I myself was to speak some days later about "Philosophy between science and theology"; my neighbour, a Swami in the orange-colored vestments of a monk, was also on the printed list of speakers with the topic "The holy mother." This was meanwhile the official name given to the wife of Ramakrishna who had died in 1920; one hymn even celebrated her as the "supreme Goddess." American Ramakrishna "converts" reared as Christians were treating her like the Virgin Mary. Ramakrishna himself was supposed to equate her with the Goddess Kali. On the other hand, Pierre Fallon told me that he knew from completely trustworthy eye and ear witnesses that in his last years Ramakrishna opposed all this talk about divinity with very extreme and almost crass words: "Do you believe I would be dying of cancer of the throat if I were a God?" So I turned to my neighbor the monk with sly innocence and asked: "Who is Ramakrishna really? He is a person from the nineteenth century, isn't he?" The Swami drew back from me a little with a gesture of visible shock and then said in the tone of at once indulgent and definite correction: "O no! Ramakrishna is not a person; he is God!"

Somewhat eagerly I attended a "service" of the Ramakrishna community. The difference from what you normally heard and saw in the temple was striking. Instead of the disordered flowing masses in which each person, with his offering in his outstretched hand, made his way to the images of the gods and symbols, to the holy trees, to the fireplaces — each one kneeling in the prayer hall, untroubled by all the others and immersed in reading his prayers aloud or reciting them off by heart — here the devout people, ordered in rows, sat completely silent until, to the sensuous sound of the harmonium, which was unknown in orthodox temples and even frowned upon on the radio for being un-Indian, a song of several verses was intoned, while at the same time a ritual server stepped in front of the altar, prostrated himself in front of the cult picture and, with incense and five-flamed lights, performed all the gestures of the worship usually reserved for the gods — although, unbelievably this cult picture was a realistic, perhaps even a photographic portrait of Ramakrishna. Never, when in the temple I watched the usual veneration of Shiva or Vishnu or the offering of the consecrated gifts (milk, honey, blossoms) in front of the lingam, the phallus united with the female vagina — never, a little to my own surprise, did the thought of "idolatry" come to mind; I always thought of these rituals, which were celebrated with uninhibited fervor, as something which in principle could be "converted" — as something which appeared to be, strictly speaking, pre-Christian. Here, however, in the fashionable "liturgy" in front of the intentionally deified Ramakrishna, I seemed to sense for the first time a hint of blasphemy.

Meantime in Calcutta the last days of the Durga festival had arrived; the city was like a bubbling kettle, which threatened to boil over at any moment. It became really serious, and this in a quite extreme way. Up to seven thousand people, also here referred to as "unreliable elements," were locked up as a precaution; voluntary helpers augmented the police force. Even the fact that in an industrial suburb three thousand workers put up barricades and that in the shootouts with the police there were deaths and many people injured — this, too, had something to do with Durga; it was about the level of the festival-day gratuity. The main streets of the city were decorated; on the colorful glass pillars which in the evenings were lit up from the inside, I discovered — hidden between flower symbols, but clear enough — the name of the shoe factory Bata, a first indication of the danger posed by commercialization here too. On the big squares, ten or twelve of which I may have visited — always led by Pierre Fallon — there was the hustle and bustle of a type of annual fair. From the loudspeakers, which were constantly too loud, both the hymns of the Vedas and the film hits of the latest kind were being played. The big wheel and the swings were always full; but you saw how on the street or in the parks "young people" were never together, never in mixed groups of boys and girls, never a couple. Regularly Pierre Fallon approached the book-sellers' stands. The sobering outcome was always the same: "Almost exclusively Soviet literature!" And yet for India, he said, the actual danger was not Communism. For that the family and the caste were too strong. Much more dangerous was the ultra-conservative "orthodoxy," which at any time could provoke a civil war. And again I heard about the frightful first years of independence. "Often enough my white soutane was red from the blood of the dead who had been killed by knife and dagger in the street, Moslems and Hindus!" — Pierre Fallon was nearly always immediately recognized by the people of the "Festival Committee" and greeted like an old friend. They brought out chairs for us and we had to write our names into the guest books, where then Pierre Fallon, who was translating the New Testament into Bengali, added a few friendly greetings in the ornamental writing of the country. Of course, we were asked everywhere what we thought of the figures of the gods in the festival marquees; that they were the main part of everything remained, no matter what, completely clear. Unfortunately, on the morning of the first main festival day we missed the moment of the "consecration"; the astrologists had corrected their first calculation during the night; so we arrived a few minutes too late. I asked the theologian Fallon if the word "consecration" was quite right. Yes, he had deliberately used the expression; in this act, so the Hindus believed, a "transformation" and metamorphosis of the physical sculpture into the godly presence really happened. The Brahman who alone was in a position to perform the ritual touched the picture of the Durga with a green branch, nine times consecutively, and with nine different branches the mouth, eyes, ears, heart, and lap, each time with the prayer: "Let the breath of life of God be the breath of life here too!" And then Pierre Fallon described to me how once, years before, he had been standing behind the closed window shutters of a house exactly at the time when the picture of the Durga on the outside wall was going to be "consecrated"; he had looked through the shutters into the faces of the people as they passed by in their large numbers and was affected by the way, at the words of the priest, the purely neutral curiosity had suddenly changed into the seriousness of religious worship.

Again and again I asked the experienced Fallon for these types of "true stories"; and indeed he told me plenty of them. I did not want opinions and "theories." He once said directly that I myself should now physically experience a "true story." For the Durga festival, just as the mythical Shiva wife visited her father's house with the children, the married daughters went home for a few days to their parents and everyone spent the festival time together. The Hindu family, friends of Fallon, were expecting us and received us hospitably. They had a fifteen-year-old daughter who was about to put on her first sari as we entered the house. With breathless joy, like "Natasha" before her first ball, she came up to us, and bowed to the ground, with the palms of her hand touched our feet and then her own forehead; it happened so quickly — as a matter of course — and so charmingly that there was not a trace of embarrassment, no time for it. Of course Fallon said the sari was beautiful; but I knew that his thoughts were already with another sari which he had asked for from the girl's parents as a present and which on the same evening would be passed on to the daughter of a refugee family. She lived at the other end of the city, however, and so we traveled over an hour by tram across Calcutta. On the way I heard more about the girl for whom the sari was intended. Of course, she was going to be married off by her father, but the boy had just gone to the army, and she wanted to wait for him. Fallon had already found out that the father, secretly of course, knew about it and was in agreement. In the wonderfully cool evening breeze, while we were waiting for a tram on another line, my guide, who knew the area, looked around and said that it was hard to believe how different this part of the city was even with regard to its spiritual atmosphere. "In the South they read Sartre, in the North they discuss Shankara." In this miserable area, however, into which we eventually arrived, neither the one nor the other was the case. It was already dark, and we proceeded carefully step by step, until we arrived in the wilderness of poverty-stricken huts to the two rat holes which served the family as a home. We looked into one of the low rooms. On the floor, which was nothing but trodden-down clay, there was a weakly lit lantern. But then, surprisingly, three or four young women came through the entrance, which was only waist high, in impeccable saris. They were the married daughters, home for the festival. They seemed to be getting on quite well; but, I was soon told that they now belonged completely to the families of their husbands and were not allowed to support the father at all, just as the father, once a teacher in Pakistan, would not accept the least thing from them. We were not able to greet him personally. In the second room, which was just as miserably lit by a stable lantern, he was sitting in deep meditation before an image of the god. The young girl delightedly received her sari, of which the donor remained unknown. He could not have brought it himself or even have been allowed to send it, as I later discovered; for this the mediation of Pierre Fallon was needed. But the astonishing story which I had been brought out to experience was not yet at an end. On the way home the Jesuit began to talk about the girl again. He had once asked her if the boy she was waiting for was a good person. Instead of an answer she said that once while walking through the streets, in order not to get separated from him, she held his hand, upon which the boy said in all earnestness: "We had better not do that, otherwise we will lose the love of God." A little bit skeptical, I remarked that surely that was not the average case. My companion hesitated a moment before he said quite firmly: "It is not the average response; but with orthodox Hindus it is also not an exception."

On the last evening of the festival we began our rambling only shortly before midnight. We were accompanied by a young Anglo-Indian Jesuit. He was living proof of the insurmountable nature of the wall which in this country separated the religious and social groups. He was born in Calcutta and had grown up there, but, like myself, he was for the first time seeing the Durga festival which was resounding through the whole city.

Meanwhile the crush around the festival squares had become frightening. I could see straightaway that here, when the crowds became excited, dozens of people could be trampled to death. Hemmed in by the crowd, we gradually pushed our way into the marquee with the image of the god. It was hardly visible because of the incense pouring out of the offering bowls so thickly. A priest swung the five-flamed light with sweeping gestures over and back in front of the goddess to the rhythm of the loudly beaten drums. Another priest stood facing the dense crowd of people; with one hand he was holding on his hip a dish of water — presumably from the sacred Ganges — while with the other hand he was sprinkling the worshippers with a palm branch. Full of fervor they stretched out their faces and hands to him. Already you could hear some ecstatic calls from the crowd, which began to sway rhythmically back and forth. A few more minutes, I said to myself, and the whole gathering would be raging in an orgiastic frenzy. But then the drums broke off; from one moment to the next everything became completely still. The priests withdrew into themselves; as we came forward through the now yielding rows, we saw the people kneeling on the ground meditating. In the cordoned-off space in front of the altar you could see that a whole crowd of children had been standing. They were now also turning to go. Five or six of them lay in a deep sleep on the floor and did not move. An old woman in a white widow's sari tottered onto the now empty square and likewise stretched out there to sleep. "Do you see the bride?" Pierre Fallon asked. His hand pointed to a slim form under the image of the gods hung with a white veil; it was the bouquet of those nine green branches, given this poetic name by the Indians, with which the "consecration" had been carried out several days ago. The next day in a cult act for which in the history of religion I think there is no analogy, it would be reversed by a Brahman: "You have visited us O Goddess during these days. We thank you for that. Now, however, you must go back to your divine abode. We ask that you graciously come back to us again next year!" What during the festival days was the truly present goddess was now changed back into a mere figure made of dried mud. The following night, as we stood among the thousands at the bank of the river, trucks came along, one after another, full of young fellows accompanying the images of the gods; some brought them on a boat into the middle of the river and sank them by torchlight. Some jumped in to grab some of the goddess's jewelry; breathing heavily, they climbed up the bank holding a glittering crown and disappeared into the crowd.

As if awakening from a long dream, I turned to my friend: "Now, mon Père, how do you judge all that? Is it simply an idolatry craze?" He sighed deeply and hesitated for a long time before answering. Finally, on the way home from the festival, which had now in fact ended, he quoted me a few lines from Paul Claudel's *Satin Slipper*: "Delusion has to do with what does not exist, longing with what is/ Going through delusion and through non-being/ Longing longs for being." This then led to a long serious night-time discussion by way of farewell. The missionary Pierre Fallon, a man of such unobtrusive and radiant priestly spirituality had had the foot of his chalice engraved with the sacred syllable of the Hindus, in the Bengali language written with three letters (a-u-m); when he spoke to me about it, he added meaningfully and yet also in a somewhat understated fashion: "Some do not like that very much." In the past weeks I had met a lot of people through him whom I otherwise would never have met; but all of them were Hindus. So I asked him, perhaps a little too directly, his opinion about the chances of the Christian mission. Again he was silent for a few moments and said then that the whole Indian culture had the stamp of their belief in God: poetry, music, dance — all of this could not be thought of without Him; and because of this he found that the thesis of one of his Indian friends was not totally incomprehensible: Whoever becomes a Christian here must die.

XIV

Hyderabad: A Thousand and One Nights — Nightly Festival in Madras — Old Indian dance — Atheistic Buddhism? — Nepal and the "living Goddess" — Death in Benares — Indescribable Taj Mahal

After Bombay, Calcutta and Darjeeling, I would never have thought that there could be a place like Hyderabad in India. Still, at the sight of this city a secretly cherished expectation connected with this "trip to the Orient" was fulfilled; when I saw the slender minarets, the mosques and tombs, the dream world of *A Thousand and One Nights* came into my mind, where neither Shiva nor the Buddha reigns but Allah and his prophet. The university where I gave my lectures was called Osmania University; until 1948, the year of the more or less imposed integration of the country into the Indian Union, the official teaching language was Urdu, a language clearly shaped by Islam with Persian script and to a large extent Persian vocabulary. While up until now I had hardly met a Hindu intellectual who was pious in the traditional way, the faculty colleague who was looking after me here was a Moslem of strict faith. In the night before a festival he led me to the graves of two holy Islam men, whose sarcophagi lay in a small chapel under a canopy. We took off our shoes; my philosophy professor put a scarf over his head, as custom demanded, and brought his gift of blossoms. Having passed the people kneeling, almost only men, old and young, who laid their foreheads on the threshold, we stepped out under an open tent ceiling, under which a large reverent community quietly began to sing the songs of Persian mystics; my companion explained the songs to me and joined in himself.

On the magnificent main street the dignitaries of the city moved with measured steps, dressed in a type of frock coat made of brown silk — copying, I was told, the former leader, "Nizam" of Hyderabad, who was still being addressed as "Your exalted Highness." A lady, hidden in a completely closed rickshaw, had the goods on offer in a shop passed in to her for her inspection. The sales room, which was waist-high and fitted with silk cushions, could be reached over some marble steps; shoes remained outside, which goes without saying.

Of course, there were also less friendly images. The entrance of the hospital for example, in which only the old Indian Ayurveda medicine was practiced, was blocked by tightly crowded groups of students sitting on the steps, who, as a banner said, had embarked on a hunger strike to enforce the academic recognition of this more or less magic medicine. My Islamic expert just shook his head; never would the Osmania University let something like this be accepted as a scientific discipline. But then he added a surprising remark: there was another, old Arabic treatment, which was similarly unrecognized by modern medicine, which he himself held as legitimate; however, its effect was mainly confined to psychological illnesses; this treatment was called Jonani, which more or less meant Ionian, and therefore Greek. And so in the middle of India you found a hint of the circuitous route which the Aristotle school had to take in the fifth century to emigrate from the Roman Empire in order to get back to the Latin West through Syria, Persia, and the Arabian countries. I also discovered that, at the beginning of their treatment and their prescriptions, the doctors of this therapy placed the sentence: "HE is the healer."

Every time I returned to the guest house of the university where I was staying and took meals I entered for the moment into a completely different world. My table companions were an American professor couple and an Indian computer scientist (if I now call him "Indian" then I am following a suggestion I heard in Bombay to use this term for all non-Islamic inhabitants of the sub-continent). The professor from Illinois was involved with the Peace Corps and had plenty to report about the selfless and demanding work of the young people entrusted to him. His wife followed, as if she were on a fasting diet, the rule which had obviously been drummed into her: never to eat something which Indian hands could have touched; when the two cheerful cooks once came in, beaming, with two magnificent, but still half-alive fish, and asked whether we wanted them boiled or fried, she almost fainted. The Indian, a man who had been all around the world, loved to shock the Americans with blunt criticism of his own government, as the Americans were far too loyal for his taste. A few days later, when we were the only guests in the house, I asked him what he thought of the activities of the American Peace Corps. I received the reply I expected, which was: nothing at all! There was much good will, and, in his view, even heroism in the work; but the overall concept was naïve. How would these students be capable of organizing something in a country which was so old and so different? Besides, America was on the whole on a lower cultural level than India if you understood culture as self-restraint. When I myself did not desist from speaking somewhat critically about the Indian intellectuals, among whom I only seldom met an orthodox Hindu, it was explained to me, with expansive gestures, that Hinduism came in many forms and that even atheism was one of them. On the day of my farewell from the Osmania University my philosophy professor gave me a nicely printed page with the "Prayer of a Moslem" which he had written himself.

On the flight to Madras I got a newspaper into my hand after several weeks of abstinence. The topic dominating the headlines was: the border conflict with the Chinese. The imploring words of the head of Government, Nehru, were almost biblical: "We must keep our loins girt!" The slogan of the soldiers, now almost tenderly called "Privates," was now, according to the lead article: Blood for blood! Presumably no soldier on the front had ever said such a thing. At the front in the icy snow fields of the Himalayas, four thousand meters high, there were obviously completely different worries. For example, you urgently needed warm clothing. And the population was called on to contribute. In fact, for a time, I even saw among my listeners people who were knitting industriously, and not just women; of course, just for a while, for after a few weeks there was no more wool in the whole of India.

I asked competent people what the Chinese had in mind with this completely unexpected attack: did they want to overrun the whole subcontinent? — which doubtless would not have been impossible to them. Oh no, was the answer, they just wanted to prove one thing, which the whole world immediately understood: that India was not capable of playing the role to which, since the Bandung Conference (1955), with partly successful rhetoric they had laid claim, of being a leading Asian power. However, as expected, the confidence in victory loudly reported in the press and in street demonstrations was not to be shaken; again and again there were reports about examples of heroic willingness to make sacrifices. Individual groups demanded that the Diwali Festival of Lights should not be celebrated and that money assigned to that be given to the war effort. However, the Hindu people ignored such unrealistic suggestions, luckily for me. After all, I had come to Madras because of this festival. As I found out, it bore hardly any resemblance to the Durga Festival which had echoed through the streets for weeks. Nobody, for example, was in a position to say anything about the point of the festival apart from the fact that it was a Festival of Lights. The biggest difference was that Diwali was less a public than a household festival. The ritual required that the festival take place before dawn, so that you did not notice any of it during the day. I left my hotel room shortly after four o'clock in the morning and went down the creaking wooden stairs; on the lowest landing the night watchman was stretching as he awoke and, with an indulgent gesture, shooed away a rat, which had been niggling at his ear and which now, in no particular hurry, hopped past me up the steps. Clearly, for Indians — and I had noticed this before — the rat was not an animal which caused Indians any sort of revulsion; rather it was viewed with the kind of friendly tolerance we have towards squirrels; and, besides, in Hindu mythology the rat was the animal ridden by a goddess.

On the dark street the Cultural Attaché and his wife awaited me in the Consulate car. They accompanied me through the city, which was secretly livened up from time to time with musicians and children carrying lights, to the professor of the Sanskrit Faculty who had invited us to his house to celebrate with him. There the festival was well underway, maybe even since midnight; we took our shoes off spontaneously and stepped somewhat blinded into the room, which was fully lit with shining lights. The host, fresh from the bath and with his bare upper body shining with oil, greeted us with ceremonious gravity and introduced us to his wife and children. The dark black loose hair of the youngest daughter, an unusually charming fourteen-year-old, was almost down to the backs of her knees; its thick fullness, parted in the middle by a thin braid, was clasped again down low with a band of blossoms. They showed us the house altar and explained it to us. On it, of course, the Lingam had its place; and again and again, while we consumed the sweets they offered us, short ritual acts were performed which the man of the house explained to us each time, not without a certain verbose, demonstrative pride. He had a small brass container filled with water brought to him, and his family formed a half circle in front of him. Silently, he first sprinkled himself with the water and drank some of it; after that he sprinkled his family and poured a little into each person's palm so that it would be drunk immediately. I was relieved that the guests were not included in this celebration because, as I had already guessed, it was water brought from the Ganges which was hundreds of kilometers away. It even came from a place far into the north, as was immediately explained to us, where a similarly holy river flowed into the Ganges — for which reason the water had a special efficaciousness and had not been cheap to deliver. The question which I had asked many times but for which I had not yet received an answer — about what the "holiness" of the Ganges meant, and what constituted it — was ignored again. However, there was plenty to ask and there were plenty of answers. Then we noticed after a while that the bench on which we were sitting and which took in almost the whole width of the living room, had no feet, but was hung up on thick hemp ropes, and was therefore a swing; then I noticed that the man of the house, while drinking his coffee, ostentatiously avoided touching the edge of the cup with his lips; this was an old Hindu custom, which required dexterity and also allowed many to use the same drinking vessel. Our host told us this in a slightly pedantic teaching tone and also, as we then immediately saw, that he was able to empty a dish full of water with his bare hand without spilling a drop, in such a way that it was finally completely dry and a second dish filled. When we were leaving, since Diwali was a festival of giving, we were all given a small valuable item; I was given a folded stole, artistically woven from the finest cloth into an unbelievably narrow band with gold embroidered borders; the woman of the house took it from the altar table and laid it around my neck with a charming gesture. And still I went back to my hotel with the ambivalent feeling that I had taken part in a type of performance rather than in a religious ceremony. At the hotel, the owner, on whose forehead the white sign of Shiva was freshly painted, greeted me with the festival wish: Happy Deepavali! Perhaps I ought to have celebrated the festival with him?

During that night of ceremonies I was sometimes disinterested. Now and then a somewhat puzzling encounter invaded my consciousness, about which I achieved clarity the following day. On my first visit to the Consulate I had been introduced to a secretary and had the distinct feeling that I knew her from somewhere; these boldly curved black eyebrows were simply familiar to me. On the other hand, there was no possible doubt that I was seeing this young girl with the typical Indian family name for the first time. So I gave the matter no more thought and did not bother mentioning it. On the way to the meal, however, my companion casually spoke about the mother of his secretary, a German-born woman, who, with much success, had founded a type of Odenwald school in the city and had recently won the Goethe Medal for it. When I then asked for the maiden name of the woman, the face with those eyebrows immediately came into my mind, although the story still seemed too improbable to me. In the mid-twenties I was attending a fairly boring art history lecture with two or three friends — for no other reason than to see a particularly attractive female student in the half-full auditorium whose beauty was a little different. Quite often we accompanied her on her half-hour walk home; of course, we did not address her. Sometimes we even went over to the other side of the street. We did not intend anything serious with her, and after one or two semesters we did not see the beauty anymore. She herself had noticed none of this admiration, as became clear at the quickly organized visit for tea in Madras. But the woman, still very charming, was visibly delighted to hear this story with all the details I could remember, and particularly with her husband present. However, she was somewhat surprised to hear she had been recognized through her daughter, and she looked for a wedding photo in which a somewhat older daughter was to be seen, about whom everyone held the view that she was really like her mother. In fact, I then felt I was actually looking at the Münster student herself, made even more beautiful by the glorious Indian wedding dress. Now it was her turn to tell me what remarkable affinity had led her to this distant land. So I found out, to my surprise — something that we could never have guessed forty years before — that she, the granddaughter of a Dorpat Indologist, had always secretly brought into the University exams, in her handbag, a small ivory figure of the elephant-shaped Hindu God of luck. When I was leaving she gave me a figurine just like it.

A completely new field of vision was opened up for me in another meeting, again unexpectedly, and similarly with a young German. The woman, who had been awarded her Doctorate of Art History, belonged to a religious community of like-minded people and, although not a nun, had with amazing courage accepted a call from the bishop of Madras, who was looking for a person to run a center — which had not yet been founded — for cultural and social work. Shortly before that, after my lecture in the University of Madras, the lecturer for German, who was also still young — an Indian who had become a Catholic during her studies in Germany — spoke to me. To her kind compliment that there was rarely anything to be heard from Germans on a theme like "contemplation" she added the complaint about her almost complete isolation. German intellectuals, she said, were hardly interested in religious matters at all and were uneducated in theology, and the Indian Catholics simply lived in closed groups according to whether they were from Kerala or Goa. So I was not altogether surprised when the art historian, having barely started to chat with me, very directly and in a tone of an almost definitive resignation, claimed that the much vaunted German-Indian dialog was not taking place at all, despite all the guest performances of orchestras and theater groups — because Indians can really only be addressed on the religious level. How little this happened where you could justifiably have expected it I had experienced a number of times. The congregations were kept silent, although the passionate praying gestures still let you know how much was missing for them in the routinely rushed Sunday Mass, whether the celebrant was Indian or not. I experienced a moving, and, at the same time, annoying confirmation of all of that on a Tuesday afternoon visit to the parish church of St. Anthony. The doctor from Bonn had warned me expressly that it had to be a Tuesday, since this weekday was specially an Anthony day, which I remembered from my childhood. And in fact the approach roads clearly announced the proximity of the place of worship itself even before it was visible: there were stalls filled with colorful garlands of flowers; there was a hardly broken chain of beggars at the side of the streets; in the proliferation of cheap devotional objects there was an indiscriminate array of tiny brass Lingams, Shiva figures with bouquets of roses, the cheapest representations of Christ, and oil prints with the picture of Anthony of Padua and other Christian saints. On the church square there were several hundred people mostly sitting on the ground, some of them since the evening before; all held their gifts ready and waited for the church to open. "Who are those people and what are they doing here?" The parish priest, who, looking at his watch, had just stepped out of his apartment, answered — not without a hint of moroseness — that they were mostly non-Christians, therefore Hindus, who saw in Anthony something of a miracle-working deity and now brought overwhelming amounts of flowers to the image, wanting to make sure of its help in this way. He said it was exceedingly difficult to contain the impending onslaught. I was let into the still empty church through a side door, and then I saw the pilgrims passing by the Anthony statue; with a fervent gesture each one passed his bouquet to a waiting sacristan who laid it at Anthony's feet. While the procession went on seemingly without end, I went out pensively and again wondered why they could not work into the liturgical celebration of the Mass such an elemental desire for physical expression of veneration and offering. While, at Mass, bread and wine were being brought as an offering and the monetary contributions of the community collected, what would be wrong if, at the same time, at the steps of the altar a mountain of fragrant blooms were to appear?

How necessary it was for these people to use their limbs in a gesture of prayer was made surprisingly clear to me again in Madras during a visit to a famous school of dance led by the still extremely beautiful Rukmini Devi. She had started out as a pupil of the almost mythical Anna Pavlova, but had long since returned to the strict tradition of old Indian dance. The most wonderful performances of her group, which was known in the capitals of the world, she told me were not seen by the public: the prayer for inspiration was danced before the image of Shiva behind the closed curtain.

There were other amazing things to see and to hear throughout the huge park of divided pavilions of this school. In a small open hall two dancers were practicing — with sweat running in streams down their naked upper bodies — a dramatic scene from one of the big epics: one of them had got food from far away for his starving village, but was satisfying his hunger secretly and ravenously from the full basket, while the second one was hidden, but was watching him in extreme anger. What was happening was unquestionably clear to everyone; but there was no basket, nor did the one hungrily eating open his mouth; and the other one expressed his violent displeasure only through a vehement twitch around his eyes, moving face muscles over which the rest of us would have no control at all. The eighty-five-year-old teacher, highly respected — as I already knew — in the whole of India as a master of precisely this type of dance, explained to me perhaps not without exaggeration that anyone who could not tell a story without speaking a word and tied hand and foot would not be considered a good dancer — not in this country. On leaving, I asked Madame Rukmini Devi if what I had heard was true — something which had seemed improbable to me — namely, that the sound of specific forms of music for the Indian listener, even for not particularly expert ones, brought to mind with complete clarity a definite season and even a time of day, for example: "six o'clock in the morning, in spring." The answer came somewhat hesitantly; more recently these things were gradually fading from experience; still, she said, once when at a wedding celebration the music and hour exactly corresponded for everyone listening, the impression was completely overwhelming; indeed, such extremely time-linked music created the feeling that one was situated completely outside of time. That is what I felt as soon as it was described to me.

Fortunately there was always someone who more or less drastically expelled you from such an enchanted garden back into the real world. This time it was a Singhalese driver, who drove me in the German Embassy's Mercedes through the tropical richness of the island of Sri Lanka, which at that time was still called Ceylon. Almost by chance I had gone deeply into the south through a casually made appointment during that remarkable festival meal in Calcutta, at which I had tried in vain to make myself intelligible to Günter Eich. It surprised me a little that my driver, an intelligent and well-educated man, who admittedly, at first, in his long buttoned coat seemed to come from an exotically colored and distant world, introduced himself to me as an "Arian," which of course I was also; but I took it as a somewhat clumsy joke. When he then, however, pointed to the South Indian Tamils at the edge of the village, and clearly expecting my complete agreement, spoke of an "Eichmann" who was needed here to clear the island of these inferior beings, then it became immediately evident again how the world in which we were living really was. It did not please my Singhalese very much that I simply ignored his remark as if I had not heard it and instead of that asked his opinion about Buddha. Some days before, I had heard a well-traveled famous Buddhist monk speak about Nirvana ("Why Nibbana?"), in a discussion group which met regularly, to which the embassies represented in Colombo used to invite speakers in turn. This time the hosts were the Ambassador of Ghana — a Protestant pastor, as I later found out. It came about that he was the only one who, besides me, refused to accept "bliss" as meaningful or even imaginable when it essentially included the notion that nobody was left who had this bliss. Precisely this, however, so the speaker explained, was the meaning of "Nirvana." More amazing to me, however, were the aggressive phrases reminiscent of Voltaire which were introduced at the beginning and which the man, dressed in his saffron-colored religious habit, employed to treat with irony the idea of God. This idea, he said, was completely foreign to Buddhism — for which reason no real Buddhist would hold the Buddha for any kind of divine being. But on our trip we had just left the huge place of worship, which could only be characterized as a temple, which was erected in Candy over a tooth of Buddha — and therefore over a relic. Although having only the least understanding of the language of human gestures, it was impossible to characterize the activity and fuss of the innumerable people who were dressed for celebration and were crowding into the temple to offer their gifts as anything other than veneration and worship. And who else should that be meant for if not for Buddha? And after, contrary to my unenlightened expectation, I had hardly met one Buddhist in India, I asked my driver what the people and he himself thought about Buddha and what type of being he was. The car stopped with a jolt; and the answer sounded almost horrified: "Buddha? That is God!" So if the monk was right, then it appeared that the "real" Buddhists were quite rare.

How much the unplanned trip to Ceylon disturbed the very carefully arranged travel plans of the German Embassy only became clear to me when the Cultural Attaché, who had come to the airport, offered me two remaining choices, both already halfway prepared and expressly thought out. The airplane had arrived hours late in New Delhi; it was almost midnight, and again I had to admire the enormous self-discipline of the professional diplomat who spoke with quiet friendliness and without any hurry, as if we were sitting together over a glass of wine. He even took time to tell me about his stay in Vienna, where he had become friendly with Reinhold Schneider in whose "Winter in Vienna" he had sometimes been mentioned under the code "K"; he assumed, as quite a few other people did, that Reinhold Schneider and I must have been particularly close, whereas in reality we had never met. So the two possibilities: either once again to carry out an unplanned excursion, perhaps to Nepal, which would not be difficult, or to be taken through the sights of the capital and its environs in the retinue of the German President who was expected on a state visit. For the next few days no one from the embassy would be available to look after me personally. Of course, I immediately decided on Nepal. When we finally got out of the car in front of the hotel my companion raised his hand: "Do you hear that?" The noise of the street was almost completely silent; and what you heard were remarkably high-pitched wails; I firstly guessed that it was a technical sound. "No, those are the jackals!" "Jackals? I thought that we were in the middle of the city of New Delhi?" "Yes, but the jungle is all around; and the jackals, which unlike hyenas are completely harmless, come out at night and roam through the streets in innumerable packs and rummage through the litter. They keep contact with one another through their wailing." Then my companion went ahead into the house, inspected my reserved room, and then conjured from the briefcase a bottle of Norman Calvados. "You will need that for Benares!" It sounded like a warning. But it was not yet time for Benares; firstly there was Nepal.

On the first day of the state visit I sat in the narrow waiting room of a small airport from which once a day a twin-motor propeller plane flew to Kathmandu, the capital of Nepal. While I was enjoying the feeling that, yet again, as a total stranger I was on the way into the completely unknown, suddenly someone addressed me by name. It was one of my students from my first American semester in Notre Dame. Having meantime advanced to becoming some sort of Peace Corps inspector, he was just returning from visiting his people in Nepal. He said that in this country, which at that time was hardly "accessible," there were only three possible ways to travel: by jeep, on a mule, or on foot. That was fine with me. A fellow traveler had overheard our conversation; he immediately introduced himself as the owner of my hotel in Kathmandu and boasted to me about the advantages of his establishment.

As it turned out, you could, in fact, see Mount Everest from the window — just the highest peak of the summit admittedly — in the middle of the glacial landscape; and also there were names I knew from reading as a child: Annapurna, Gaurisankar, etc. Otherwise my "room with a bath" was adventurously primitive. The spirit stove under the worn-out carbide barrel was hardly capable of heating its contents and before the water had the bath half-filled through the soldered-in tap it was already cold again. So, shivering with the cold, I ordered a hot water bottle for the bed. I was all the more surprised when next morning, with my first look out the window, I saw palm trees, bananas, and fruit-laden citrus trees. The people on the street were happily enjoying the midday warmth of the protected high valley; a grandfather was using a carrying frame like weighing scales, one side packed full of pottery, and on the other was his beaming grandchild, and he went laughing on his way to the market. Young women, busy with the shelling of pods, had taken their clothes off as far as the hips and offered themselves without embarrassment to the sun's rays. Even those carrying the loads, although groaning under the weight they were bearing using cords stretched across their foreheads, were wearing highly attractive jewellery: with every step their split skirts gaped almost up to the backs of the knees and a filigree type of fine tattoo was to be seen on their naked calves. Besides jeeps and animals there was thankfully the rickshaw; and so I was able to see quite a lot of the hustle and bustle of the market in the city — with its almost six hundred temples — and even of the numerous shrines in the surrounding area. The amount of honored deities appeared to be legion; and clearly they were not too exact about it; so I discovered among the images of deities an Art Nouveau "Flora," who surely at some stage had adorned the steps of a commercial villa; but she too was honored with the red mark on her forehead, the same as Shiva. At a nighttime temple celebration to which I had walked quite a long way with hundreds of pilgrims there were fairly strict regulations. They looked at my camera with a gesture of rejection and denied me access at the gate; but it gradually dawned on me was that it was not the camera but just the leather bag; it implied the killing of a "sacred cow." For more than an hour, I walked through the rows of people camping outside and the throngs singing and feasting in the light of torches which were also warming them, and finally, under a sky bespangled with stars which seemed unbelievably near I went home on my rick-shaw.

In Nepal at that time (1962) there was as yet no printed or illustrated brochure for tourists. Still, a few hectographed pages drew your attention to what would be worth seeing. Here there was mention of the "living goddess" who now and then showed herself to visitors. I myself, of course, even by the second-to-last day of my visit, had still not seen her. So I went to His Majesty's Government of Nepal Tourist Office and stated my wish with a certain amount of urgency. Immediately a ten- to twelve-year-old boy was summoned to accompany me. We entered into the small inner courtyard of the temple of the goddess where an old woman was hanging out washing. After a short conversation with the boy, in a loud voice and with no hint of respect she shouted something up to the upper floor. And shortly after that a girl of about four years old appeared on the covered balcony, dressed festively and wearing a lot of make-up; looking somewhat bored she raised her hand, clearly in greeting, and soon withdrew again. The assured seriousness with which this child was viewed and venerated as a genuine goddess was for me simply horrifying. On several occasions it had been said to me with pride that, while Tibet only had the Dalai Lama, a mere "incarnation" of the Buddha, Nepal was the only country in the world where a living deity existed in person. Meantime I knew that by means of a really crude method of testing among the three- to four-year-old girls of distinguished families the chosen one was usually found and then declared a goddess. She was isolated from all natural company of parents, siblings, and friends, and brought to the temple whose upper floor she could not leave from now on because her foot could not touch the ground again, apart from going once a year to a festive parade through the city — until the end of her childhood was signaled by her first menstrual period, and a new "living goddess" had to be sought and would, of course, also be found. Until that point, day after day, for eight to ten years, a specially chosen "priest" carried out a ritual in her honor; even the king appeared for it once a month. In New Delhi I sought information about the later fate of the "goddesses" from a person who had expert knowledge of Nepalese traditions. The information was shattering: no man wanted to marry a goddess, not even someone who had been one; so these girls could consider themselves lucky if — as did happen now and then — an American family adopted them; often enough, however, the end was prostitution. On my return to the hotel, when in pure innocence I spoke spontaneously to my host about the "poor girls," to my complete amazement this widely traveled man, married to a Canadian, was wounded in his "holiest feelings."

For Benares — that was how it was called when I was greeted that night in New Delhi — I would need the Calvados. Of course, the whys and wherefores were not totally beyond my imagination. And when I stepped out of the hotel and a dozen rickshaw drivers stormed up to me, all of whom wanted to bring me to the "dead bodies," I remembered the sentence which I had heard many times: the Hindu went to Benares, if possible, to die at the banks of the holy Ganges which would then immediately take his ashes. But I wanted to take my time in exploring this city, which I already knew was incomparable. Besides, I had some duties. The times and places for my guest lectures still had to be agreed with the university, which was situated quite far away from the city. And soon I began to suspect that the publicity of these events had been consciously reduced so as not to endanger the orthodoxy of the students; after all, this was the Benares Hindu University. But then the crowd and the interest were such that, beyond what was planned, three partly public symposia were spontaneously organized; the topics arose from the discussions which followed each lecture. It was left to me to give the precise formulation of the subject matter; and, of course, I had in mind to learn a lot from this, although I had only partial success. I had, for example, read in Radhakrishnan that an orthodox Hindu was one who accepted the Vedas as revelation, as *shruti*; and I wanted a precise definition of the concept of *shruti*, which literally means "that which is heard."

The spacious office which the professor of Sanskrit had made available to me was over-full and I had to step over stored materials to reach the chair which was put there for me. From a corner, a little cloud of smoke smelling of sandalwood was rising. On the seat of honor, dressed in white and with his feet pulled up under him, was a long-bearded south Indian Sadhu, about whom the host said he had all the verses of the Rig-Veda in his head. To begin with he wanted to recite a hymn in the old form of incantation. He started, of course, with the specially long drawn-out holy syllable OM, and then he beat the rhythm of the archaic text with his hands. The atmosphere crackled with suspense. I was next with my question about what it really meant to call the Vedas a document of revelation. The answer brought many voices into the discussion: everything known is basically "revelation." The Vedas are just a special case. I then wanted to know in what way they were special. For a long time the discussion raged back and forth; there was no clarification in sight. At last I asked if the Vedas had the same authority as a physics textbook. The answer: Yes! Here I made an attempt in a roundabout way to achieve clarity by means of an analogy: there was clearly a difference between the veneration you showed your mother or your teacher and the veneration shown to the God Shiva. The answer: No, there was no difference! I went back again to Radhakrishnan: How can you speak of orthodoxy at all and differentiate it from heterodoxy? The answer: There is no such difference! Somewhat despairingly I gave up and ended the conversation. There was only a point in holding a discussion if differences were acknowledged and retained. Overheated by the discussion, we suddenly found ourselves standing outside in a small circle, where it became clear that the Europeans were all together in a group; there was an American there and he felt that he belonged with us. A young Sanskrit researcher from Poland threw out the angry remark that in the concrete practical things like caste division there was very strict differentiation. And a Belgian Jesuit added: "Oh, and when a person becomes a Christian suddenly it is in no way all the same!" In fact, it was strange — and I had thought that many times — that in all the discussions in this country no Indian person had ever posed the question about how Christians saw things. On the other hand, it made you wonder when you heard that the very close relationship between America and Communist Russia was hardly noticeable to people in the "West" but was clear from an Indian perspective.

Much more exciting and also more convincing than all the academic discussion was the city of Benares itself. Admittedly it needed to be embraced with all the senses; above all, you had to smell it. For that reason you could only sympathize with the organized groups of travelers who climbed into the limousines standing by in front of the hotel. In the showcases of the hotel I found a perfume recommended, which was called Morning in Benares. Somewhat skeptically, I wondered what smells would have had to be mixed together in the perfume if it were really to reflect reality: the freshness of the early fog from the Ganges, the smell of the camels, but particularly the spicy smell of smoke which came not only from the thousand burning sandalwood sticks of the wayside shrines and street altars, not only from the innumerable open fireplaces of the houses kept burning with cow dung, but also from the funeral pyres of the dead which were blazing day and night.

I seldom went through the city by rickshaw without meeting a group of people bringing a corpse to the cremation site.

You could hardly call them funeral corteges; often it was just two expressly hired men who, with a business-like lack of ceremony, carried on their shoulders two strong bamboo poles to which the body, wrapped in a cloth, was fastened. Once I passed another rickshaw on which two young men were have a lively chat together; but between them stood, as I then realised with shock, the bamboo rods, similarly loaded, leaning against the seat.

At the cremation site, the now evident finality of the "last act" and particularly the closeness of the holy river necessitated greater ritual gravity, even though the brutality of the process could not remain concealed from anyone. With horror you saw now and then a stray dog that knew how to scavenge. There was always a delay until a fireplace became free and a new funeral pyre was built up. The dead, sometimes four or five of them at a time, rested in the meantime on the steps leading down into the Ganges, with the stream already washing against their feet. The regular, beautiful face of an old woman was, contrary to the usual tradition, uncovered; her bright blue sari was decorated with floral wreaths and small bouquets. One of her sons was preparing a last rice dish on a tiny fire lit beside her; another, still very young, showed me, in a white linen bag, a few grains of gold which were to be placed in the mouth of the deceased. When the funeral pyre was prepared, the blooms and wreaths were carefully placed on the surface of the water of the Ganges, which carried them slowly away. Then the eldest son, who had in his hand a sheaf of reeds already glowing like a torch, stepped several times around the pyre, pausing each time at the head of the dead, and lowered the flame until it almost touched the face. Only after that did he light the pyre.

In the city of Benares the banks of the Ganges bordered by temples and cremation sites radiated something so strong and almost sensually palpable that you were hardly able to avoid it. And I did not want to do so; and so I spent many hours there, a not completely disinterested onlooker, and tried to take in whatever was happening. Today I sometimes ask myself if the "year of the dead" which still lay before me would have been too much for me had it not been for these experiences.

Of course, I did not just visit funeral pyres. Anything but. Right along the glistening surface, as far as the eye could see, the Ganges did appear to transform people a little. Already at sunrise you saw them making a pilgrimage to the river with measured steps and very upright, a bouquet of blooms around their necks, a brass pot in their hands, reciting prayers, and totally imperturbable. And at dusk you still saw in the evenings countless people sitting on the steps, motionless, sunk in meditation. Some had descended a few steps into the river and were putting hand-sized rafts made of plaited leaves with a light on them into the gentle undulating stream; and again you heard them praying while doing this. The prayers were, as I knew from Pierre Fallon in Calcutta, for the most part not requests, but words of praise for the divine power. There was more than enough superstition, as was to be expected. And the actions of the ascetics often seemed simply absurd. I saw one who repeatedly brought a bamboo cudgel crashing down on his head; he was already reeling and was nearly falling over. Another whose naked body was covered in grey ashes was pulling, with a rope behind him, quite a heavy looking shrine made of metal and on wheels; as he was at the same time using both hands to hold a container on his head it was not clear how it was working — until I noticed, horrified, that there was a type of meat hook stuck in his back to which the rope was attached. For me as a European, the fact that these religious people begged and did nothing became more and more of a problem. On the other hand, when I sent away a well-fed young man who hung around me and constantly repeated that he was "holy, but poor" with the brusque words: "Holy man must work" — I found myself, to my subsequent surprise, unexpectedly embroiled in the old mendicant debate and thought of the arguments brought by Thomas of Aquinas in the defense of the mendicant order.

But leaving all reasoning aside, you are always fascinated anew when religious feeling is simply lived out. On one of my last evenings in Benares, stumbling in the dark, I chanced on the sound of an individual singing voice, which, as it turned out, was coming from a poor hovel, a storeroom. I opened the gap of the roughly timbered door and someone came out immediately and compelled me to take a seat on a box inside. Clearly not altogether sober, he whispered to me several times: "here is God, but not China!" The enemy attacker at the Himalayan border had meantime become a total nightmare. There were between ten and twelve men sitting in the room, which was only lit by a single candle. They were all simple folk, perhaps burden carriers, who were quietly listening to a singer accompanying himself with a type of rattle; from time to time one or two hand drums sounded from the darkness near me. I asked my neighbor what was being sung. He listened for a while and said: "God, you are always yourself; and the world is before you like a two-day game!"

The danger from China was also a topic of conversation when I eventually met with the Catholic bishop. Here I also heard something authentic about the Second Vatican Council which had recently begun. The bishop himself had been too sick to take part in it, which perhaps explained his deep pessimism in the assessment not just of the military situation, but also of the hopes of the Christian mission. "Anyone who becomes a Catholic here is a hero; I admire him." I was reminded of a statement by Pierre Fallon and again, for my part, admired the courage of the missionaries. When we came to speak about the border conflict with China the bishop looked really worried; he talked about a senior officer with the border troops who told his family that they should prepare to evacuate.

Meantime the newspapers were full of heroic rhetoric; and there were already some measures in force which drastically affected the individual. For example, to save fuel, inland flights were almost entirely canceled.

So one evening I traveled to New Delhi by train. In the sleeping car I shared a cabin with a senior security police officer; his name and rank could be read on his suitcase. The breakfast was respectfully brought to us in the compartment with the morning newspaper. I anticipated a discussion about the situation in the Himalayas; but then, completely out of the blue, the officer asked me: "What do you think about life after death?" This reminded me that I was still not quite free of Benares.

When you leave the dense atmosphere of this unique community with its throngs of people, Delhi seems at first to be not so much a city as an extensive landscape over which the inhabitants actually say "seven Delhis" are scattered, and on whose area a mammoth city like Los Angeles could be accommodated. This time I was accommodated in the International Center from which I looked out on the Lodi Park, an area with a thin scattering of tombs and old trees allowing of wide vistas such as you could not imagine existing in Benares. As soon as it was dark, herds of jackals romped in front of my window, their dreadful howls continuing through the night. For my few remaining days I had been presented by the German Embassy with an almost too full sight-seeing program which, besides New Delhi and Old Delhi, Ara and the Taj Mahal, also included the grave of the great Akbar. Meantime, however, I was at a stage where saturation point had almost been reached. Still, I set out on my travels again, somewhat tired and with a good measure of serenity. Then, confronted with something completely new, the delight which, as Chesterton said, is intrinsic to all experience was enkindled afresh. Compared to all I had seen until now the new was really spectacular. On this round trip we visited nothing but tombs. Tombs are completely un-Indian or more exactly un-Hindu. This came as a surprise to some foreigners, particularly at the point where, unsuspectingly, they inquired about Gandhi's grave. Of course, his corpse had been cremated, and all that was to be seen was the piece of ground which this special funeral pyre had covered for an hour — perhaps like other funeral pyres before it. Still, many years later, the place had been made recognizable by means of a black marble stone, which, of course, was not a tombstone. Wherever you come across real graves in India they are Moslem graves. And tombs, as works of architecture, are always signs of Moslem rule. Mostly they are, even in their size alone, of a magnificence with which hardly anything in the Western world compares. And yet the impression is not only one of colossal size; the often immense square surrounding the actual gravesite is always softened and literally "tempered" to a measured form, while in the inner room the blossoming diversity of the forms and shapes seems absolutely inexhaustible. In Sikandra under the perfectly shaped cupola exactly at the intersection of the axes pointing from gate to gate in the four directions of the compass stands the snow white sarcophagus made from one piece of marble, which looks less like the ton weight block which it is than like a carved network of feather-light ornaments. The shrine contained, they thought, the corpse of Akbar the Great; but then you were directed to the crypt, in which perpendicularly under the first sarcophagus there was a second one, also a perfect work of stonemasonry; and under that again, deep in the ground, was the real grave of the descendant of Tamerlane. A strangely moving thing for me was my first sight of the Taj Mahal, the most famous of all Indian tombs. It was one of the obligatory tourist attractions — for which reason I had almost neglected traveling to it. Before that, my knowledgeable companion had led me to a "fort," a similarly admirable example of Islamic architecture. From a narrow tower room of this fortress where he was imprisoned for life, the builder of the Taj Mahal was allowed to look at the tomb of his beloved wife which was visible from afar — in a mirror which was fixed to the outer wall of the tower. And for the first time I saw the extremely famous construction in this mirror, with the terrible story giving me food for thought. And shortly afterwards, when I went over to it, the way it presented itself in the glistening sunshine made me lose all trace of snobbery; and the mere attempt to describe this incomprehensible juxtaposition of simplicity and splendor disarmed the viewer and rendered him silent.

At the end of the Indian trip I had a fine meal with Italian red wine: at the residence of the Papal Nuncio. The *chargé d'affaires* was the host; the Nuncio himself was in Rome at the Second Vatican Council. Again there was some first-hand news: Pope John was very ill; a date for his operation had been set for immediately after the Vatican Council and the cardinals were asked not to leave. They did not yet know that the solemn final session would take place three years later under a new pope.

My assumption that there would still be tropical heat in Delhi in December proved to be completely wrong. So my return to the north German winter would not be a completely sudden change of climate, and the stopover in Egypt as a transition would not have been necessary at all. But my wife and I had just decided on it. And again the old experience that something completely superfluous can be really fine proved true again. For me, in any case, the infinitely relaxing walk through another strange world — that of Luxor, Karnak and the Valley of the Kings — was as refreshing as a deep sleep.

All of these things of beauty floated one by one past the eyes of your soul as if you were seeing them from behind a pane of glass; at the same time, I noticed how another person at my side devoured things never seen before with a virginal ability to be amazed.

Two days before Christmas we set off home on different flight routes, one via Athens and Vienna and the other via Vienna and Brussels. But when I arrived in Düsseldorf, my wife, exactly according to plan, had landed fifteen minutes earlier and was already waiting for me with the children.

XV

What is a University? — My reader John XXIII
— The "Year of the Dead" begins — Departure
to East Asia – "Where is Gloria?" — Japan and
the Nô play — "Face to face with my enemy" —
Saigon: All Souls 1963 — Wonderful Thailand
— The return home of my son

The turn of the year 1962/3; the first half of the lecture-free
sabbatical semester is used up; the other, like a blank sheet
with nothing written on it, lies in front of me. I was impatient
to use this time for the writing of the "Theory of Festivals"
which had been going through my mind for twenty years. In
two winter lectures I had managed a preliminary formulation
of it, and the experiences which had sparked the thesis which
now needed pinning down, stretched from a sinister military
"Christmas celebration" in the war, through Corpus Christi
in Toledo, to the big Hindu festivals in Calcutta and Madras.
However, my usual meditative "pencil sharpening" phase of
preparation was interrupted by another necessary job which
was also close to my heart.

In our country at that time universities were being
founded. It was a new undertaking with far-reaching consequences. As was to be expected, the question about the meaning of the university as an institution was posed with hitherto
unknown urgency. Immediately, of course, conflicting ideas
came to the fore. In the hall of the Bochum Kammerspiele, for
example, one of the initiators of the "Ruhr University" which
was now being built put forward as an absolute requirement

that in this day and age only the exact sciences should define the face of the university. When I returned from India there was an express letter awaiting me from the Bishop of Essen appealing to me, as soon as possible, in a public speech in the same place, to oppose this challenge — where he himself was planning to be the organizer. To his complete surprise I assented only on condition that I would not be speaking as a representative of the Church or at any event organized by the Bishop, but that I would only speak for myself as J.P. Of course, the slight friction which this caused was cleared up in good humor in a personal conversation. And so in the first month of the year, in the overfilled Bochum Kammerspiele, I tried to expound the Western idea of the university as I understood it. As I went into the theater I noticed in the darkness the radio recording-car; of course, none other than Carl Linfert had sent it over.

"Openness to the totality of things": this title clearly formulated a claim, but not one to be insisted on. It was a claim you were to face and to deal with. I particularly wanted to make it plausible to the audience that only the philosophical view took the whole of reality into account and that, furthermore, in the words of John Henry Newman, it would be simply unphilosophical to shut theology out of the university. It was clear that the applause given to such ideas unfortunately did not mean much in the face of subsequent events. The turbulence of the late sixties, in which the inner fabric of the university was to be shaken to its foundations, still lay in the future; and even today (1978) no one is really in a position to see what will develop. Of course, it is comforting that no one knows where words seemingly spoken in the wind might eventually be carried by the same wind.

A few days after the Bochum lecture I retreated to the cloister of my garden house, wrote the title "Consent to the world" on the first page of the manuscript, and in one session wrote *opusculum*, which had for so long lain dormant. Its theory: to celebrate a feast meant on a special occasion performing and showing, in a not everyday fashion, one's already established affirmation of the world and of existence. When I returned from my second Asia trip in the late autumn, the first copy of the small book lay on my desk. There was as yet no talk of this trip at all. In an amazingly short time the friendly inspiration of my Japanese publisher turned into a lecture tour which would lead me to a half a dozen countries east of India. But quite a lot happened before that.

After the unexpectedly laborious drudgery of writing the book I had traveled with my wife to a southern sunny beach for a quick break before the beginning of the semester. We were hardly back when Antonius, my brother from Fulda, arrived at the house; in keeping with the custom of the Münster region we used to call him "Tönne." We were really surprised to hear that he was just dropping by from the nearby University Clinic where he was seeking therapeutic advice; the urologist however, one of his peers, had advised a thorough check-up which would take its time. The matter seemed to be not particularly serious. The day before Easter — in the Spring — we took a pensive stroll together in the garden of the clinic, and no-one could have known that it was to be the last walk of his life. But it happened that a good three weeks after that his eldest daughter and my youngest son, his godchild — both students of the University of Münster — spoke the prayers for the dying at his bedside.

Pope John died on 3 June 1963, hardly a month later. It was an excruciatingly long and at the same time terribly public death. I was thinking of his wonderful words which, later, beside Sartre's dreadful sentence about the absurdity both of being born and of dying, would serve as an appropriate heading to my small book about *Death and immortality*: "Every day is a good day to be born; every day is a good day to die."

And also the audience in Saint Peter's Basilica came to my mind. I had been there with Monika and Michael in the spring of 1961 without any premonition of the future. The Regensburg Cathedral Boys' Choir were guests and had sung a song at the beginning, after which the Pope, with vigorous gestures and not heeding the microphone which was erected in front of him, spoke about singing: the Church was a lover who was always singing; even the Requiem was also song. Strangely I felt a certain personal bond with this Pope, which, at that time, I was only partially aware of. In Morcote at Lake Lugano where, on 28 October 1958, with my wife and Hilde Schürk-Frisch I heard about the decision of the cardinals I said spontaneously and with a certain disappointment: "Dear God, that is such an old Pope!" Both of them asked: "How do you know?" So I told them about the last trip I had been on with my friend Schranz. In September 1957 we had wanted to go by boat from Venice to Athens and then on to Rhodes. The Venetian summer morning was so wonderfully clear that we decided to have, not just our luggage, but also our coats and jackets, sent on to the ship which was to leave in the evening. But then we were surprised in the early afternoon by a violent storm. Already feeling very shivery, we sneaked around the arcades of Saint Mark's Square during the endless roaring downpour, and luckily we discovered there an Indian art exhibition, the opening celebration of which was just beginning. A little embarrassed but not put off, we stepped into the clearly exclusive circle of invited guests being greeted by the ambassador of the Indian Union who was there as an honored guest of the patriarch of Venice, Angelo Roncalli. Roncalli's fatherly, benevolent smile seemed to me not at all different from what was normal with bishops. Still, I must say that everything set in motion by the Pope of the Vatican Council fitted perfectly with the confident simplicity of this man's expression. Some years afterwards when I read in his *Spiritual Diary* that every year he withdrew into seclusion for spiritual exercises, and that one of the last topics was the cardinal virtues, the thought went through my mind that perhaps he had brought with him into his retreat the Italian editions of my four small books on this topic. But then I forgot about the matter again, until I later mentioned it in passing as a postscript in a letter I was writing anyway to Dieter Sattler, the ambassador to the Vatican. He took up the question immediately, as he was very interested himself, and passed it on to the former private secretary of the pope. But the now Archbishop Capovilla wrote to me that he would have to see the books if he were to give accurate information about the matter. So I sent him a copy; all my books which appeared in the Morcelliana (Brescia) Publishing House had the same format. And then the confirmation came quickly that it could *certainly* be said that these *opuscula* had really belonged to the private library of the Pope, a reader, therefore, whom many an author would wish to have.

In the middle of the semester's work which meanwhile continued in Essen and in Münster with lectures and seminars about Plato, Thomas Aquinas, and J.-P. Sartre, I was surprised by a somewhat unusual telephone call. A spokesman for the German Federation of Trade Unions put the hasty and even "illegal" question to me whether, should the occasion arise, I would accept the "big cultural prize of the Federation." I said that I would first have to take a deep breath and reflect; I would in any case want to know who else had already received this prize. The answer: up until now no one; this year, at the end of the Ruhr Festival Games it would be awarded for the first time. Then I remembered the speech with which I had, years ago, once opened the art exhibition of the Ruhr Festival, something which, of course, I was not going to forget. Suddenly the person I was speaking to had to go; he gave me a few more facts: it was planned to give the prize both to Ernst Bloch and myself; probably I would find out more in about an hour; the jury was now gathering. When in answer to my question he named some of its members, I already knew that these people would never award me a prize. And that is exactly what happened; after that strange telephone conversation with a person I did not know, I never heard another word. The summer Ruhr Festival was coming to an end without any mention of the "big cultural prize"; the jury presumably could not agree. Just before Christmas it was in the newspaper that the honor had been awarded to Ernst Bloch and the soci0-critical graphic artist Frans Masereel.

The summer semester had not yet ended when my wife told me that a woman had rung up wanting to speak to me very urgently. Her name seemed vaguely familiar to me; it was late in the evening; I had just returned from Essen. On the following morning a registered letter arrived from the caller, a secretary in the University administration. A flat key fell out of the letter when I opened it; it was the key to her apartment, which I alone was allowed to enter; she was going to take her own life that night. When I contacted the University administration I was told in the usual way that they would call Fräulein S. immediately. At this point I suspected she might have thought better of it. But then she could not be found. I spoke briefly with the director of the bureau and requested that he accompany me to the apartment on the highest floor of a high-rise building. The young woman lay dead in her bed; on the table beside her was the message that she was donating her corpse to the anatomical institute. There was also a will of which I was the benefactor. On the narrow bookshelf above the bed was my book *What is Philosophizing?* After the protracted and difficult processing of the formalities, I donated the not inconsiderable proceeds from her estate to a fantastic, despairingly heroic enterprise which promised to help unmarried women to find an escape from their deadly loneliness.

Chapter XV

The East Asian trip was taking shape in those weeks and the preparations were in full swing. Dieter Sattler in the Foreign Office opened all doors with his friendly willingness to help me. And so I said goodbye to my eldest son Thomas, who, as I myself had done a good forty years previously, was beginning with carefree decisiveness to take leave of his father and fence off his own separate existence. More or less by chance he had just come into the house after having, for some time, not wanted to live there. So, standing in the hall on 8 September 1963, I said farewell to the twenty-seven-year-old who had just finished his final examinations in physics: "All the best then and take care!" Thomas had a USA research scholarship in his pocket and was going to set off only a few weeks after me on his first big trip, to the University of Berkeley, in the far, far west — at first for a year, but perhaps even for two. Then the starkness of our farewell depressed me considerably at the thought of the long separation; and so I sent a warm greeting to welcome the newcomer to the California which I knew well. He responded with a thank you and a cheerful report from the other hemisphere. And since neither he nor I would have ever dreamed that we would not see one another "here" again, we both set off completely light-heartedly and full of curiosity to what for each of us was a new world.

The stop in Calcutta, despite the feeling of uneasiness, went without a hitch, while unbelievably at the same time my soothsayer was proven correct, having said a year previously in Bombay that I would never again set foot on Indian soil. Astonished and relieved at the same time, I arrived a few hours later in Hong Kong. My curiosity about the specifics of Chinese Buddhism and about the border to Red China was at first completely washed away in a flood by completely different and unexpected matters: by the incredible beauty of these bays and islands which literally took my breath away; particularly, however, by the vehement attention with which the topic of the headlines was being discussed everywhere: "Where is Gloria?" This girl's name had been given to the unusually deadly typhoon which was making its way at great speed northwards from the South China Sea. In Hong Kong they were afraid of it and at the same time wanted it to come, because, while it would perhaps bring destruction, it would also bring rain. The water shortage had meantime become a stinking scourge in this densely populated city with over a million inhabitants. For a European this elemental emergency gave rise to immense consternation and yet, at the same time, to surprise at how naturally life seemed to continue as normal. So, of course, even in the spacious apartment of the General Consul there was water only every fourth day for three hours; but we drank our tea in a relaxed way as if there was no "Gloria" and as if there was enough water. It was also possible to speak with open objectivity about the puzzlingly porous "Bamboo Curtain." In Europe at that time there was the unpleasant rumour that those who escaped from the Maoist dictatorship were not let in by the British Crown Colony but forcibly sent back into the prison from which they had fled with unbelievable effort. In that tea-drinking group was the Hungarian Jesuit Ladanyi who was rightly seen as the best informed expert about Red China; the *China News Analysis,* which was not only published by him, but also solely written by him, was read in all Diplomatic Missions in the world. P. Ladanyi firstly confirmed to me that there were a hundred thousand refugees forcefully sent back to the Mainland, as they called it here, in the same goods trains as those in which the beef for Hong Kong was transported here every day from China. But you could not avoid uttering a deeply ashamed "but" about how the "Westerners" could do it. The communists in power had in fact let the refugees escape because of starvation in the country; the Governor of Hong Kong, which was overflowing with people, had more or less accommodated them in camps and fed them for weeks, during which time governments all over the world had been asked about their willingness to take refugees and how many. The answer from the USA was fifty to sixty! Finally, of necessity, they had sent the people back to Red China. So, of course, the claim of the Chinese that they were allowed to leave their country, whereas the "free world" refused to take anyone in, was a propaganda lie, but nevertheless, in a sense, true. On the way home I asked the knowledgeable priest for his opinion about the possibility of a war between Russia and China. He stopped, and said very seriously that even thinking of war should be forbidden, but he feared that in the long term it would come to that.

Two days later, before dawn, the seventy-year-old president of the Lotos Association was waiting for me at the ferry. He wanted to bring me to the sparsely populated island of Laan Tau which rose like a beacon out of the sea and on whose peak there was a Buddhist monastery. Clearly he had decided to introduce me, without delay or respite, to Zen Buddhism; and I have seldom spent a whole day taken up with such laborious conversation. It started when, out of pure politeness, I enquired about some philosophical interest or other. Magisterially he said that philosophy interested him a lot and at the same time not at all: "yes and no!" But that was just the beginning. While climbing, I asked at a hardly discernible fork in the narrow path, which was the correct way. "Yes, what is a way? A way that's not a way." And so on. Or suddenly my guide would stop and declaim: "What is truth? It is true and not true: exactly that is the truth" — at which he elbowed me in the side with a guffaw. In the large meditation hall of the monastery, which was almost empty, he forced me to sit on one of the benches and immediately spoke with monotonous repetition: "You are nobody, you are nothing." A young monk had entered the room unnoticed; he listened and laughed, showing a perfect set of flashing white teeth; but that was all visual — just for the eyes. You did not hear a sound. Somewhat tired, I began to feel the seductive attraction of being nothing; but then, in a kind necessary self-defense, I slapped the palm of my hand on the bench and exclaimed: "I am absolutely someone; because God created me!" — to which the president of the Lotos Society again responded with his enigmatic laughter. On the horizontal beams of the symbolic gate, through which we then left the monastic settlement I read the English inscription: "There is no time; what is memory?"

Compared with such arduous and puzzling subtlety, how refreshing was Sister Euphemia (or some name like that) who had the glorious inspiration of badgering an Italian company into leaving to the Caritas Hong Kong a macaroni machine which had been shown at an international industry exhibition. With the wheaten flour, which the Americans sent in plentiful quantities, the Chinese, as they did not bake bread, thought of nothing better than to bring it all to the black market. But now the resolute nun stood with her helpers at the point where the huge machine expelled the noodles in a single complex process. Beaming, she distributed the noodles to her charges who were waiting around in colorful throngs.

Because in Korea the number "four" means death, it is avoided as far as possible or simply omitted altogether — with the result that, for instance, in the lift, the fifth floor immediately followed the third. And for that very reason, when I visited the German Embassy in Seoul I ended up not with the Cultural Department but first with the Military Attaché, a young Colonel who was standing in front of a map of the world which covered the whole wall. It suited me to be immediately confronted in such a way with the sharply outlined political reality of this part of the world. There was a ceasefire in operation here; but strictly speaking there was still a war going on. And I quickly understood why the Iron Curtain in Korea was more impenetrable than in other areas. Anyone wanting to send a message to his brother north of the 38th parallel could only do this through a dependable intermediary, let us say, in Tokyo; still he would hardly dare to do it; he might all too easily come under suspicion in his own country.

I found out from the Cultural Officer that five or six of the almost dozen universities in the city were interested in a lecture from me; but we immediately agreed that two would be enough. My reply to the next question about what I myself would like to see or do resulted in a bewildered shaking of the head; in all politeness I was just being laughed at. "Shamanism? Necromancy?" No, no; there was no such thing here and certainly not in Seoul, which after all was an almost American city. But then the secretary shyly said that she remembered that the Embassy driver, a Mr. Kim, had occasionally mentioned such things. And indeed after some hesitation and fussing, this Mr. Kim drove me to a place which was clearly well known to him on the edge of the city, where on the odd occasion something of that nature took place. But behold! We stepped into an inner courtyard away from the street. It was surrounded at a high level, as is usual in Korean houses, by seven or eight open rooms; and here the rituals of necromancy were in full swing. The "shamans" were all older women. One of them was just putting on her multi-colored cult garments to the sound of drums and bamboo flute and was already beginning to move rhythmically back and forth. And gradually this movement increased, accompanied by strange throbbing singing. It became a frantic hopping dance, with the dancer springing higher and higher from the floor, going wildly out of control until she could hardly draw breath. Suddenly the dance and the music stopped for a while; the Shaman turned to the bystanders, hugged one or other of them and excitedly whispered to them the messages of the dead, which were listened to with deep emotion and sometimes with tears. It was always a family which gathered at such an event — and also paid for it (as Mr. Kim, who explained it all to me, gave me to understand with expressive gestures); clearly the Shaman demanded really precious gifts and above all a lot of money. In some of the rooms you saw families having a festive meal while still waiting for news from their dead. Sometimes these rituals lasted the whole day and perhaps half the night as well.

Still totally fascinated, I spoke about these remarkable things at the farewell dinner to which the ambassador had invited some guests. Nobody at the table had ever heard of it. The host himself, however, a qualified sinologist, confirmed to the astonishment of everyone and perhaps on the basis of purely theoretical knowledge, that "nature cults" of this type could nowadays only be seen in Korea. And Mr. Kim, who brought me to the airport, accepted from me a special token of thanks, not without a hint of secret complicity.

During the five weeks in Japan that followed I had many experiences for which I had to search for a name to cover the at once fascinating and enormously disconcerting events — until, years afterwards, the thought came to me that this key word could be: Nô play. Of course, I also found the modern Japan amazing enough — this perfection of electronic devices already in daily use, the automated high garage above a Kabuki Theatre. But all of this was not entirely unfamiliar. Many a time I had been amazed at the incomparable inventiveness of Japanese cuisine. I had been charmed by the sight of a festive meal and by their ability to make even the smallest area, like a little colored plate on which there were two slices of aubergine, into an ornamental work of art. But really there was nothing mysterious about it. And yet, again and again, unexpectedly and surprisingly, I encountered something quite difficult to decipher, something hardly comprehensible to me, which the Japanese accepted as completely normal and appropriate.

Chapter XV

It already started on my first visit to these archaic mask games which are called *Nô-gaku*. It was only to be expected that I would understand nothing of the plot; without the explanations of my companion, a university professor of theater studies, I would not have known how to interpret a single gesture. In the Nô play there is only strictly ritualized gesture, nothing spontaneous, not even an instinctive hand movement. How were you to know that a measured raising and lowering of the open fan symbolized a courtly dance festival? When we entered, the play was already in progress on the completely unadorned stage. There was a choir, sitting still and upright in a dead straight line, just singing a somewhat monotonous recitative, accompanied by a similarly motionless "orchestra" crouching on the floor; the music was produced not just by the instruments but also by the human voice of some of the musicians; the tone generated in this way was not seen as singing, as was expressly explained to me. It was a sound more comparable to the howling of an animal or of the wind; singing was exclusively a matter for the choir. How strange, I thought. But already there were much stranger things in store for me. In the distance, a prolonged lament was being intoned by a booming bass voice with a gurgling quality; and my companion, who was, at this stage, quite excited himself, whispered to me that it was the famous actor playing the main role, a girl, now ready for her big scene. And then in ceremonially slow gliding steps, still lamenting and sighing, the man came onstage with his face hidden behind the mask of a young woman. And clearly the audience, caught up — even breathless — were simply unaware of anything except a pretty girl racked with pain.

Every time I expressed my amazement about it my Japanese friends listened to me attentively; but they did not really understand what I meant. Such strange encounters were legion. There was the young philosophy professor who had translated some of my books into Japanese, who only ever spoke the English he had learned in Harvard, but never German. He had invited me for a meal in his house; on the way there he began, to my amazement, to excuse himself; his house was such a wretched hut that it was impossible for him to receive there a guest such as me. But, as it turned out, his house was completely normal. His wife and mother-in-law knelt down in greeting on the threshold with their foreheads to the floor, and the meal was, as ever, excellent. Then, because of his expertise I gained some unexpected information. "Do you hear the noise?" he asked me once as we were approaching a Shinto Temple through the tangle of paths in the park. For no particular reason I thought for a moment of the jackals of Delhi; but my companion pointed to our feet under which the pebbles were crunching; and he told me that these pebbles had been especially brought here from far away so that their trickling sound would encourage the pilgrim to meditate. To my casual question as to why Japanese school pupils wore uniforms until they became students I was given the surprising answer that difference in clothing could be a cause of shame to poorer people, and it was an essential point of Japanese social morality not to embarrass people. I myself felt a little embarrassed while wandering through one of the large warehouses of Tokyo and being welcomed on each floor at the bottom of the escalator by a white-gloved girl wearing a kimono and making a deep bow. The "soft and sexy voice" particularly impressed a *Newsweek* reporter who estimated the average daily quota of bows at two and a half thousand; for me it was all reminiscent of the strictly standardized gestures of the Nô play.

On a rainy day in Kyoto, when I wanted to postpone the planned visit to the imperial gardens, I was taken aback to hear the reproachful question as to whether it were possible for the weather to be more suitable? Right now the colors could be seen in all their freshness and splendor! And really there was much more to see than the already autumnal colorfulness of the park — for example, the snow white gravel piled up a meter high on a carefully raked rectangular surface large enough to cover half a tennis court. A visitor who noticed my astonishment came up to me and pointed to a wooded hilly area on the other side of the garden: "Do you see the forest path where the trees have been felled? When the full moon shines on this exact spot, we gather down here and watch its reflection on the bright stones; they glisten like the sea!" — Unbelievably it was Canadian Dominicans who praised the wet day to me. They themselves, I was told, were wont on St. Thomas's day, if it were not raining, to sprinkle water on the artistically set stone path to the teahouse; that was when it really gleamed the most.

Some puzzling aspects were better explained by the stranger — once he had been initiated into the mysteries of the country — than by the native, who, understandably, could not see what was so different. So I would not have understood anything about Japanese music without patient instruction from Eta Harich-Schneider, the German harpsichordist. Overtaken by the war, she had remained in Tokyo and had now, in the employ of the University of Chicago, done the first transcription of the courtly and ritual music of old Japan into the musical notation familiar to us. One of her friends, a Buddhist abbot in what was earlier the imperial city of Nara, once celebrated alone in the spacious temple a particular archaic liturgy; he himself sang the old texts with an exactly modulating voice, viewing us both clearly not as listeners, but as participants; so he suddenly demanded of us with an authoritative gesture that we sprinkle incense into the glowing charcoal in the basin in front of which we were kneeling. I could not resist whispering to my neighbor, who was now fully concentrating on the singing, asking if she knew that the early

Christians had been thrown to the lions for such things. Somewhat alarmed, she still sprinkled the scented grains as I did.

In Hiroshima, the Germanist who, full of pride, showed me a masterly printed block book with German Baroque poems along with their Japanese translation which he had done himself, remarkably did not yet know that the reading evening with Ernst Ginsberg, for which the printing had been specially done at high cost, would never take place. He was completely distraught and did not want to believe that the actor, having just arrived in Tokyo, had become very ill and had immediately departed again. I myself, in memory of our first meetings in Basel, had been looking forward to seeing him again. But already a good three months later, Ernst Ginsberg, who was not just paralyzed in his arms and legs, but also was not able to speak anymore, sent to his Zurich friends gathered to celebrate his sixtieth birthday the moving "message of greeting" whose last paragraph read: "Matthias Claudius ends his famous letter to his son Johannes with the words: 'Be joyful and have courage and don't leave this world without giving public witness to your love and honor for the founder of Christianity.' Permit me, here before you, publicly, to close with this demonstration of love."

My departure from Tokyo was a veritable Nô play and there was even a role in it for me. I had got it into my head that I wanted to bring home the mask of a beautiful girl; and of course, what the stores had to offer was out of the question. My theater scholar was friendly with the author of a book about Nô masks and he in turn with one of the best mask makers in the city. Shortly before my departure the difficult business was done: the price was agreed; I was even to receive my mask directly from the hands of the master himself. So three of us went to the apartment of the mask maker where we met other guests, among them a famous Nô actor. The room into which we were brought looked like the inside of a

shrine made of cedar wood; the master said it was his workshop, but there was neither a tool to be seen nor even the tini-
est trace of anything like wood shavings; even this word seem
in retrospect to be too coarse. The old man in the black kimono, with a face which looked as if it had been carved from
some light-colored wood, had a low, black lacquered table
brought in, and we sat down for tea. His wife served us while
kneeling and always remained nearby; her part in the game
was, as became clear, of special importance. In the first half-
hour there was no talk of masks, and there was nothing like
that in evidence. Finally the tea things were cleared and a shallow box, a work of art in itself, was placed on the table. Some
of the masks, however, which were taken out with the greatest
of care, were three hundred years old and of course were not
for sale. They were hugely admired by everyone; the Nô actor
kept turning them around in the lamplight, and their expressions constantly changed. Fine, I thought to myself, at least
this is the first act. But then to my horror the master said that
he simply could no longer exhibit the masks he had carved as
they were nothing but botched jobs. I cast an enquiring look
at my neighbor; his answer was a calm look advising patience.
Everyone began to press the host and praise his art which had
brought him considerable fame — and so on. Then we saw
five or six masks, all masks of girls; my wish was therefore
well known. I immediately liked two of the masks particularly
well and already put them, perhaps a little hastily, on my
shortlist. The master said, however, that he could not give me
those two; they would have to remain with him a little longer
to become completely beautiful. He recommended another
mask to me which would become prettier and prettier; he
knew this from experience. I agreed and, with my European
impatience, in a whisper brought up through the mediation of
my theater scholar and his friend the question of the price. But
suddenly the master drew back. The mask was badly made;

he could not take any money for it at all — out of the question! There were protests and appeasements from all sides; but no one said anything; no one got excited; things took their natural course. The price had now long since been agreed. But clearly there was to be a whispered conversation with the wife of the master. And then, again along the line of mediators, a specially tied-up white envelope was passed to me like contraband. I turned shyly away, wrote a check, and put it into the envelope. But the game was by no means over yet. This mask had to have a brocade cover of a particular color; and this could not be found. When I pointed to a charming reed-green and silver bag, it was explained to me gently but firmly that for a girl's mask only a red and gold lacquered cover was possible; but that I would receive this before my departure — which did then happen.

It is said that anyone who gets to see Fuji when leaving the country, which apparently is not altogether usual, can be sure of a return to Japan. So on the last day I wrote the *Haiku* into the visitors' book:

On my departure will the snow-capped Fuji herald my return?

And in fact Japan's holy mountain, one of the most beautiful mountain peaks in the world, revealed itself to me in all its splendor when I took off. But similarly, Ernst Ginsberg, on his homeward trip to death wrote that he saw it "in all its glory."

To have to travel directly to the National Taiwan University for my lecture immediately after landing in Taipei at first displeased me utterly. But then the midday tiredness and reluctance fell away at a stroke. The amazing mental vigor and vitality radiated by the American faculty colleague who greeted me with this demand, made me immediately wide awake; what I did not know was that he held in his quiver a special arrow which was only to be taken out a few days later. Besides, in the

Chapter XV

University a large auditorium awaited me. It was bristling with expectation. I had hardly finished speaking (about "Philosophy between science and theology"), when already there were four or five spontaneous requests to speak, and a vehement discussion began. Something like this had never happened in Japan; it had always depressed me that a conversation or even a debate could not be started; their applause was polite, sometimes even very lively, but they remained silent. But these were now Chinese students! Probably here too the elastic tension which was characteristic of public life in Taiwan was in evidence, comparable only with the intensity of life which I later came across in Israel — both similarly shaped by the passionate will to rebuild an extremely threatened political community. In any case, it was almost impossible to avoid this hectic pace. My days have seldom been as full as in Taiwan. The time for sleeping was short. Only long after midnight could I release myself from my fascination with Chinese opera, which I had looked for in vain in Hong Kong. Admittedly, without a companion I would neither have understood the wonderfully alienating symbolic language of the gestures nor have been able to interpret the faces of the actors which were made almost unrecognizable — not by masks but by wild, painted-on ornaments. A highly political, if also understandably fruitless night discussion followed the sumptuous exotic meal in the house of the son of Chiang Kai Shek; after all, the marshal had just now, for the first time, publicly proclaimed that the attack on the mainland could begin at any time.

The car trip from the capital city to the south port of Kaohsiung took the whole day. There again in the evening I was to hold a lecture — where a German doctor paid me a rather dubious compliment in expressing her joy about my "Westphalian English." On our trip, every view of the blooming country confirmed why the island was called "the beautiful" (Formosa); destroyed bridges and paddy fields covered with sand and stones reminded me of "Gloria," the typhoon with which I, too, was familiar. The most exciting thing was the report of a missionary traveling with me about the three years of his imprisonment in Red China. This came up in conversation by chance, but then it was as if a dam had burst. The man was sitting beside the driver; he was therefore not looking anyone in the eye, and so he spoke uninhibitedly — as if to himself, and perhaps for the first time — of the dreadful things which had happened to him. I was careful not to interrupt him by asking a question. He did not speak much about the physical maltreatment which was always a threat. He spoke much more about the horrors of "brainwashing," of the merciless pressure to see every fellow prisoner as an enemy of the state and to treat him as such. The result was complete isolation of everyone from everyone. He spoke of the pressure of, for weeks, spending ten-hour days, with a fixed lunch-break, discussing under constant supervision by the guards one's own failings against Mao, whether there were such failings or not. The whole thing was not set up for conversion to communism, but to "break" every person individually, without exception, and to make them open to manipulation and thereby be forced to do something through which he would lose his self-respect. One day the "eldest" ordered all cellmates to spit in the face of a fellow prisoner where there was no reason for it at all. In the beginning the missionary himself was the only person who had refused to do it, but then, out of fear, he was unable to continue with his refusal and in the end he spat as well — and at this moment he lost his self-respect. It was not possible for anyone not to capitulate. After a long silence which nobody dared to break, this passionate sentence was blurted out: "If someone had asked me what was preferable to me, the prison cell or crucifixion, I would without hesitation have chosen crucifixion!" The car stopped in front of the priest's home; in the falling darkness I bade him farewell almost without a word and also a little embarrassed at being the involuntary witness of a confession which was really meant for someone else.

On my departure from Taiwan the same American who had collected me on my arrival now brought me back to the airport. While he was shaking my hand, he gave me a book which he had written and about which he wanted my opinion. "Some time or other. Take your time!" I immediately translated the title *In the presence of my enemies* into the familiar verse of the psalm: "You prepare a table for me in the presence of my enemies." To my surprise the book was also a report about his three-year imprisonment in a Chinese prison; in our conversations he had never mentioned this. The thesis of the author, John W. Clifford, implied that it was *not* impossible to offer resistance. He had heard many times that brainwashing was a type of mystical technique which nobody was able to withstand. "It is, however, neither mysterious nor impossible to withstand. *I know.*"

I spent my first evening in Manila reading newspapers in my hotel room. A maxim which I had heard more than thirty years previously from my teacher Plenge came to mind; above all, I followed the advice already given to me by the head of the German Cultural Institute on the short journey from the airport to the hotel: not to go out alone at night even by taxi. It was better to ask for a car and an escort from the German Embassy — whose driver, however, had just been attacked and was lying in hospital with stab wounds. I was tired anyway and limited myself to an afternoon walk through the shopping area and to some churches in the inner city — during which the malicious saying was partly confirmed that the Philippines had moved from the strict seclusion of a Spanish Monastery directly into the amusement atmosphere of Las Vegas. I saw an All Souls campaign on posters with the request to enter the names of the dead on a list for whom the "first intentions" Mass was to be celebrated. And in some shop windows there were the coarsest vulgarities, manufactured in bulk and carved from the finest woods. At the entrance to many restaurants there were signs not permitting pistols and "deadly weapons." In front of my hotel there were children advertising smuggled cigarettes at the top of their voices, while on the other side of the street a policeman was walking up and down clearly seeing and hearing nothing. The daily newspapers were anything but bedtime reading. An election campaign in the Philippines had a character all of its own. The President claimed that during meetings of the Opposition there was a minute's silence during which they prayed for his murder. Since the beginning of the year there had been one hundred and forty-four politically motivated murders in one single province, where, for this reason, the election, so the President threatened, would perhaps be suspended indefinitely. Lily Abegg, Far East correspondent of the *Frankfurter Zeitung* who had come to the German Cultural Institute for the lecture, said very definitely that this country simply needed a type of dictatorship; "but then along come the Americans always with their democracy." Although in general I was of the same opinion, I had to make the point that they had also "come along" to free the island kingdom from Japanese occupation and that they did this at the cost of massive sacrifices. I had never seen such a huge military cemetery as the American one on a hill in the outskirts of Manila.

The four or five (Catholic) universities of the city of a million people were taken up with examinations for a week, so that a guest lecture for students was not possible. So they came up with something much more volatile: I was to speak to the professors about Thomas Aquinas. Several hundred had arrived in the lecture room of the seminary and, it seemed to me, were interested above all in holding a discussion. It began immediately with the aggressive question about what there was to object to in Thomism; clearly the thesis about which I had lectured a decade before in Madrid was not unknown to the questioner. For better or for worse I had to nail my colors to the mast. The positive result for me was that the slightly polemic inquisitorial tone of the challenge had mobilized me too. And so I said it was, firstly, not only an error, but a falsification, to call an "Aristotelian and Thomistic philosophy" separated from theology a philosophical world view of Thomas Aquinas; and secondly, that Thomas does not express himself in artificial "terminology" but in "language" which is alive and has a liquid clarity; because of that, it was impossible to bring what he says about the world into the form of a closed system of propositions; and, thirdly, the Thomism of the schools lacked the element of the *philosophia negativa* which characterized the master, the first sentence of which, in its authentic formulation, says: "The essences of things are unknown to us." As was to be expected, a lively, many-sided debate ensued, in which the wonderful but rare combination of passion and objectivity was preserved — which was as refreshing as a swim in the sea. And also the president of the Spanish Dominican University Santo Tomas, whom I had not exactly been able fully to convince, handed me my fee at the end with obvious respect: two artistically worked silver sets of rosary beads, one for Madame and one for me. But, as he added on purpose, both were not yet consecrated — so there would be no problem about making them later into two necklaces.

The following day, after a long sleep and waking up late, I had a call from the German Embassy: "Do you really want to go to Saigon today?" "Why not?" "Have you not seen the newspaper yet?" I could only see a corner of the newspaper, as it was still under the door. "The Head of State Diem is said to have been overthrown and has left the country on a foreign warship. There are no details available." I did not want to decide yet and enquired in the Pan Am office. "No, we are *not* flying to Saigon today! But Air France has a flight at about the same time." So I arrived in the South Vietnamese capital in the afternoon on an Air France aircraft, at this stage not without some concern. When I landed, the sight of a good dozen American military aircraft lined up in an impressive row calmed me. Otherwise, however, the situation at the airport was quite uncomfortable. Revolutionary soldiers roaming around with their carbines casually shouldered and the barrels facing forward is not what you want to see.

When, after some exhausting telephone calls, I finally traveled with the young head of the Goethe Institute into the city, which was crowded with curious and restless people, one of his acquaintances called out to us very excitedly that the curfew had been brought forward that evening to seven o'-clock. In the remaining half an hour we quickly looked around a little: there was barbed-wire barriers all around the badly damaged presidential palace and two or three tanks on the squares; on almost every street corner there was a machine gun in position. Every now and then you could hear the roar of artillery fire in the distance. I looked up questioningly, but my companion said: "That is normal; that is the border." Okay ...

In the hotel the wildest rumors were circulating. Only twenty-four hours later did the truth become known: on the morning of this All Saints Day in 1963 they had taken the Head of State Diem — who had mysteriously escaped from the locked palace — and his brother Nhu out of a church during Mass and killed them in a barbaric way while they were still on the transport truck.

The following day was Sunday. My morning walk through the almost empty deathly quiet streets led me coincidentally to the huge shell of an empty platform from where Diem had, three or four days previously, watched a parade celebrating the ninth anniversary of his rise to power. Standing beside the tanks and machine guns the soldiers chatted with a group of young people who were somewhat bleary-eyed and clearly showing off a little. Already the first churchgoers were appearing and heading towards the cathedral. I followed them and stepped into the high transept of the undamaged neo-gothic building and watched from one of the back benches as the space filled little by little with people festively dressed for Sunday High Mass — as if it were a Sunday like any other. The bare black hair of the young women fell loosely over the tight-fitting silk robe slit from the hip. Under the robe shiny dark trousers reached down to the ankles, below which slim heels of golden sandals could be seen. A hint of Paris, I thought. Almost everything here reminded me of Paris: croissants for breakfast; the diagonally cut sticks of white bread, the *baguettes;* in the hotel room the double bed, the long bolsters, and even the loose contact of the lighting wire running along the wall to the switch. The elegantly printed invitation was, of course, in French announcing my lecture with its English title. The lecture, of course, understandably never took place at all, and so I set out hunting for the most exact and complete information possible. The German Ambassador had angrily spoken about the press which never tired of reporting about the self-cremation of Buddhist monks or about the extravagances of Madame Nhu; he said it gave a completely false picture; above all, this was anything but a religious war. So what was it about? In Taipei I had been told that there was no better informed man than a Belgian priest, Diem's personal adviser. But when I mentioned this clearly well-known name to the ambassador, he immediately demurred. Regretfully, he could not possibly put me in contact with him, at least not now; he was probably not in the city anymore, possibly even dead. I then tried to contact him myself, and to my surprise this courageous man suggested a meeting place for the following day — where he would be visible literally to "the whole world": in the journalists' restaurant near the parliament. On this my last afternoon in Saigon I learned more — admittedly very confusing things — than in all the earlier conversations: whether with Germans who knew the country, or American Caritas workers, or Vietnamese — among them two Buddhist monks who had just been released from prison. What I heard was the story of the attempt, doomed from the start, to free the country from the after-effects of colonialism, without seeing it immediately fall into a new dependence on Soviet Russia or Red China. This attempt met with resistance from their largely corrupt upper class, who were both fascinated by and dependent on Paris. However, this liberation simply could not be achieved without "dictatorship," without control of foreign exchange, without invasive and perhaps even secret surveillance — and so on. This was something which again did not fit in with the completely un-historical American notion of "democracy." All this and still more (e.g. family politics, the opium trade, the rivalry of religious groups) had, at that time, before the actual American Vietnam war, become tangled into such an impenetrable jungle that I could only feel surprised when someone claimed that you only needed to do this or that, and already everything would be smoothed out. On the contrary, I began to suspect — not, of course, what horrors were going to befall this country — but that from now it would be less and less possible to extricate all the parties concerned from this frightening entanglement, and that the end would be an unthinkable catastrophe.

Among the letters which awaited me in Bangkok was news of a death. Weeks previously Kurt Wolff had died in a ghastly way. The seventy-six-year-old had been living for quite some time in Switzerland and had traveled to the Frankfurt Book Fair. On the way home he had chosen to travel via Marbach on the Neckar where the German literature archive was holding an exhibition of literary expressionism, and in it, as was to be expected, there was a fairly comprehensive collection of his own publishing company's earlier publications.

Chapter XV

During his quiet afternoon stroll through the small town, a truck started backing up and crushed him against a wall before his wife's eyes; he died a few hours later. Helen Wolff, who moved back to New York shortly afterwards, wrote to me that she had found open on his night table in the hotel my little book about the Platonic myths. In it he had marked the quotation from a late dialogue: "For us it is like when a person who knew everything in a dream knows nothing when he wakes."

Dream — this key word thrown to me in such a remarkable way kept coming into my mind as I walked through the holy district of Bangkok. Only gradually did it become clear to me what was, in fact, the reason for the dreamlike and almost unreal nature of this city: it lay not so much in the golden sheen of the towers nor the preciousness of the sculptures and fixtures suffused with light but in the fact that the often completely unusually large dimensions were, so to speak, denied and the merely quantitative aspect suppressed by the delicate filigree ornamentation. The four-meter-high ebony black doors of the royal temple, for example, were covered with inlaid mother of pearl in such a way that they looked more like the lids of jewellery boxes. And the forty-eight-meter-long figure of the Buddha stretched out in sleep was covered with gold leaf, and they had divided each of the huge soles of the feet into one hundred and eight panels, each panel again displaying a mother of pearl symbol. Anyone who innocently stepped into one of the temples and with closed eyes listened to the chanting of the monks might think for a while that he was not in Bangkok but, say, in Maria Laach. The countless monks who walked in their light saffron vestments through the streets where ordinary life went on were like figures from a dream. It was said that there were two hundred thousand of them in this country. "Begging" for a meal, which was really a duty for them, was a story in itself. Every family, I was told, saw it as an honor when a monk took specially prepared food from them. Almost every young man who thought anything of himself spent some time as a monk — for example, before his marriage. At an evening gathering at table my neighbor, who had just been appointed state secretary of a ministry, pointed to his shaved head and whispered to me that he had been a monk for a hundred days before taking up office. When I said I assumed he would not have been treated too strictly, he answered with a laugh that was also a definite contradiction. And I was quickly taught about the daily routine of the monks: rise at 5 a.m.; meditation; communal recitation of the Sutras; begging around lunchtime for food which was to be consumed by twelve noon; after that, only drinking was allowed; in the afternoons an hour of choir duty; return to the cloister before dark. I could not resist asking about the subject of the meditations and received the well-known and expected — yet still each time strange — answer: "Oh, that is all the same; anyone who wants to can also count his breaths."

On the way to the Thai PEN Club I was emphatically made aware of the fact that I was to address my audience in the following way: "Highnesses, Ladies and Gentlemen!" — because some members of royalty would be present; besides, the chairman was a Royal Prince. Not without amazement, this democratic European saw how, as a matter of course, the audience who gradually began to fill the room — professors, journalists, intellectuals — all knelt down on the threshold. This, as then became clear, certainly did not at all inhibit the liveliness and openness of the following discussion. In my lecture about the concept of tradition I had not repressed my notion of the "holiness" of tradition and its status. Again, one last time I was clearly given to understand that to Buddhists the thought of a divine being was completely foreign. To my outspoken political comment that in Saigon it was often said that in this decisive point there was no essential difference between Buddhism and communism, they chose to give no answer. On the following evening on the way to the airport, when I told the cultural attaché about this conversation, I found out that also in Bangkok a leading Buddhist was in custody because of communist activities.

In the Lufthansa airplane I suddenly felt that I was already in Germany, which had for months seemed so far away. It was only one more night until I would land in Düsseldorf — a very long night of course, since we were flying ahead of the sun which was rising behind us. The darkness lasted for a full nineteen hours. I asked the stewardess for a German newspaper; but the most recent one that she could lend me was the most recent edition of *Spiegel*. So I took up the magazine not without some misgivings. In the ephemeral drab pages I came across a report of the Second Vatican Council. It had begun its second session a few weeks before under the new pope. I already knew about it through objective and informative articles in the American *Time Magazine*. I read only the first words of the *Spiegel* report and then I put it aside. "Cardinal Ottaviani, the Catholic Church's chief guardian of the faith and morals . . ." — I did not want to be informed in this tone, and certainly not about a topic such as this.

Barely a fortnight after my return, John F. Kennedy was murdered in a manner which still remains a mystery to this day. You can hardly imagine now the shocked reaction of the students in the autumn of 1963 to the death of this man, who was after all a representative of political power, of the establishment. My son Thomas described in his Californian diary the immense dismay which paralyzed life on the University of Berkeley campus. For my part, I said to myself: the "year of the dead" was continuing. It had still not come to an end. And dates of death and dates of birth are often close to one another.

In May 1964, on the occasion of my sixtieth birthday I was to be conferred with an honorary doctorate in theology

— this was what Michael Schmaus, Dean of the Faculty of Theology, wrote to me from Munich. On my birthday I always thought of my mother in a particular way, not only because she gave birth to me but also because she was more or less exactly twenty years older than me. Her eightieth birthday, soon to be celebrated, was to be her last, as we all knew; she lived only a little time after it. When I asked her on the day itself how she saw the past she did not understand the sense of my question at first. So I had to say it again: "Was life good for you?" After some hesitation came the answer in Low German: "Ah, I was always able to put up with it."

The Honorary Doctorate in the Auditorium Maximum of Munich University was, in accordance with the passage of time, a quite sober affair, as the academic magnificence of former times had been significantly reduced. Still, the listeners were expected to listen to the reading of a document written in Latin; and the festival garb of the Dean was so rich in folds that it could only be donned with the skillful assistance of a woman specially appointed for the task. At the beginning of the festival act something happened which was not part of the planned proceedings: the Dean, instead of stepping up to the lectern, immediately went over to Karl Rahner, who was conspicuously sitting in the front row, and shook his hand to resounding applause from the auditorium — with which, as I learned only later, a disagreement between the two men generally known about in Munich was settled. A spontaneous gesture of this type suited the generous nonchalance of Michael Schmaus, and on the other hand it meant you could not be resentful that a written copy of his well formulated *Laudatio* remained simply untraceable after he had read it out. My publisher would have liked to publish it in *Hochland* along with the lecture which I held on this occasion ("Theology – philosophically viewed").

Chapter XV

Clearly, I thought, while my hearing was being tested audiometrically in the clinic, you did not cross the threshold into the seventh decade of your life with impunity. The doctors spoke quite seriously about "one-sided deafness," which recently was not altogether rare. Neither they nor I knew how quickly and through which merciless invasion I would be freed from this affliction —forever, it appeared, and with one blow. On the way to the clinic again, I was already standing at the hall door when the telephone rang. An English voice asked for me, and I thought for a moment that it was about the placement of a German housekeeper which my wife and her London brother had discussed several times. But then an overseas call was announced and the daughter of the London brother announced the bad news that her cousin Thomas, our son Thomas, had suddenly become very ill and was in hospital in Seattle in Washington State; she herself was going to fly there immediately. I asked: "A car accident?" No, not an accident, but a brain haemorrhage; it would be a while before I would grasp the unfamiliar word haemorrhage: cerebral haemorrhage. "But why Seattle?" But did we not know that Thomas was on a trip with two German friends? There must surely be a letter on the way to us.

It was 24 July 1964, late on Friday afternoon shortly before the beginning of the weekend, that I got this disturbing news. I immediately reserved a seat on the earliest possible flight to Seattle the following morning. The American Consulate in Düsseldorf spontaneously assured me that, as an exception, there would be an official there on Saturday especially to issue me the visa. But by midnight there was already a second call, again from Seattle. Thomas was unconscious; his face had an expression of deep astonishment; he was going "rapidly downhill," the doctor said, and he expressly advised me *not* to travel, as there was no point. Before the night ended we were informed that he had died.

On the evening after spending a wonderful, almost boisterously happy summer's day, Thomas had suddenly collapsed into unconsciousness at the campsite on the slope of Mount Rainier. Then, accompanied to Seattle by a doctor who had also been camping, he was brought to the King County Hospital and died twenty-four hours later, after a priest from the cathedral, called by the thoughtful cousin, had administered the last sacrament.

It was good, at the first onslaught of pain, to have to deal with practical matters — for example, the difficulty of chasing up a printing firm which worked on a Saturday, or finding a way to make money available to my niece in America. And when, after inquiring about the approximate cost of transferring the body by air the amount "per kilogram" was mentioned, there was no danger of losing the ground under your feet; then you were casually informed that this special freight had, "naturally," to be prepared in such a way that no one would guess it was a coffin — and that made the matter more expensive. And at this stage I did not yet know about the adventures a young girl had to undergo in her battle with two competing funeral parlors; otherwise the unbelievable sentence would have come to mind which Werner Bergengruen had used to preface one of his books: Every death had its funny side.

A letter from Thomas really had been on its way; it reached us two days after the news of his death. It was a long letter to me, started before he set off on the trip and then continued several times. I was taken aback by the first sentence: "Fortune has smiled upon me again for a short time; I hope that it wasn't black Fate." But his formulation, which sounded like a premonition of death, was, as became immediately clear, actually based on the recent purchase of a used car. I had contributed a considerable "loan" for it; but the gratitude which was now seeking expression far outweighed this. The letter had a new tone which had long since been missing between us; suddenly I could hear the language of trust, of devotion, of humor; very early forms of address were there again as if a matter of course. Clearly it had been necessary to travel to the other side of the world to make this return possible.

I do not think Thomas knew anything about my story "F for Fortuna." So the first sentence not just of his last letter but also of his American diary entries which I saw much later was all the more remarkable: "I would like best to start this diary with *O Fortuna, velut luna.* But we'll see."

The death notice published in the newspaper reads, even if you have written it yourself, like something finally confirmed by someone else. It was read by a student friend of Thomas whom we only knew by name; he had been in Berkeley for a while and had only returned from there two or three weeks previously. He rang us up completely distraught; he simply could not believe that Thomas, to whom he had just bade farewell, was no longer alive. He was particularly upset that he had not yet visited us and told us about Thomas, although he had been urgently asked to do so. He asked when the funeral was going to be held; but we did not yet know that ourselves because the transfer of the body had not yet taken place. So I told him the place and time of the requiem in case he wanted to take part — something I could not know. He said yes with such outright and almost reproachful vehemence that I said if he did not mind I would like to ask him something else — to which he immediately replied that he could imagine what it would be. And then I was again amazed at the wonderful blunt directness of young people. He said he would catch up on his visit soon; but now he wanted to say something concrete to me: his friend Thomas had gone to Mass and communion with him at Easter for the first time in a long time, and then regularly; Thomas had requested him to tell us this personally, and it was very painful for him now to have done this too late.

But of course it was not at all "too late." The message about my son's homecoming — a much deeper homecoming than to his father — still came at the right time.

And so the "Year of the dead" ended abruptly. Things would never be the same again. Meanwhile the world continued on its course. Which course? — no one knew.

Index

Index

Index

Index